LIVING COLOR

Console-ing Passions: Television and Cultural Power

A series edited by Lynn Spigel

LIVING

RACE AND TELEVISION IN THE UNITED STATES

COLOR

Edited by Sasha Torres

Duke University Press

Durham and London

1998

© 1998 Duke University Press

All rights reserved

Printed in the United States of America

on acid-free paper ∞

Typeset in Minion by Tseng Information Systems, Inc.

Library of Congress Cataloging-in-Publication Data

appear on the last printed page of this book.

CONTENTS

Amos 'n' Andy

INTRODUCTION

Sasha Torres

I.

What does race *look like* on television? Given the centrality of racial representation to television's representational practices, it is remarkable how little
attention this question has received from television scholars. One of the early
exceptions to this rule is J. Fred MacDonald's *Blacks and White TV*, first published in 1983, which argues that television reneged on its early promise to
"be almost color-blind," substituting this commitment with "persistent stereotyping, reluctance to develop or star black talent and exclusion of minorities
from the production side of the industry."[1] *Blacks and White TV* remains the
only book-length study to survey the presence of African Americans in and on
television throughout the medium's history. It provides a wealth of historical
information and correctly points to the necessity for minority representation
in the television industry. But its premises and conclusions now seem problematic in light of recent scholarship on race and representation. New work
on the national history of race relations and on the mass mediation of race
suggests that MacDonald's assumption that television *ever* sought to produce
"prejudice-free . . . popular entertainment" is at least overstated, particularly
if we take into account TV's pre–civil rights era origins, its virtually total sub-
mission to the interests of corporate capital, and its generic inheritances from

The Single Guy's Trudy and Sam

cinema and radio, themselves both heavily indebted to the legacy of min-strelsy.[2] MacDonald's faith in the "liberal" media notwithstanding, the fail-ures of liberalism with respect to the divides of race in America have by now been thoroughly documented.[3] Further, his emphasis on the stereotype divides "good" from "bad" programming too neatly and projects their social conse-quences too confidently.

In MacDonald's wake, as Herman Gray has pointed out, "critical studies of television have kept the matter of race at arm's length . . . consigning it to foot-notes and suggestions, acknowledging its thorny complexity all the while at-tending more directly to the way that the formal television apparatus operates to produce meanings, position subjects, narrate stories and organize logics."[4] Despite recent interventions—by Gray and others—that counter this trend, I believe that *Living Color*'s publication is a timely one, as the necessity of re-examining the field's scant attention to race becomes increasingly urgent.[5] The end of the century finds the U.S. in a moment of accelerating racial crisis that requires the sustained attention of every engaged intellectual. Even those of us suspicious of empiricist claims should be given pause by the overwhelming social-scientific evidence that race structures economic, political, and every-day life in this country in punitive and inhumane ways. In the realm of culture, these divergences are everywhere evident and nowhere as obvious these days as on television, which is increasingly dependent on racial difference to organize its images, narratives, and discursive flows. This nexus of race, representation, and television arises in a context in which people of color figure crucially in the calculus of audience measurement and in which "multiculturalism" is as much a visual as a political logic.

It is therefore far from coincidental that *all* of the definitionally televisual events of this decade—Anita Hill's intervention into the confirmation hearings

Little Rock

of Clarence Thomas, the video-fest accruing to the beating of Rodney King, O. J. Simpson's trials for murder — have involved, if not centered on, persons of color. And in its more quotidian modes, television is no less apt to deploy race in the most cynical possible ways in pursuit of its material and ideological goals. Consider the role of model minority Trudy (Ming-Na Wen), a regular character on *The Single Guy* and the only character of color to grace NBC's fantastically successful "Must-See" Thursday night sitcom lineup regularly during the 1995–96 season.[6] In four shows targeted to GenX-ers and set in a fantastic and virtually all-white Manhattan, Trudy's Asianness introduces the perfect amount of racial "spice." Hypercompetent and occasionally ruthless with dull white husband Sam, Trudy manages to evoke the tropes of the geisha girl and the dragon lady simultaneously.[7] In the process, she and her white cohort participate in the ideological repackaging of New York City and the invigoration of Manhattan's tourist and real estate markets.[8]

Obviously, the stakes are high in Gray's implicit call for a new television criticism that would displace the opposition between race and the televisual apparatus — indeed, that would theorize precisely the imbrications of the "thorny complexity" of race with the apparatus's capacity to "produce meanings, position subjects, narrate stories and organize logics." This call must be heeded if television scholars are to produce adequate accounts of *either* television *or* race. Certain historical facts here become relevant. At least since network news organizations covered the 1957 explosion over Orval Faubus's resistance to desegregation at Little Rock, the question of race has had determining effects on every major industrial shift, programming cycle, and reconceptualization of the audience undertaken by television in the United States.[9] Similarly, since this moment, every major struggle for racial justice in this country has had to confront the question of its televisual mediation, has had to appeal to, struggle against, perform for, and otherwise contend with television and its power to shape national policy, public opinion, and the politics of everyday life.[10]

II.

Each of the essays in this collection takes up Gray's challenge, investigating the intricate relation between the medium's most commonplace modes of making meaning and describing how television's seemingly boundless appetite for racial image and narrative is crucial to its capacity to signify at all. It is my hope that, taken together, the work in *Living Color: Race and Television in the United States* will resituate questions of race as central to the theoretical and political projects of television studies by demonstrating how, across genre, racial formation, and historical moment, race has been constitutive of TV's cultural work.

The essays are arranged in a rough chronology corresponding to the historical appearance of their central object of analysis. However, this arrangement should not be taken to imply a faith in a teleological "improvement" in TV's racial politics. Quite the contrary. The advantage of this arrangement is rather that the essays, individually and as a whole, work against such an evolutionary narrative. In addition, the juxtapositions that arise from this chronology spark internal dialogues within the collection, while its chronological gaps invite readers to undertake new work on the questions the book investigates.

The first two essays discuss some of television's early attempts to explore the implications of racial difference for both informational and entertainment programming. In "Entertaining 'Difference': Strains of Orientalism in Early Los Angeles Television," Mark Williams examines two of the shows aired on early Los Angeles television that featured musicians of color: *Harry Owens and His Royal Hawaiians* and *Musical Adventure with Korla Pandit*. Working from rare kinescopes of these programs, Williams reads their Orientalist tendencies, but also locates points of resistance to those tendencies, especially in *Musical Adventure*. Williams argues for the ideological complexity of early local television's racial representations, even as he insists that these programs participate in "a displacement . . . of race relations in Los Angeles during this period," by featuring South Asian and Pacific Island performers rather than African American or Latino ones. Williams's essay thus demonstrates how L.A. television's early constitution of locality necessarily both represented and effaced the social, political, and cultural differences present in its imagined community.

In the second essay, "Confronting 'the Indian Problem': Media Discourses of Race, Ethnicity, Nation, and Empire in 1950s America," Pamela Wilson chronicles the uses, during the 1950s, of print and broadcast media by Native Americans and their non-Indian supporters to fight the U.S. government's proposed withdrawal from "the Indian business." This policy, called "termination," would have had devastating effects on Indian culture by dissolving tribal structures and sending many into urban ghettos. Termination was effectively defeated by the public outcry following the broadcast of a 1958 NBC documentary about the issue called *The American Stranger*. Wilson's readings of this and other such programs, situated within a richly documented account of the struggles over "the Indian problem" in the 1950s, ably demonstrates how racial representation served as a sign, even before the heyday of television documentary in the 1960s, of the form's social utility and seriousness of purpose.

The third essay takes up the complex politics of African American televisual representation during the 1960s. Phillip Brian Harper's "Extra-Special Effects: Televisual Representation and the Claims of 'the Black Experience' " offers an important distinction between the two conflicting demands often placed on such representation by audiences and critics. On one hand, Harper notes the imperative toward "simulacral realism," representation that "would improve the objective conditions characterizing daily life for the mass of African Americans living within the scope of television's influence." On the other hand, Harper identifies the contradictory demand for "relevance" or "*mimetic* realism . . . whereby television would 'reflect' the social reality on which it was implicitly modeled." This analytic distinction between simulacral and mimetic realism undergirds Harper's reading of the anxieties produced by intraracial division—particularly class difference—that inform both critical assessments of black televisual performance in the 1960s and the structure of *Room 222*, which Harper discusses in detail.

The next two essays brings us to the 1980s (a gap that I hope will invite students of 1970s television and racial politics to enter the conversation). The first of this pair is Hamid Naficy's study of "Narrowcasting in Diaspora: Middle Eastern Television in Los Angeles." This essay theorizes the potential for television to soften the blows of everyday exilic or diasporic existence for Iranian immigrants to the U.S. Distinguishing between "diaspora television," which is "made in the host country by liminars and exiles as a response to and in tandem with their own transitional . . . status," and other kinds of "minority television," Naficy argues that diaspora television constitutes a new televisual genre that "helps the communities in diaspora negotiate between the two states of exile: the rule-bound structures of the home and host societies . . . and the formlessness of liminality. . . ." Naficy's work on diaspora television renders visible a number of crucial aspects and functions of ethnic programming. In the process, it pushes us to rethink the putative coherence of racial, ethnic, and religious identity, national origin, language, and address implied by the phrase "U.S. television."

The next essay is Jimmie L. Reeves's "Re-Covering Racism: Crack Mothers, Reaganism, and the Network News." Reeves demonstrates how race determined the shape of TV coverage of the "cocaine problem," shifting it from an early '80s "discourse of recovery," in which cocaine users are imagined to be middle-class white professionals, to a post-crack "discourse of discrimination," which demonized the so-called urban underclass and particularly the "crack mother." In addition to its usefulness as a reading of 1980s news texts, Reeves's analysis also reminds us of reportorial convention's vulnerability to the pressures of racial ideology.

Mimi White's " 'Reliving the Past Over and Over Again': Race, Gender, and Popular Memory in *Homefront* and *I'll Fly Away*" examines the intersections of racial representation with historical realism. White considers two dramatic series first aired in 1991 and set in the recent historical past. Both *Homefront,* with its rendering of the late 1940s, and *I'll Fly Away,* with its depiction of the early 1960s, situate racism and sexism centrally within their plot lines. And both, White argues, use "history" and historical drama as an "alibi" or "safety net," implying that "the problems they address in narrative terms, in particular regarding race and gender, were worse 'back then,'" even as they exploit the representational charge afforded by their graphic depictions *in the present* of racially and sexually motivated violence. With its careful assessment of how these programs deploy "an algebra of difference" — playing characters, political problems, and narrative developments off one another in a political zero-sum game — White's essay models the uses of close textual analysis to intervene in the mediated political rhetorics organizing the prime-time drama.

The next two essays deal with televisual texts produced around the beating of Rodney King. My essay, "King TV," interrogates the collision of race, historical event, and television's representational practices. In particular, I examine the role of "liveness" in a disparate set of texts that depict and renarrativize the beating of Rodney King and the uprisings following the Simi Valley verdict. I argue that the texts of "King TV" — the Halliday video, CNN's April 29, 1992, coverage of reactions to the verdict, and the 1992 season premiers of *L.A. Law* and *Doogie Howser, M.D.* — are crucially organized by what Jane Feuer has called "the ideology of liveness," the false promise of television's immediate access to and transmission of the real. More particularly, I argue that liveness, in news and fictional representations, serves to authorize a textual racism often energized by the heteronormative white masculinity that is U.S. television's stock in trade.

John Caldwell's "Televisual Politics: Negotiating Race in the L.A. Rebellion" examines the intersection of race with televisual "style" in the coverage of Rodney King's beating, the Simi Valley verdict, and the Los Angeles uprising. Caldwell attends to seldom scrutinized representational detritus — the digital graphics, framing devices, and pre- and postcommercial bumpers used by local and national news to process and reprocess images of the beating and the rebellion — as well as to more oft-analyzed genres like the sitcom and prime-time drama. In so doing, Caldwell argues that televisual style was deployed in the wake of the Simi Valley verdict as a form of ideological and visual "crisis management," that served to "manag[e] difference, build . . . consensus and stylistically packag[e] the dangerous other." Given the extent to which the Simi Valley verdict problematized the political value of close reading, bloodying it "by legal precedent," Caldwell's essay usefully cautions us not to "flee to more naïve conceptions of extratextual reality" by itself performing the efficacy of textual analysis.

José Esteban Muñoz's "Pedro Zamora's *Real World* of Counterpublicity: Performing an Ethics of the Self" also relies on close readings of the text of MTV's *The Real World,* but reads the collision of textuality with the "real" somewhat more optimistically than Caldwell's essay does. Muñoz situates HIV + AIDS activist Pedro Zamora's performances of his queer and Latino identities as producing a televisual counterpublic that contests and revises the racist and homophobic discourses of the majoritarian public sphere. In addition, Muñoz sees Zamora's counterpublicity as a strategy "that resist[s], . . . through performances that insist on local specificities and historicity, the pull of reductive multicultural pluralism." Throughout the essay, Muñoz makes strong claims for Zamora's agency, as a "cultural worker," in producing a televised performance that advances his progressive political agenda with respect to AIDS.

The final two essays take up some of the issues arising from O. J. Simpson's murder trial. Stephen Michael Best, in "Game Theory: Racial Embodiment and Media Crisis," situates the Simpson case in the context of other recent "scandals" involving African American celebrities, including Clarence Thomas, Michael Jackson, Michael Jordan, and Magic Johnson. Best elaborates the intimate connection between certain key televisual modes—liveness, flow, replay—and the insistent cultural representation of black masculinity in crisis. In the process, he brings various theories of the television apparatus into productive dialogue with important recent work on race, the body, and visuality.

The last essay in the collection reminds us of the often overlooked complexity of the racial politics of the Simpson case. Brian Locke's "Here Comes the Judge: The Dancing Itos and the Televisual Construction of the Enemy Asian Male" suggests that The Dancing Itos—who appeared frequently on NBC's *The Tonight Show with Jay Leno* during the Simpson trial—functioned as "nonracial" within what he calls "the black-and-white binary of contemporary racial discourse in the United States." It is only within this binary logic, he points out, that the outrageous racism of The Dancing Itos' version of Asianness could pass almost without comment. Locke's essay situates contemporary late-night television as a prime site in which the racialized conventions that govern media depictions of Asian and African Americans reinforce and undo each other. It also illuminates Leno's reliance on racial and racist discourse to produce formal and ideological coherence among *The Tonight Show*'s highly fragmented address.

III.

Having introduced each of the essays, I would like now to underscore some of the conceptual and political imperatives that have guided the processes of their selection. First, despite their diversity of objects, theoretical approaches, and practical methodologies, most of the essays in the collection attend centrally to television texts and, to a lesser extent, to their context in the political economy of the television industry. That is, they understand their objects to be primarily textual representation and its industrial conditions of possibility, and secondarily the reception of these texts by audiences.

Second, the collection as a whole tries to destabilize the black/white binary that so persistently structures racial discourse both in the United States and on U.S. television. Despite the fact that U.S. television generally underrepresents Native Americans, Asian Americans, and Latina/os, *Living Color* takes for granted that a study of racial representation on television must address tele-visual discourse about race as broadly as possible. The essays by Wilson and Muñoz, in particular, attend to some frame-breaking moments in TV history, moments in which Native Americans are represented outside the conventions of the Western, and Latinos exceed and confound racist and heteronormative assumptions about Latino masculinity. In addition, the articles by Williams, Caldwell, and Locke all work to theorize how and why different racial identity formations are balkanized and pitted against one another on television.

Third, the essays in *Living Color* consistently underscore the necessity of thinking race in relation to the other categories rending the social in the United States, especially gender, sexuality, and class; implicitly, they insist on the political and conceptual importance of keeping a number of analytic balls in the air at once. In particular, careful attention to the intersections of race and gender may be found in the essays by Williams, Reeves, White, and Best. The essays by Torres, Muñoz, and Locke focus on the imbrications of race and sexuality. And the essays by Harper and Reeves provide particularly useful analyses of class and its relation to race.

Fourth, *Living Color* sees race everywhere on television, refusing to limit its scope to particular televisual genres. The volume thus seeks to correct the field's tendency to undertheorize the effects of racial representation in forms other than the sitcom and the documentary. Naficy's focus on the generic complexity of diasporic television, Caldwell's attention to computer graphics, Muñoz's scrutiny of MTV's pseudo-documentary *The Real World* all help widen the field of vision in which race and television collide.

Finally, as I've already suggested, the essays take up a variety of positions on television's capacity to operate counterhegemonically in the interests of ag-grieved collectivities, underthought ideas, and progressive racial formations. In this respect, the articles in *Living Color* represent both sides of a split in tele-vision studies, a split Lynn Spigel and Michael Curtin have recently described in relation to the study of sixties programming: "While some critics might in-sist that the hegemonic processes of incorporation simply rob evolutionary movements of their political meaning, others . . . are more interested in how revolutionary impulses seem to stubbornly resist total incorporation and re-emerge in new ways in a continual pursuit to be heard."[11]

IV.

I have a number of people to thank for their intellectual comradeship during the preparation of this manuscript. In particular, Elizabeth Alexander,
Lauren Berlant, Amanda Berry, Stephen Michael Best, Julie D'Acci, Elizabeth Francis, Phillip Brian Harper, José Esteban Muñoz, and Sharon Willis
were adept sounding boards during the editorial process. In addition, the following persons and institutions afforded various kinds of crucial assistance:
Bryan Shepp and the Dean of Faculty's Office at Brown University provided
much-needed funds for research and editing; Brown's Department of Modern Culture and Media sustained this endeavor in many ways; the advisory
board for Console-ing Passions, especially Lynn Spigel and Lauren Rabino-
vitz, nurtured this project through its earliest stages; my editor, Ken Wissoker,
displayed remarkable stamina and forbearance; and the contributors were un-
failingly patient, good-humored, and thoughtful. Marianne Costa provided
crucial help with very little notice and did a masterful job, as usual. Chris Cagle
proved an excellent relief pitcher in the book's final innings. Last and most,
Chris Amirault provided a keen editorial eye, a rigorous understanding of the
shape and scope of the project, and indispensable moral support. This book
might have been finished without him, but it wouldn't be nearly as good.

Living Color: Race and Television in the United States is dedicated to the
memory of my grandparents — Dorothy Clarke, John J. Clarke, Bentina Torres,
and John Torres Sr. — whose relations to me and to each other inscribed both
the failures and the promises of race relations in the United States.

Notes

1 J. Fred MacDonald, *Blacks and White TV: African Americans in Television Since 1948*
(Chicago: Nelson Hall Publishers, 1983); I quote here from pp. 3 and xvii of the second edition, published in 1992.

2 To follow this thread, one might proceed from David Roediger's *The Wages of
Whiteness: Race and the Making of the American Working Class* (New York: Verso,
1991) and Eric Lott's *Love and Theft: Blackface Minstrelsy and the American Work-
ing Class* (New York: Oxford University Press, 1995) to Melvin Patrick Ely's *The
Adventures of Amos 'n' Andy: A Social History of an American Phenomenon* (New
York: Free Press, 1991).

3 See, for example, Michael Omi and Howard Winant, *Racial Formation in the United
States: From the 1960s to the 1990s*, 2d ed. (New York: Routledge, 1994).

4 Herman Gray, "The Endless Slide of Difference: Critical Television Studies, Television and the Question of Race," *Critical Studies in Mass Communication* 10, no. 2 (1993): 193.

5 Thankfully, the bibliography of work on race and television is growing. Relevant texts include Jannette L. Dates and William Barlow, eds., *Split Image: African Americans in the Mass Media* (Washington, DC: Howard University Press, 1990); Jacqueline Bobo and Ellen Seiter, "Black Feminism and Media Criticism: The Women of Brewster Place," *Screen* 32, no. 3 (1991): 286–302; Aniko Bodroghkozy, " 'Is This What You Mean by Color TV?': Race, Gender and Contested Meanings in NBC's *Julia,*" in *Private Screenings: Television and the Female Consumer,* ed. Lynn Spigel and Denise Mann (Minneapolis: University of Minnesota Press, 1992), 143–168; John Fiske, *Media Matters: Everyday Culture and Political Change* (Minneapolis: University of Minnesota Press, 1994); Darrell Y. Hamamoto, *Monitored Peril: Asian Americans and the Politics of TV Representation* (Minneapolis: University of Minnesota Press, 1994); Patricia A. Turner, *Ceramic Uncles and Celluloid Mammies: Black Images and Their Influences on Culture* (New York: Anchor Books, 1994); and Herman Gray, *Watching Race: Television and the Struggle for "Blackness"* (Minneapolis: University of Minnesota Press, 1995).

6 This lineup included *Friends, The Single Guy, Caroline in the City,* and *Seinfeld.*

7 To its credit, *The Single Guy* in its next season introduced an African American member of the ensemble (a dreadlocked law student), thus becoming the first of this elite group of NBC comedies to integrate fully and removing some of the representational burden from Trudy.

8 On the Manhattan real estate market, see Thomas M. Lueck, "Stirrings of Renewed Strength in Northeast," *New York Times,* 2 January 1996. A short package that aired in April 1996 on NBC's short-lived daytime magazine *Real Life* explicitly attributed the New York tourist industry's rebound to shows "like *Friends* and *Seinfeld,* which make New York seem like a nice place."

9 The Museum of Broadcast Communications in Chicago archives two programs on Little Rock that suggest the density and complexity of this coverage. See *The Mike Wallace Interview* with Faubus (ABC, 1957) and *The Clete Roberts Special Report,* "The Human Explosion" (KNXT-TV, Los Angeles, 26 September 1957).

10 For a discussion of how television factored into the strategies of the civil rights movement, see Mary Ann Watson, "The Chosen Instrument of the Revolution," in *The Expanding Vista: American Television in the Kennedy Years* (Durham, NC: Duke University Press, 1994), 90–111.

11 Lynn Spigel and Michael Curtin, introduction to *The Revolution Wasn't Televised: Sixties Television and Social Conflict,* ed. Lynn Spigel and Michael Curtin (New York: Routledge, 1997), 9.

ENTERTAINING "DIFFERENCE"

Strains of Orientalism in Early Los Angeles Television

Mark Williams

The historical study of the representation of racial difference in popular media can benefit greatly from an attention to specificity: specificity of medium, specificity of historical context, and specificity of representational practices. This paper examines the representation of "nonwhite" and non-American performers on local television, an aspect of early television history that has been largely ignored. Los Angeles was the most independent, distinct market in early television. Physically separated from the network formulations in the East, it was dominated by local unaffiliated stations for several years, especially before transcontinental microwave relay and coaxial cable "linked" the two coasts in late 1951, which allowed for "live" network programs and national advertising practices and rates. As a result, there was a certain flexibility in the barriers to entry for performers on early television in Los Angeles, including barriers to "nonwhite" performers. Los Angeles television therefore provides a unique site for researching early and local television practices, some of which proved to be among the less continuous practices of early television history.

Although Los Angeles has been and continues to grow more culturally diverse, the historical address toward and representation of this cultural diversity have been little discussed. This essay cannot presume to offer an exhaustive account of ethnic and racial representation in early Los Angeles television, since it is conditioned by the limited programming, archival resources, and documentation available regarding this early period. Demographic information for television ratings in this period is also scarce; one can only extrapolate the culturally diverse viewership within the Los Angeles audience from general census figures. What this paper will specifically address, within the industrial and regional contexts of the time, are the textual questions and potential viewing positions afforded by two rare, prevideotape examples of perhaps the most popular Los Angeles programs to feature "nonwhite" performers in this era: an episode each of *Harry Owens and His Royal Hawaiians* and *Musical Adventure with Korla Pandit*. These programs share similarities and present differences in their depictions of race and ethnicity, often in terms of mode of address and resultant viewer positions. Examined together, they delineate many of the issues surrounding the representation of social and racial "difference" in this period and suggest general parameters of such representation.

Central to the analysis of these programs is the concept of Orientalism, a somewhat amorphous but quite useful term that refers to the institutionalized tropes of representation that have been employed by the West in figuring and positing the East as a fetishized, mysterious Other. Rooted in colonialism and typically brimming with masculinist fantasy and dread, these practices of representation are generally charged with both explicit and implicit racial and sexual stereotypes. Edward Said posits a dichotomy between overt and inferential modes of racism, describing "manifest Orientalism" as "the various stated views about Oriental society" (the changes in the West's "knowledge" of the Orient) and "latent Orientalism" as "an almost unconscious (and certainly an untouchable) positivity."[1] These latent attributes are more or less constant: what remains intact are "the separateness of the Orient, its eccentricity, its backwardness, its silent indifference, its feminine penetrability, its supine malleability . . . the Orient as a locale requiring Western attention, reconstruction, even redemption. . . . Thus whatever good or bad values were imputed to the Orient appeared to be functions of some highly specialized Western interest in the Orient."[2]

Such an interest is readily apparent in the television programs discussed below, which each enact some of the premises and strategies of Orientalism, but in different registers (especially gendered registers) and with different results. The related and yet distinct modes of address of each show provide problematic opportunities for marginalized discourse to be articulated, yet only within paradigms of "entertainment" and "performance."

Harry Owens and His Royal Hawaiians

One of several early programs in Los Angeles to feature a dance band that had demonstrated a strong regional following, the Owens show is formally allied with traditions of musical variety, spectacle, and entertainment programming. Varied autonomous segments of musical performance (in radio and vaudeville formats) are addressed to both a surrogate studio audience and the home viewer, which lends the program a charge of "live" performance as well as a social sense of viewership. Paramount's Los Angeles television station KTLA specialized in such programs, which generally were telecast as remotes from either the venue at which the band regularly appeared or from a theater down the street from the station. These shows surveyed a variety of musical genres, all tailored toward the stylings and standards of big band "swing," itself characterized in some critical histories of music as an imitation and assimilation of African American music aimed toward a white and middle-class palate.[3] For example, Lawrence Welk, Ina Ray Hutton, and Spade Cooley all fronted swing orchestras on KTLA programs in the same era that Harry Owens did.

The Owens show, of course, primarily offered a survey of "Hawaiian" talent and culture, though it also included specialty numbers by several white members of the band. As is indicated by the kinescoped episode of the show (the final telecast of the 1951 season), the program's exoticism is securely "contained" by the discursive centrality of Owens as master of ceremonies and mediator to a foreign culture, a role and persona he had long cultivated.

Owens had established himself as a bandleader, composer, and radio and motion picture performer for many years prior to his television show debut on KTLA in 1949. Employed as a band member and a bandleader since the 1920s (he co-wrote the hit "Linger Awhile" in 1923), he was playing in Hollywood in the early 1930s when the visiting manager of the Royal Hawaiian Hotel invited Owens to organize the resort's house orchestra, which he did in 1934. Forming his orchestra from mostly Hawaiian musicians, he named it after the hotel, which identified where the band performed but also connoted a legacy of "true" Hawaiian patronage and identity. Owens began writing and adapting ballads based on traditional Hawaiian songs and soon became one of the chief proponents of Hawaiian music in the United States.[4] He eventually also worked in motion pictures, composing songs for films such as *Waikiki Wedding* (1937) and *Cocoanut Grove* (1938), the latter of which was one of several films in which he appeared.

Owens's wider notoriety was established by his association with perhaps the most important conduit for the popularization of Hawaiian music: the radio program *Hawaii Calls,* broadcast Saturdays before a live audience, often from the Moana Hotel. Webley E. Edwards, a car salesman who came to the islands in the 1920s, created the program in 1935 and selected Owens as musical director. (First broadcast to the West Coast via shortwave, the program ultimately grew to its apex of 750 stations worldwide in 1952.) Edwards had been displeased by the "jazzed-up" versions of Hawaiian music he heard in San Francisco nightclubs and suggested that his program offered more genuine island music, even though he insisted that several *hapa haole,* or English-language songs, be included on each program. Procuring the world's largest assortment of "island"-styled songs, including many by Owens but many more by Charles E. King ("Dean of Hawaiian Music") and Sonny Cunha disciple Johnny Noble (a specialist in *hapa haole*), Edwards encouraged a "spontaneous" performing style that was "rehearsed to sound unrehearsed" and regularly changed the musical personnel. He also sought institutional support to resolve the show's lack of sponsors, and in 1936 received the first of annual stipends from the Hawaiian government, which recognized the show's role in promoting tourism to the islands.[5]

Owens left the radio show in 1937 to tour with the Royal Hawaiians to New York and then to the Beverly Wilshire Hotel in 1938. Between scheduled engagements back on the islands, they continued to tour the mainland with some regularity until 1944. (Their return to Hawaii was often delayed or even curtailed after the U.S. entry into World War II.) Owens's recordings and performances consolidated his position as a principal source of Hawaiian music and introduced audiences to Hawaiian musicians and performers such as Hilo Hattie, Ray Kinney, and Eddie Bush while further popularizing *hapa haole* music in a big band sound that was rhythmic and danceable and that regularly featured a steel guitar glissando. After extensive tours during the war, he reorganized the band in 1947 and played primarily on the West Coast before his debut on Los Angeles television in October 1949.

One important context in which to understand the success of Owens's television show, therefore, is the familiarity of its performers and its nostalgic resonance for many ex-GIs and their families in the post-WWII Los Angeles audience. L.A. was, of course, a principal site for relocation for many servicemen who had passed through the area during tours of duty, one reason for its postwar growth into a suburban sprawl. Both in its evocation of Hawaii—

quite literally the U.S. base of Pacific operations and also of entertainment for the servicemen — and in the theatrical array of specialty acts it assembled, the Owens TV show registered a special appeal to this audience.[6] Local appropriations of and nostalgia for island culture were also indicated in the so-called tiki subculture that had existed since the 1930s and flourished in the postwar era. As detailed by Brian King and Stuart Swezey, suburban L.A. homes often featured bamboo, tiki torches, or other island iconography in dens, basements, and backyards, and several restaurants and bars adopted Hawaiian decor. At least some of the popularity for these appropriations is attributed to their "pagan" allure. This more lurid, Dionysian aspect of postwar Orientalism may be less apparent in the work of Owens than in the renderings of later "island" stylists such as Arthur Lyman and Martin Denny, though class and gender fantasies inflected by masculinist ideals remain central to the Orientalist discourse of this program.[7]

The vaudevillian presentational format of the Owens show confirms Said's concept of Orientalism, in which, as James Clifford suggests, "the Orient functions as a theater, a stage on which a performance is repeated, to be seen from a privileged standpoint. . . . For Said, the Orient is 'textualized': its multiple, divergent stories and existential predicaments are woven as a body of signs susceptible of virtuoso reading . . . occulted and fragile. . . ."[8]

From its very opening, the Owens show makes literal this notion of a "staged" access to the Orient, coded by the dissolves to breaking waves that serve as transition from the title card to the site of performance. Throughout the telecast, this dissolve serves to textually separate Owens and orchestra from the appearance of "native" (usually hula) performers on a second stage area, even though the actual distance from the main stage is only a few feet. The iconography of the waves appears to be an adaptation of a characteristic feature of the *Hawaii Calls* radio program, which featured "sounds of the surf accompanying Owens' music. The ocean's roar was considered so vital to the program's authenticity that one sound engineer was stationed at water's edge with a microphone."[9] On television, this practice instills an economical yet significantly visual means of suggesting an expansive performance space, but it also establishes a hierarchy of these spaces. When members of Owens's band step up to perform specialty numbers, no such visual transition is utilized. The "other" site of the adjacent stage becomes coded as alternately savage or feminine, but in any case Oriental.

Several of these numbers feature young women dancing the hula, and an-

A chorus of band members sings as transition begins. Mid-dissolve to hula dancer on other stage. The hula dancer.

other highlights a young man's daring choreography with a sword. Serving principally as eroticized spectacle, they seem to embody the "Native," one base image of colonialist literature as described by Stuart Hall. For Hall, the displays of the "rhythmic grace" of such performers "always contain both a nostalgia for an innocence lost forever to the civilized, and the threat of civilization being over-run or undermined by the recurrence of savagery, which is lurking just below the surface; or by an untutored sexuality, threatening to 'break out.' Both are aspects—the good and the bad sides—of *primitivism*."[10] These numbers function to evoke a potential for such brazen uncivility, and some latitude in the degree of "primitiveness" of these acts is allowed by the bracketed performative space and quasi-ethnographic tenor of the Owens show.

But they are ensconced within a consistent, familiar, and "familial" discursive register. Owens's friendly composure when addressing both his performers and the spokesperson for the show's sponsors conveys a genuine affection for his televisual "family." But the inferred family relationships become overdetermined to the point of fluidity. The orchestra's very name plays on the notion of a privileged lineage, and features Prince Kawohi, a male hula dancer who also sings a specialty song and who claimed literal relations to Hawaiian royalty.[11] Perhaps most important in this regard is the presence of Hilo Hattie, whom Owens had called the Hawaiian Sophie Tucker, and clearly the most privileged of the featured performers: she is the only female "native" to span the full space of the stage with Owens. A singer and a clown, Hattie's persona is grounded in having the countenance of a grandmother. She is respected and foregrounded, yet she is positioned as comically asexual in the context of the more eroticized hula dancers. (Her signature song, "When Hilo Hattie Does the Hilo Hop," ironically figures her as the ultimate siren.) Although she is clearly a maternal presence, Owens refers to Hattie during the program as his adopted daugh-

"Hilo Hattie Does the Hilo Hop"

ter, and later, in perhaps the most beautiful moment of the show, she sings a duet of "The Hawaiian Wedding Song" with Eddie Bush. Ultimately, the sense of "family" affection is even inclusive of all of KTLA: the culmination of this season-ending program is the presentation of an ornate and enormous bouquet for Owens, who waxes his appreciation for everyone at the station.

All of these relations are coordinated and centered around Owens himself. Regularly employing direct address to the audience(s), he possesses a comfortable combination of personal and discursive qualities that allows for an assured degree of mastery over the program's spatial and temporal flow. This aggregate quality is recognized in contemporary critical discourse as "whiteness," a category of ethnic and racial identity that appears to subsume all such categories at the same time that it denies itself as such a category.[12] His access to the phrases, language, and manners of Hawaii—which significantly extend this sense of mastery—complement his own performing talent, especially as a bandleader but also as an egalitarian part of an ensemble during certain numbers. In short, Owens is an unassuming but nevertheless ideal great white father, and the show is significantly framed by the performance of "Sweet Leilani," a song he wrote to commemorate the birth of his daughter (whose name is obviously drawn from the island culture) and his biggest hit as a songwriter, winning an Academy Award and selling some 26 million copies of records and sheet music.

Couched within a fatherly, panethnic, and humanist effacement of cultural "differences," yet relying on coded character "types" that Western culture has promulgated, the show's tone becomes imbued with a romanticism and nostalgia for an exotic idealization of Hawaii as transcendent paradise—in this context, as the ultimate suburban leisure experience and lifestyle—an idealization that the show's major sponsor, United Airlines, hoped to promote. As a result, the show can unashamedly foreground its economic agendas, both

Owens plays "Sweet Leilani"

within the commercials for United in which Owens participates (discussing his past and impending trips to the islands on the airline, and the comforts and accoutrements of the flights) and within the general patter between numbers; among the many phrases used to evoke the yearning for a paradise of the other, the one that recurs most often is that of "the trade winds."

There is a reciprocal aspect to the show's comfortable posturing, for it also functions as a romanticized commercial for the tourism that the Hawaiian economy was at this time increasingly reliant upon and, more important, for the efforts to finally achieve statehood.[13] Hearings concerning Hawaiian statehood had been in process since 1935 (virtually coterminous with the *Hawaii Calls* program) but were continually stalled by a perceived threat in the race and class structure of the islands. Comprised of a large "nonwhite" population, and especially characterized in the immediate postwar period by labor unrest that had led by the late 1940s to a restructuring of Hawaii's economic superstructure, the islands had become a hard sell for statehood in Congress.[14]

In contrast, the overall impression of the islands emphasized on the Owens show is that of a most calm and relaxing paradise, a "natural" site for business and pleasure, unaffected by the upheavals of the rest of the world. Such a representation of course effaces the historical intrusion and economic imperialism enacted by the West in Hawaii. Upon immigrating to the islands in the late 1880s, whites had systematically assumed political and economic power in Hawaii, importing foreign labor from other regions in the Pacific to fulfill the demand of Hawaii's expanding major industries, especially the sugar industry. The labor shortage during wwii had opened higher-wage positions to "nonwhites," though whites still comprised a majority of the upper economic classes; most Hawaiians occupied the lowest classes. Native Hawaiians therefore found themselves not only economically disadvantaged but also an increasingly smaller minority among a polyglot population of Asian, Pacific, and *haole* islanders. From this perspective, working to promote statehood can be positioned within larger, more imperialistic agendas that have given rise to significant movements of identity politics on the islands.[15]

The show furthermore ironically positions the West, personified by Owens, as the effective guarantor of indigenous Hawaiian culture. Owens is depicted as preserving, maintaining, and promoting the transient and endangered "primitive" (i.e., oral and performance-based) history and legacy of the islands.[16] In a baldly melodramatic example of such an impulse, Owens presents a scenario of benevolence in his recounting of the monies he will be able to personally deliver to "Little Blind Sammy," a leper on Molokai whose song, "Sunset of Kalaupapa," the band has recorded. At one level, this incident was genuinely altruistic: as described in his autobiography, Owens personally transcribed and paid to publish the song, performed and promoted it on the show, and collected and forwarded revenues to the leper colony.[17] At another level (compounded by the copious detailing of the incident in his book), the incident is self-serving in its promotion of Owens as ethnographic savior and economic Good Samaritan. More important, it crystallizes several of the agendas that the program's Orientalism serves, in romanticizing the islands (even a blind leper can appreciate its sunsets), suggesting the untapped resources that seem primed for Western "realization," displacing attention from the issues of the indigenous underclass in Hawaii, and coating all within a charitable light. Situating the indigenous culture as passive and innocent—in Said's terms, as feminine and penetrable in its "primitive" beauty and allure—the program positions Hawaii as an ideal and accommodating site for both personal (especially male) comfort, if not hedonism, and benevolent commercial exploitation.

Musical Adventure with Korla Pandit

Musical Adventure with Korla Pandit has a distinct relationship to the allure of Orientalism, but within a very different register of textual dynamics and mode of address. Korla Pandit was a surprise phenomenon of early Los Angeles television, prodigiously talented as a keyboard performer but also mysterious and exotic in his self-presentation. Always attired in a turban, Pandit was best known for his silent and intense direct address to the camera. In the various television programs on which he performed, over a period of several years for different TV stations and in syndicated filmed programs,[18] he allegedly never spoke.

Details about his career are somewhat spotty, and my information is based largely on conversations with Pandit and written sources of varied reliability.[19] Pandit was born in New Delhi to one of India's upper-caste families; his father was a government official and a scholar of English and history, a Hindi Brahmin who converted to Christianity; his mother was a coloratura soprano opera singer of French descent. Recognizing their son's musical abilities at a young age, they sent him to England for tutoring. He later moved to the U.S. and continued his education at the University of Chicago. Throughout this early period he appeared in occasional concerts. While attending college, he learned to play the organ (reportedly not a common instrument in India) and began experimenting with intricate tonal settings and performance styles previously unheard on the Hammond organ.

In the mid-1940s he came to Los Angeles and worked as a staff musician for local radio programmers as well as the NBC and Mutual radio networks, working in support of a wide spectrum of musical styles that included big band and country-western programs. (The Sons of the Pioneers nicknamed him "Cactus Pandit.") Especially in a nonvisual medium, Pandit's musical versatility lent itself to play with his ethnic and racial identification; one of his more regular assignments included providing musical accompaniment for two years on Mutual's *Chandu, the Magician,* on which he appeared as "Juan Rolando." [20]

Pandit drew the attention of local TV producers as television grew in the late 1940s. After performing at a benefit concert being televised locally by KTLA, he was approached by that station's manager and director of operations, Klaus Landsberg. As it happened, Pandit had already conceived the visual scheme and format for a television program featuring his talents. The local NBC affiliate had been courting him, offering wide exposure but only a provisional twelve-week series. KTLA offered a one-year contract for a show of his own, provided he perform background music for other of the station's shows; he would therefore receive more work and more money. (For example, his music was heard regularly on KTLA's *Time for Beany,* the nationally syndicated fifteen-minute puppet show created by Bob Clampett.)

On KTLA, Pandit established a considerable following for his fifteen-minute weekday evening shows and soon began an additional sixty-minute Sunday afternoon show—the first L.A. program to air in this weekend daypart. Soon expanded to two hours and staffed by only one technician (as opposed to the narrator, camera and lighting crew, etc., for the evening show), this program was also a surprise popular success. (Pandit recalls one station wag predicting, "Watch this turkey die.")²¹ As his legion of fans—reportedly mostly female—grew in number, Pandit recorded albums and began to perform publicly in concert. But even though his popularity became increasingly apparent, his television opportunities seemed to recede: when his contract at KTLA expired, he moved to ABC affiliate KECA-TV for about six months, and Los Angeles Times station KTTV for five months in 1952. This pattern was apparently related to problems in continuing sponsorship for his shows, a seemingly odd circumstance for a performer with such a notable following.²²

Indeed, the kinescope of *Musical Adventure with Korla Pandit* to be considered here—the only extant episode of the weekday evening KTLA program of which I am aware—contains no mention or sign of a sponsor, and will be assumed to be a sustaining program. Comprised of a sequence of musical numbers that vary in national/ethnic connotation and performance style (using different keyboard instruments and diverse percussive techniques), the show also features a voice-over narrator (Ken Graue), visual effects such as dissolves and overhead shots, and a guest appearance by singer Geraldine Garcia.

This program, often seen as campy, both demonstrates and makes problematic discursive and representational strategies revolving around questions of race, particularly in their resemblance to those found within the strategies of colonialism and imperialism. Pandit intended the show to be a celebration of music's capacity for panethnic/racial communication and pleasure and deliberately mixed and matched the sources and styles of music presented. Yet even though the show clearly provides opportunities for the representation and enunciation of culturally diverse images and discourses, privileging the abilities of a third-world performer, it also adheres to cultural stereotypes both in the representation of Pandit and in the dominant thematic tone that purveys the songs and narration. What's more, although the music represents one level of interplay of cultural voices, the only direct verbal discourse offered is the "framed" address of the disembodied station announcer's introductions and descriptions. Such an address can be seen to evoke a subtle subordination or sense of "effortless" superiority toward ethnic and racial difference: Pandit is "spoken for," and his expressions of culturally derived entertainment are described and contained within Western definitions of primitivism and exoticism.

Musical Adventure

In addition, the show is manifestly presentational: it seems to offer itself as a conduit to exotic culture in action, or at least performance. At the show's start, the voice-over presents an invitation to the viewer: "come with us through melody to the four corners of the earth. Hear music exotic and familiar spring from the amazing hands of Korla Pandit, on a musical adventure." The "adventure" promised in the show's title connotes what Hall identifies as the literature of imperialism, "the male-dominated world of imperial adventure, which takes *empire* . . . as its microcosm." [23] Adventure is one of the principal categories of this literature, for " 'Adventure' is one way in which we *encounter* race without having to *confront* the racism of the perspective in use. Another, even more complex one is 'entertainment' . . . which we watch because it is pleasurable." [24]

The Pandit show does not evidence the first of the base images of imperialist literature ("the familiar slave-figure"), since Pandit more nearly resembles the base image of the "Native" — especially the "good side" of this figure, "portrayed in a certain primitive nobility and simple dignity." [25] This aspect of the representation is further complicated by Pandit's attire: his natty Western suit, shirt, and tie would seem to indicate non-"primitive" connotations. But the presence of and visual emphasis on his turban and jewel — "native" and yet upper-class accoutrements — predominate.

The show and Pandit's representation seem most closely aligned with the base image of the "entertainer" or "clown," which, as Hall states, "captures the 'innate' humour, as well as the physical grace of the licensed entertainer — putting on a show for The Others. It is never quite clear whether we are laughing with or at this figure: admiring the physical and rhythmic grace, the open expressivity and emotionality of the 'entertainer,' or put off by the clown's stupidity." [26]

Pandit's presentation and performance do not, it seems to me, entail any qualities of stupidity. Such qualities might be imputed to certain acts in the Owens show, but Pandit's maintenance of his "native" nobility and dignity eclipses such a connotation. Nevertheless, the admiration of his musical abilities and simultaneous distancing afforded by the cultural otherness of his representation do involve us in an ambivalent position like the one Hall describes; even today, the show is received as entailing a complex allure of mysticism, camp, and genuine achievement of performance.[27]

The show's representation of Pandit insists on this ambivalence. On one hand, the figure of Pandit combines nobility and rhythmic grace. On the other, the show attempts to engage a kind of psychic "primitivism," corresponding to longings not foregrounded in "civilized" everyday life; the songs, we are told, convey states and emotions not constrained by rationality: taboo, envy, sweet melancholy, accelerated passion. The importance of such a charged appeal to the show's success was readily evident, as indicated in a 1951 cover story on Pandit in the local Los Angeles magazine *Television-Radio Life:* "We were determined to find out what was so different about him and why his appeal was mounting to such phenomenal heights. . . . The unique enchantment of his music is beyond words . . . as he explained, subtle, insistent basic rhythmic patterns appeal to men and women. They stimulate pleasant emotions which everyone likes to experience. We pondered a moment and then agreed with his explanation that the emotional appeal of his music was the secret of his popularity. The drum and the flute are supposed to have the strongest erotic influence, and Korla simulates both instruments on the electric organ."[28]

Pandit's access to "savagery" seems resolutely cultured—closer to Nature perhaps, yet hardly untutored or ill-mannered. Indeed, the connotation of "adventure" registered in the show's title seems more related to a travelogue than some charged exploration involving physical risks and thrills. The more passive and contemplative engagement of the program both allows for and is allowed by the less stridently threatening representation of Pandit. Nevertheless, the ultimate function of the show's depiction and evocation of race and ethnicity is allied to the functions of the adventure genre and Orientalism.

These aspects of latent Orientalism agree with what has already been suggested as a preferred "reading" of the discursive elements of the Pandit show. Pandit is silent, the (Western) voice-over describes and interprets the music, and the principle of inclusion for the music is some U.S.-derived connotation of foreignness or exoticism. From the Orient, to Western island culture, to Spanish and South American cultures, the songs that are featured in the show evidence loose national and ethnic boundaries. Even Pandit's androgyny can be seen as congruent with the more unconscious aspects of colonialism that Said defines as Orientalism.

But, as Homi Bhabha suggests, the security of such a privileged and seemingly static vantage point—even the stability of continually employed stereotypes—should not be assumed. Bhabha emphasizes the dynamism and repetition of Hall's ambivalences and Said's poles of racism, suggesting that stereotypes should be recognized as fetishes, "affixing the unfamiliar to something established, in a form repetitious, vacillating between delight and fear." [29] Ethnic and racial stereotypes are not the same as sexual fetishes, but "within the apparatus of colonial power, the discourses of sexuality and race relate in a process of *functional overdetermination*. . . ." [30] The stereotype, functioning as the primary point of subjectification in colonial discourse, "is the scene of a similar fantasy and defense" to that of the scene of sexual fetishism, "the desire for an originality which is again threatened by the differences of race, color, and culture." [31] The stereotype is an arrested, fixated form of representation, denying the play of difference and returning the colonial subject to "its identification of an ideal ego that is white and whole." [32] The stereotype functions, in other words, as part of the hegemonic process by which dominant, white subjectivity is continually reinscribed. As Bhabha points out, the shifting fixity and phantasmatic qualities of the stereotype generally exist to exercise dominant power relations by containing an arranged and manageable threat to them. Nevertheless, especially because fetishes of this type must be "seen" rather than hidden or made secret (a quality of many sexual fetishes), they participate in a "regime of visibility" deployed in colonialism. The visibility of the racial/colonial other is at once a point of identity and a problem for attempted closure within discourse: "The taking up of any one position, within a specific discursive form, in a particular historical conjuncture, is thus always problematic—the site of both fixity and fantasy. . . . The process by which the metaphoric 'masking' is inscribed on a lack which must then be concealed gives the stereotype both its fixity and its phantasmatic quality—the *same old* stories of the Negro's animality, the Coolie's inscrutability or the stupidity of the Irish *must* be told (compulsively) again and afresh, and are differently gratifying and terrifying every time." [33]

It is within this regime of visibility that the Pandit show becomes untraditional, and potentially less recuperable. Despite the discursive containment of his performance, and beyond the adherence of much of the program's format

Korla Pandit

to colonialism and Orientalism, the show disrupts one of the primary subjective tendencies of these discourses in its excessive employment of visual direct address. As Said points out, Orientalism has an important specular aspect: "Orientals were rarely seen or looked at; they were seen through, analyzed not as citizens, or even people, but as problems to be solved or confined or— as the colonial powers openly coveted their territory—taken over."[34] Clifford picks up on the voyeuristic implications of this colonialist regime when he notes, in reference to Said's study, that "The effect of domination in such spatial/temporal deployments (not limited, of course to Orientalism proper) is that they confer on the other a discrete identity, while also providing the knowing observer with a standpoint from which to see without being seen, to read without interruption."[35]

The visual framing device that opened all of the Pandit shows—the camera pulling back from the shimmering, blurred circles of dancing light on the jewel affixed to his turban, into a focused medium shot of Pandit, who stares in direct address throughout—evokes a desire to "see" that is met by the uninterrupted gaze of the other. The voyeuristic regime more typical of the representation of racial and ethnic difference is refused, and the privileged viewer position that usually allows for a reading or analysis of the other is frustrated. To be sure, the subject position offered by the direct address of an other is variable, depending on the degree of attention of the viewer, any variety of social factors impinging on the viewing, and the viewer's own subjective determinants. It is even possibly fully recuperable, read as merely the "inscrutability" of the other. But such viewer variability is not so easily managed here as it is in most depictions of stereotypes.

The specular arrangement of Pandit's opening confers on the other a discrete identity, but not one that can be "read" through and "known" as a stable recognition of the other. The disavowal of the fetish of the stereotyped other is not securely masked, and the underlying threat is not so immediately contained. As Bhabha points out, "in the objectification of the scopic drive there is always the threatened return of the look . . . in that form of substitution and fixation that is fetishism there is always the trace of loss, absence."[36] The direct address of Pandit in these sequences—heightened, I think, because he does not speak, and undisturbed by any other visual information in the shot, which is further aestheticized by the smooth trucking motion of the camera—forces a potential confrontation with the desire of an other. The "inscrutability" of this gaze is less recuperable because it plays on television's more traditional use of direct address to offer the impression of a subjective presence.[37] Pandit's direct address, which meets the erotic investment of the viewer's gaze instilled by the fetish of the jewel, compounds the regularized system of subjective crises that stereotypes usually disavow. The desire of the viewer's gaze, trained within the traditional regimes of colonialism, is confronted by a mirror of the racial, ethnic, gendered (androgynous) other—Is this gaze one of desire? identity? hypnotic control?—so that the viewer may recognize and experience difference without the closure ensured by positioning the other as fetishized object.

Whatever threat this direct address may entail is not maintained, however, and the renegotiation of Pandit's gaze takes on significantly gendered aspects within this episode of the program. In evidence of Bhabha's claim that the fetish of the stereotype is not identical with that of the sexual object, the image of Pandit as exotic other becomes specularly unhinged from that of Pandit as erotic other: his gaze becomes heterosexually ineffectual and therefore colonially regularized in terms of the representation of a woman. Within the context of a song entitled "Envy" (described by the announcer as "An emotion which is black, a mood that twists the spirit, that makes a lover suffer and wonder if love is worth the price"), the image of a woman (Geraldine Garcia) enters the frame, fragmented and hovering above Pandit like a thought balloon or an apparition. But rather than engage in the traditional heterosexual scopic regime anticipated by such an arrangement—the aggressive or even possessive gaze toward this gendered object of desire—Pandit's gaze becomes increasingly unfocused and undirected.

As Garcia sings the words to the song ("I envy anyone you happen to meet . . ."), the grounding of her discursive relation to Pandit—the positionality of the shifters "I" and "you"—is left nebulous and unestablished. It remains unclear to whom and about whom she is singing: Is she supposed to

Pandit and Garcia

be an acquaintance of Pandit? a memory? part of his consciousness? part of ours? Rather than partake in the gendered position offered by such a visual schema, Pandit's gaze is passionate but furtive, gazing at Garcia no more than he does at the audience or, perhaps more important, at an unfocused some- where which indicates his self-absorption within his own performance. When the prospect of a more gendered animalistic desire presents itself, Pandit's gaze—which introduces him to us in a potentially problematic way—refuses a metonymic schema of aggressive heterosexual address and is positioned in- stead as engaged within a more narcissistic object choice. We are presented with two fetishes, one sexual and one colonial, in a relationship that positions them as dual metaphors rather than in a metonymic exchange of desire. Such a recuperation of the potentially radical otherness of Pandit's opening gaze repositions the impact of his closing gaze at show's end, which enacts the ob- verse of its opening: slow truck in to Pandit's stoic, direct gaze, then unfocus on the jewel in his turban. The open-ended otherness of his gaze remains, but is inflected by his apparent narcissism. His relation to desire, and especially to primitive sexual aggressivity, is more securely contained.

Positions resistant to those that seem offered by the show are of course possible, and any real engagement of an Other's desire is not wholly recuper- able. Pandit's own intentions for his music and its effects are philosophical and humanistic, devoted to transcending "difference" via the universality of the ap- peal of music.[38] But the dynamics of the representation of Pandit's "otherness" are for the most part complicit with television's overall address toward race and gender construction and the general commercial consumption of television. The Pandit show, by offering a regularized access to the more exotic, primi- tive aspects of subjectivity not seen as readily accessible in everyday "civilized" life, codes these attractions within the more "primitive" cultures the show presumes to survey. At least in this episode, Pandit's potentially "threatening" allure as a "nonwhite" performer with a dedicated white female audience is conceivably mitigated.

In conclusion, let me reiterate that this analysis does not presume to be exhaustive or totalizing in its analysis of historical representations of race and ethnicity. Performers from a wide range of racial and ethnic groups appeared on Los Angeles television in this period, and I assume that I am not aware of all of them. Variety shows occasionally featured "guest" appearances by performers of color who were in town. At least one short-lived program was premised on featuring African American musical performers: *Adam's Alley,* hosted by Joe Adams, L.A.'s lone "Negro radio" deejay, premiered on KLAC channel 13 in September 1949 and featured many major artists in guest appearances as well as a choir performing spirituals and an occasional pop standard.[39]

A few other performers of color appeared with some regularity on local Los Angeles shows. Scatman Crothers, for example, played guitar and sang on KTLA's *Dixie Showboat* (a show that doubtless featured a regular display of racial and ethnic "types"), and on Larry Finley's *Sell-a-Thon* (a precursor to the *Home Shopping Network*). Iron Eyes Cody was a regular on Tim McCoy's Western program, which of course revolved around McCoy's old movies but reportedly also focused on American Indian culture and folklore in order to dispel the inaccuracies of their portrayal in many of the Western TV shows and films so popular at the time.[40] In a more anticipated and perhaps compromised vein, Leo Carillo, a veteran actor best known as the sidekick Pancho on the syndicated TV series *The Cisco Kid* but also a member of a famous and long-standing Southern California family, hosted a variety show on channel 13 in the early 1950s on which he would deliver a closing monologue directed to "Mom and Dad" that occasionally featured the vitriolic anticommunist discourse of the era.[41] At a more general level, William Stulla, best known as the host of *Engineer Bill,* a popular kids' show on independent station channel 9 after it became KHJ, related to me his shock and embarrassment at the racist imagery found in the old animated cartoons purchased to be telecast in those days.[42] As is true for so many aspects of early television study, access to print and especially program materials featuring these performers is at best limited and partial.

Furthermore, this analysis precludes neither oppositional readings nor the potential in these shows for empowerment to suppressed or repressed social voices — these performers *are* represented, after all. George Lipsitz points out, for example, that early television did, in some instances, actually contribute to the cultural pluralism of postwar Los Angeles, particularly in sports and music programs, such as the one hosted by deejay Johnny Otis.[43] My intention is to point out the essentially "safe" positioning of these alternative discourses, as represented by the two programs considered in this paper.

Above all, these shows are indicative of a displacement in the local representation of the demographics of race relations in Los Angeles during this period. In 1950, with an area population of some 4.6 million people, the "nonwhite" population numbered about 580,000. Over 300,000 of these were Hispanics, and over 200,000 were blacks. Those remaining made up little more than 1 percent of the total population, and the vast majority of these were of Japanese (rather than Hawaiian or East Indian) descent. Hispanics and blacks, the most numerous of non-Anglo groups in the city, were seen sparingly on television at this time. This corresponded in a casual, effortless way to the housing and real estate restrictions so prevalent in the burgeoning L.A. County and metropolitan areas.[44] The two programs discussed in this essay, which to my knowledge were L.A.'s most prominent and enduring shows to feature "nonwhite" performers in this era, help to demonstrate that if Los Angeles television history is itself marginalized within the larger discourse of media history, in matters of race and ethnicity L.A. was as Anglo-centered, that is to say was itself as "marginalizing," as any region in the country.

Finally, it should be noted that the regional issues raised here are determined more by the social and industrial history of Los Angeles than by a regionally specific discursive or linguistic function. Pandit was in Los Angeles as part of the network radio talent concentration of this period; Owens was an L.A. regular because of both the city's proximity to Hawaii and its plentiful postwar live-music audiences. Nevertheless, I would suggest that the regularly scheduled representation of racial minorities on these shows, as well as their still surprising qualities of address and so forth, were related to or at least "allowed" by their displacement away from national network practices.[45] My analysis is an attempt to introduce both the range of questions and the complications inherent in work in these previously underrecognized areas of this history.

Notes

1 Edward W. Said, *Orientalism* (New York: Vintage Books, 1978), 206.

2 Ibid.

3 See LeRoi Jones, *Blues People* (New York: William Morrow, 1963).

4 This history is detailed in Owens's congenial (at times quasi-spiritual) autobiography, *Sweet Leilani: The Story behind the Song* (Pacific Palisades: Hula House, 1970). His orchestra is not to be confused with the long-standing military band known as the Royal Hawaiian Band; see David W. Bandy, "Bandmaster Henry Berger and the Royal Hawaiian Band," *Hawaiian Journal of History* 24 (1990): 69–90.

5 George S. Kanahele, ed., *Hawaiian Music and Musicians: An Illustrated History* (Honolulu: University Press of Hawaii, 1979), 109–114. This book has a deserved reputation for excellence as a reference text. For an overview of the rise to popularity of Hawaiian music on the mainland, see Gene Santoro's "Lilt," *Atlantic Monthly* 274, no. 5 (November 1994): 128–132.

6 For an extensive overview of the u.s.o. entertainment provided during the war, and its potential conditioning of the serviceman audience for postwar television variety/vaudeville formats, see Teresa D. Tynes, "A Theater Worth Fighting For: The Stage and American Democracy in World War II" Ph.D. diss. (forthcoming), Department of American Civilization, University of Texas.

7 See "AMOK," in *Incredibly Strange Music, Volume I*, ed. V. Vale and Andrea Juno (San Francisco: Re/Search Publications, 1993), 164–187. This interview also contains information on Korla Pandit, though some of the dates and details of his career are inaccurate.

8 James Clifford, "Introduction: Partial Truths," in *Writing Culture*, ed. James Clifford and George E. Marcus (Berkeley: University of California Press, 1986), 12.

9 Burt A. Folkart, "Harry Owens of 'Hawaii Calls' Dies at 84," *Los Angeles Times*, 13 December 1986.

10 Stuart Hall, "The Whites of Their Eyes," in *The Media Reader*, ed. Manuel Alvarado and John O. Thompson (London: British Film Institute, 1990), 7–23.

11 "How 'Royal' Are the Hawaiians?" *Television-Radio Life*, 9 January 1953.

12 See Richard Dyer, "White," *Screen* 29, no. 4 (autumn 1988): 44–64, and Robert Young, *White Mythologies: Writing History and the West* (New York: Routledge, 1990).

13 Indeed, Owens noted that the Royal Hawaiian Hotel had been a key player in the movement toward Hawaiian statehood, and Owens himself was commended by the Legislature of the Territory of Hawaii for his efforts on behalf of Hawaiian statehood in March 1959. See Owens, *Sweet Leilani*.

14 For an overview of the process toward statehood, see Roger Bell, *Last among Equals: Hawaiian Statehood and American Politics* (Honolulu: University of Hawaii

Press, 1984), especially chap. 5, "Issues Confused, 1946–1950: Civil Rights, Party Politics, and Communism," 120–179. Much of the congressional resistance to statehood was from the South, which saw Hawaii as threatening not only because of its racial composition (arguing that such a "mixed" population could not be assimilated into "American" society), but because Hawaii would probably supplement the challenge to the South's segregation laws, which were under contention in the postwar Congress. Nevertheless, resistance to Hawaiian statehood rooted in racial intolerance was not restricted to the South. Another site of resistance was anticommunist rhetoric, such as that of Nebraska's Republican senator Hugh Butler, who feared Hawaii's closeness to Asia but especially the strength of its chapter of the International Longshoremen's and Warehousemen's Union. See Justus F. Paul, "The Power of Seniority: Senator Hugh Butler and Statehood for Hawaii," *Hawaiian Journal of History* 9 (1975): 140–147.

15   Notable among revisionist histories of Hawaii is Theon Wright's *The Disenchanted Isles* (New York: Dial Press, 1972). For a polemical introduction to native Hawaiian identity politics, see Poka Laenui, "The Rediscovery of Hawaiian Sovereignty," *American Indian Culture and Research Journal* 17, no. 1 (1993): 79–101.

16   An exemplary study of the issues related to Hawaiian history and culture(s) in the wake of Western contact and domination is Elizabeth Buck's *Paradise Remade: The Politics of Culture and History in Hawai'i* (Philadelphia: Temple University Press, 1993). My thanks to Janet Francendese for recommending this source to me.

17   Owens, 237–249. Included are script excerpts from the programs on which the song was introduced and press clippings about the song's success.

18   Pandit appeared with some regularity on local Los Angeles stations KTLA (Paramount, channel 5) from 1949 to 1951, KECA (ABC, channel 7) in 1951, and KTTV (*Los Angeles Times,* channel 11) in 1952. He made several short performance films known as "telescriptions" for Lou Snader in 1951, which played in syndication for many years and reportedly induced great fan mail response. Although he never spoke on his television shows, he did sometimes speak when on radio and often granted interviews with print journalists.

19   These sources include an essay in a fan magazine: Leo Gavallete, "The Mysterious Korla Pandit," *Videosonic Arts,* no. 2 (n.d.): 10–16. After a career overview, including excerpts from an alleged interview with Pandit, the article discusses Pandit's experiences with "the science of induction," which Pandit denied was a brand of hypnosis. The most detailed biographical and career information available is the long interview that appears in *Incredibly Strange Music, Volume I,* 112–121, though many names and broadcast stations are misidentified. I should also mention that one individual I talked to during my research questioned Pandit's background and

even his ethnicity. But this was the least corroborated perspective on Pandit, and in any case demonstrates one aspect of the "ambivalence" projected onto his representation.

20   "Men of Music," *Radio-Television Life*, 21 November 1948, 37.

21   *KTLA 40th Anniversary Special* (1987).

22   Ted Hilgenstuhler, "What Happened to Korla Pandit?" *Television-Radio Life*, 6 March 1953, 36, 39.

23   Hall, 15.

24   Ibid., 17.

25   Ibid.

26   Ibid., 16.

27   A June 1987 Pandit concert that I attended at the Park Plaza Hotel in downtown Los Angeles (sponsored by the AMOK bookstore in Silver Lake, mentioned above and known nationally for their catalogue of the bizarre) brought together a genuinely eclectic audience: a variety of New Age followers, Melrose hipsters, many older fans, and the occasional early television historian. Pandit also accompanies silent films at special screenings in Southern California and performed at the 1993 Console-ing Passions Conference in Los Angeles. He also appears in the Tim Burton bio-pic *Ed Wood* (1993) as the musical performer at a wrap party.

28   Mildred Ross, "What Makes Korla Click?" *Television-Radio Life*, 6 April 1951, 39.

29   Homi K. Bhabha, "The Other Question . . . ," *Screen* 24, no. 6 (November–December 1983): 25.

30   Ibid., 26.

31   Ibid., 27.

32   Ibid., 28.

33   Ibid., 29.

34   Said, 207.

35   Clifford, 12.

36   Bhabha, 33.

37   See Margaret Morse, "Talk, Talk, Talk," *Screen* 26, no. 2 (March–April 1985): 2–15.

38   In Pandit's own words, a metaphysics of music, TV, and spirituality is indicated:

> What I'm trying to communicate through music is true love and the divine consciousness (regardless of religious belief—*that* doesn't matter). TV isn't real, it's just light, and in my programs I was expressing love through *sound and light vibrations*—actually, that's what *we* are. We reflect light, and that's what determines what color we are. . . .
>
> The key to my television programs was: I was able to project this music into the hearts of listeners. I concentrated on playing music of transcendence—that

was the whole basis of my programs on TV, recordings, and live performances. It didn't matter whether I was playing rock, jazz or classical—I captured the true feeling of what that song was supposed to do. (Vale and Juno, 113, 119)

39   Charles Emge, "Coast Station Launches First All-Negro TV Show," *Down Beat,* 7 October 1949, 9. I am grateful to Rick Wojcik for recommending this source to me.

40   See Jane Pelgram, "A Colonel Calls the General Wrong!" *Television-Radio Life,* 16 November 1951, 35.

41   Rudy Behlmer, interview with author, 9 November 1990.

42   William Stulla, interview with author, 26 October 1989.

43   George Lipsitz, "From Chester Himes to Nursery Rhymes: Local Television and the Politics of Cultural Space in Postwar Los Angeles," unpublished paper, n.d. See also Johnny Otis's recent book, *Upside Your Head! Rhythm and Blues on Central Avenue* (Hanover: Wesleyan University Press, 1993), for an anecdotal survey of the music scene in postwar L.A.

44   For details of these restrictions and their impact, see Mike Davis, *City of Quartz* (New York: Verso, 1990), especially chap. 3.

45   Both shows did have some wider exposure, Pandit via the Snader telescriptions and Owens on a Western states CBS mininetwork, but neither could be said to have achieved success on TV at a "national" level.

CONFRONTING "THE INDIAN PROBLEM"

Media Discourses of Race, Ethnicity, Nation, and

Empire in 1950s America

Pamela Wilson

Journalistic media discourses about American Indians in the decades following World War II depicted a crucial turning point in the relationship between the U.S. government and indigenous American peoples. Newspaper articles and television reports of this period marked both a growing politicization among the American Indian population and an increasing reflectiveness among non-Indian Americans about their responsibilities to America's tribal population. This dual politicization — of tribal peoples and of the mainstream "public" — reflected an increasing awareness by Native Americans about how to use the "master's tools" to counter white political hegemony and work toward autonomy and self-determination. Two of the most powerful tools Native Americans and their non-Indian allies appropriated during this period were the American legal system, through which they fought for treaty-based tribal justice on legal grounds, and the mainstream journalistic media, through which they fought for changes in public policy and increased cultural understanding. This essay examines some of the representational practices of the American mass media of the 1950s, particularly the new medium of nonfiction television, as attempts to articulate the cultural politics of what today might be considered "Native America" and its relationship to the cultural, political, and economic hegemony of American society.[1]

Specifically, I am interested in the discursive construction of "Indianness" in the 1950s, within the context of both the prevalent global political climate and the domestic civil rights struggle. Recent trends in cultural analysis have indicated the need to reconceptualize our critical examination of dominant media representations of "the Other" by exploring how such images serve various interests in larger cultural and political economies. Media stories during the 1950s frequently problematized the construction of *American Indian* as a sociopolitical category and situated the cultural politics of American Indian tribes and peoples in the context of broader issues of race, ethnicity, nationalism, and empire. These media discourses exhibited a profound ambivalence about race: on the one hand, popular classification of Native Americans as "red" placed them outside the "black" versus "white" struggle, but on the other hand, their positioning as nonwhites allied them with other nonwhites against a common oppressive and colonial regime. For these reasons, the relation of Native Americans to issues of race was ambiguous and constantly shifting.

I would like to address a few of the critical challenges of historical cultural analysis, which involves reading the past through the visions of contemporary critical interventions. Historians must filter, order, and interpret myriad data; traditionally, this has been done through the construction of a narrative that structures events based upon historiographical conventions such as chronological sequence and the assumption of a single historical truth. In contrast, the contemporary intervention of critical cultural analysis into the historiographical process has resulted in new ways of processing the information or "evidence" gathered from historical materials. In this process, historians strive not to automatically reduce the events of the past to a single truth narrative, but to explore both the multiple and contested knowledges that reflect competing and conflicted political, cultural, and socioeconomic interests and how those knowledges are used in relations of power and structures of social difference.

This concern with *difference* leads poststructuralist historians to seek sources that expose different ways of knowing, different perceptions of truth, and the way these differences become contested issues. In an attempt to redefine historiography, feminist historian Joan Wallach Scott has written: "The story . . . is no longer about the things that have happened . . . and how [people] have reacted to them; instead, [history] is about how the subjective and collective meanings of . . . categories of identity have been constructed."[2] Scott also defines politics as the process by which power and knowledge constitute identity and experience, which are discursively organized in particular contexts or configurations. Recent cultural critics have noted that racial or ethnic "difference" in American culture, though traditionally constructed as extra-normative, must be understood as a constitutive element of white America's national identity. This is particularly relevant in the case of indigenous American peoples, whose presence both historically and in the American mythic imagination has shaped America's national master narrative.[3] Here, I use the case study of Native American politics and the media in the 1950s as a basis for interrogating some of these theoretical and historiographical challenges—in particular, the contested construction of categories of identity. An examination of the issues that crystallized around the production and reception of nonfictional media representations of indigenous Americans can provide contemporary scholars of media and culture with new insights into the media's role in the social construction of "difference," variously articulated in terms of race, ethnicity, nationhood, class, and gender.

At midcentury, white America was still plagued by the recurring "Indian problem": how to understand "them," what to do with "them," how to justify or recompense for past treatment of "them," and how to conceptualize "them" economically, politically, socially, and culturally. The years following World War II saw an increasing public awareness of the problems engendered by the "special" (i.e., colonial) relationship between American Indians and the American nation. As the nation's primary internally colonized cultural group, Indians were acknowledged to occupy a status historically distinct from other racial and ethnic minorities. The ambivalent and contradictory frames of both perception and action toward American Indians were rooted in the multiple differences that "Indianness" presented to white America: differences rooted in race, in culture, in tenacious resistance to assimilation at both corporate/tribal levels and individual ones, and especially in the ongoing problem of dual citizenship (i.e., how indigenous governments or nations could coexist within the structure of local, state, and federal governing bodies). The construction and intersection of many of these axes of sociopolitical difference can best be understood within a framework of imperialism.

The persistent "Indian problem" has been rooted in multiple and complex ideological differences between colonizing and colonized cultures, at the center of which is land ownership. "Land," Ward Churchill has written, "is the absolutely essential issue defining viable conceptions of Native America," noting that "contests for control of territory . . . underlie the virtually uninterrupted (and ongoing) pattern of genocide suffered by American Indians. . . ."[4]

Many whites considered communal tribalism, particularly the joint owner-ship of land and tribal assertions of sovereignty, to be antithetical to America's ideological principles of private property and individual ownership—and, during the cold war, to be potentially communist. The dominant white argu-ment that, to become citizens, Indians needed to assimilate by forswearing their tribal rights was institutionalized in nineteenth-century policies reward-ing individual land ownership with U.S. citizenship. Thus, the official solution to the "Indian problem" was based for nearly a century upon a proposition of assimilation; all federal policies and practices were directed to that end.

The postwar decades were a period of increasing dissatisfaction (on both sides) with the colonial relationship between the U.S. government and Native America. All parties acknowledged, in particular, the shortfalls of the cum-bersome colonial administration (the Bureau of Indian Affairs, an arm of the U.S. Department of the Interior), which was frequently considered one of the most inept and ineffective of federal bureaucracies. At the same time, both liberals and conservatives increasingly pressured Congress to dismantle this deteriorating federal system. A growing sense of white guilt on the Left over both the historical practices of brutal imperialism and the disgraceful present-day socioeconomic conditions on many Indian reservations intersected with economic pressures on the Right to "get the United States out of the Indian business." Finally, non-Indian corporations in the West (and their conservative political allies) strongly pressured Congress to grant them access to the lucra-tive Indian land and natural resources held in federal trust. Despite this wide-spread dissatisfaction with an existing system that adequately served neither the government nor tribal peoples, there were sharply divergent views as to what should replace the century-old colonial structures to which both sides had become accustomed.

Although many Indians considered the federal trusteeship system to be paternalistic, they realized the system minimally provided them with a de-lineated land base that they could occupy, if not necessarily manage. Liberal non-Indians were extremely ambivalent about how to end the corrupt colonial administration as well as the substandard status of American Indians. Conser-vatives, building upon a century of assimilation effort, now called for *termi-nation* or federal withdrawal—that is, full and immediate assimilation of indi-vidual American Indians through the legal removal of institutionalized rights, privileges, and federal services, the dissolution of federally recognized tribal structures, and the liquidation of tribal land holdings.[5] In 1953, Congress passed the major legislative action toward termination, House Concurrent Resolution 108. The bill called for the "freeing" of Indians from federal supervision and control, the text of the resolution framing the legislation as if serving the interests of the Indians rather than those of the federal government: "It is the policy of Congress, as rapidly as possible, to make the Indians within the territorial limits of the United States subject to the same laws and entitled to the same privileges and responsibilities as are applicable to other citizens of the United States, to end their status as wards of the United States, and to grant them all of the rights and prerogatives pertaining to American citizenship . . . [to] assume their full responsibilities as American citizens." The terms of HCR 108 included removal of federal administrative supervision over certain tribes in California, Florida, New York, and Texas, as well as the termination of the Flathead Tribe of Montana, the Klamaths of Oregon, the Menominee of Wisconsin, the Potawatomi of Kansas and Nebraska, and the Turtle Mountain Chippewas of North Dakota. (The Klamath and Menominee were considered two "of the most economically and socially advanced Indian tribes in the country," each with timber assets worth many millions of dollars.) BIA Commissioner Glenn Emmons defensively noted that "there is nothing here to suggest that Congress is engaged, as some have contended, in a massive drive to break up the tribal estates and destroy the foundations of Indian tribal life." Yet historian Donald Fixico claims that "anger at . . . H.C.R. 108 was prevalent throughout Indian country." There was little to no media coverage of the quiet passage of this measure.[6]

Various rhetorical strategies shaped the termination debate. Many conservative white politicians cast the termination issue in terms of *liberation*, framing termination as a way to more fully incorporate individual Indians into the American democratic system. The leading proponent of termination in Congress was Republican Senator Arthur V. Watkins of Utah, who used a rhetoric of democracy and liberation to justify the legislation, appealing to "ideal or universal truth[s]" of freedom: "[We] endorse the principle that 'as rapidly as possible' we should end the status of Indians as wards of the government and grant them all of the rights and prerogatives pertaining to American citizenship. With the aim of 'equality before the law' in mind our course should rightly be no other. . . . Following in the footsteps of the Emancipation Proclamation of ninety-four years ago, I see the following words emblazoned in letters of fire above the heads of the Indians — THESE PEOPLE SHALL BE FREE!"[7] After releasing American Indian tribes and individuals from their "disabilities and limitations," the congressional resolution would eliminate all BIA branch offices and personnel in targeted areas.[8] Concurrently, the BIA implemented its controversial relocation program, which "assisted" individual Indians with one-way transportation incentives to relocate from the reservations to urban areas—a federal assimilationist move to break up and disperse Native American communities and incorporate individual Indians into the urban workforce, regardless of the estrangement from community and family that resulted from such a diaspora.

In response to this cultural and political threat, a confederation of tribal peoples was in the process of joining together to construct a political and cultural body that today is often called "Native America": a consolidation of more than 500 distinct tribal groups unified for political purposes to counter the forces of white capitalist hegemony. Stephen Cornell points out that the agenda of Native America was, first and foremost, tribal survival and the maintenance of distinct cultural and political autonomy in the face of political and cultural imperialism.[9] The efforts of intertribal regional groups and national pro-Indian interest groups to gain an "Indian" voice in the mainstream media enabled this nascent Native American nationalism.

The major pro-Indian interest groups of the 1950s were the National Congress of American Indians (NCAI), the Association on American Indian Affairs (AAIA), and the Indian Rights Association (IRA). Usually working in cooperation with tribal peoples, the latter two organizations were both run primarily by liberal white lawyers and anthropologists who considered themselves "friends of the Indians" rather than agents of cultural or religious hegemony. These groups also collaborated with the NCAI, which was the only nationwide organization whose tribal-affiliated membership was limited to American Indians, and which represented Native America as a national body of associated tribes. Through their public relations divisions and their national networks of members who provided contributions, political letter writing, and local community activism, pro-Indian interest groups contributed a great deal to shaping and defining the media discourses about American Indian politics in the early 1950s.[10]

The mass media, particularly local newspapers and the new medium of television, played a crucial role in shaping the terms of the termination conflict as legitimate political debate and informing the non-Indian public about previously little-known local and regional issues. However, even at their most progressive, dominant media representations of the 1950s offered an ideologically contradictory portrayal of American Indian issues—a conjuncture of discourses that tell us as much or more about the cultural anxieties of a white, masculinist, bourgeois colonial culture nearing the end of its comfortable regime than about Native American life. Yet, these representations also provide us with insights into the confluence of counterhegemonic forces that were working to deepen cracks in the dominant regime, particularly with regard to strategies for gaining increments of control over media representations.

One of the most important ramifications of media representation during this era was the breakthrough of Native voices onto America's television screens, with increasing opportunities for Native American tribes and organizations to present their cases directly to the American public. The ability to use persuasive media messages to increase public awareness had the potential to shape public policy on Indian affairs issues. Tribal leaders' incipient awareness of television's power to garner the support of the American people — culminating in the controversy and public policy debates following the 1958 broadcast of the NBC documentary *The American Stranger* — laid the groundwork for media events staged by the next generation of Native Americans. Both the acquisition of access to and the experience of manipulating the media of the late 1950s set powerful precedents for the young American Indian activists who occupied Alcatraz in 1969, expropriated the BIA headquarters (the "Trail of Broken Treaties") in 1972, and seized Wounded Knee in 1973, all strategies that made optimum use of the glaring floodlights of television news cameras.

Prior to the congressional passage of HCR 108 in 1953, national media coverage of issues relating to the crisis in Indian Affairs was scant.[11] What little attention was given to the changing tide in federal attitudes and policies regarding Indian status resulted from campaigns by pro-Indian groups and influential individuals to get these issues out from the ghettoized corridors of Congress and the BIA and into the public arena. Until the late 1950s, most of non-Indian America was unaware that a battle was brewing on the reservations and in the House and Senate chambers regarding the future of American Indian tribes. At this time, the primary images of "Indianness" among most non-Indian Americans were provided by the myths writ large by Hollywood Westerns: the dual nineteenth-century romanticized and masculinist stereotypes of Indians as either noble relics of a vanishing race or as savage warriors. In fact, the popularity of the Hollywood-produced Western genre was at its height in the mid-fifties, when the cowboy-and-Indian dramas dominated the television screen and the entertainment ratings. In contrast, the infrequent nonfiction media reports on tribes in the early 1950s were concerned with such modern issues as land claims and federal government pressures to abandon traditional lifestyles and assimilate into mainstream American society; these reports presented a jolting cognitive dissonance. As Vine Deloria Jr. comments, it was difficult for most non-Indian Americans "to connect the[se multiple] perceptions of Indians in any single and comprehensible reality." As a result, interest groups such as the AAIA and the NCAI sought to intervene in prevalent media images of Indians, acknowledging and critiquing the powerful influence of Hollywood representations on the national imagination.[12]

Much of the rhetoric of the very early media coverage of the impending termination policies minimized the potentially disruptive impact of termination on Native culture and naturalized federal withdrawal from Indian Affairs as an "inevitable" stage in the "maturation" and "development" of American Indians in modernity. A tone of ambivalence and resignation about the seemingly predestined course of history was common during this period. Yet the early media stories exhibited a confusion among non-Indians about how to conceptualize Native America as a political and social category, and usually constructed American Indians as *individuals* "between two worlds" — portraying "the Indian" as an individual social subject requiring protection or needing to take responsibility for "him"self. At this point, the question became one of *when* and *how,* rather than *if,* termination and assimilation would take place. The concern expressed by many non-Indians over the "incompetency" of Indians to handle their own business affairs served as a justification for continued paternalistic imperialism.

The first wave of termination-related media coverage swept the nation's newspapers in the fall of 1953 with a wire service editorial, carried by newspapers across the nation, that opened, "It is the apparent intention of the administration in Washington to put the American Indian on his own, and stop baby-sitting for the 400,000 members of the various tribes." Incensed by this infantilization of tribal peoples, the AAIA jumped to counter these editorials by blanketing newspapers nationwide with its own series of press releases that charged Congress with producing "a crisis more acute than any that has faced the Indian in our time." This first major antitermination public relations campaign stirred up public opinion and established relationships with sympathetic media contacts, adding fuel to the efforts of pro-Indian groups to use the media as a tool to gain public support.[13]

Prior to this time, very few newspapers had covered the *tribal* response to the proposed federal policy changes, in spite of mounting Indian opposition. (An AAIA poll of tribal councils showed that most roundly rejected proposed federal withdrawal.) Newspaper editorials in the following months began to comment upon the "gathering storm" and the "chorus of outrage" over the emerging Indian Affairs policies.[14] Late that year, the NCAI got involved in the public relations machinery, distributing to the press the antitermination resolutions passed at their annual convention.[15] The U.S. secretary of the interior responded to the growing controversy with a *Nation's Business* article explaining the termination policies as Eisenhower administration efforts to "weld a working partnership with the people" regarding access to the nation's natural resources, "to restore to the American Indian his rights and privileges as a first-class citizen," and "to participate in the management of his own affairs. . . ." In contrast, Oglala Sioux Tribal Council President Charles Under Baggage explained in the tribal newspaper: "We are in a critical condition. Hardship is facing us. If we are to stand our grounds, we must all take a firm grip and all together Fight For Our Rights. We are being pressed from all sides. Our determination to Save Our Reservation For Indians Has Now Arrived." The newspaper's publisher, William G. Pugh ("the Voice of the Sioux People"), further argued against discourses of assimilation and termination: "We oppose the assimmilation [*sic*] program now being studied by experts in their line of thought, but ignorant as far as the line of Indian thought is concerned. If by Assimilation you mean the Opening of Indian Reservations, the complete integration of the American Indian into the remaining American population, the loss of Indian identity and Indian traditions. Then we are further opposed. . . ."[16] Unfortunately, such strong expressions of tribal dismay over the prospect of termination were rarely able to find a national media forum, circulating instead in tribal or regional publications.

In early 1954, delegates representing 183,000 tribal members convened in Washington for an emergency conference sponsored by the NCAI. NCAI President Joseph Garry wrote to President Dwight Eisenhower, asking him to join Native peoples in opposing "what they believe to be a hasty and ill-considered termination of Federal responsibility to Indians, . . . legislation which would violate their sacred treaties with the federal government." The Declaration of Indian Rights, drafted and approved at the conference, promoted discourses of tribal nationalism:

The government of the United States first dealt with our tribal governments as sovereign equals. In exchange for federal protection and the promise of certain benefits our ancestors gave forever to the people of the United States title to the very soil of our beloved country. . . .

Today the Federal Government is threatening to withdraw this protection and these benefits. We believe that the American people will not permit our government to *act in this way if they know that these proposals do not have Indian consent;* that these proposals, if adopted, will tend to destroy our tribal governments, that they may well leave our older people destitute; and that the effect of many of these proposals will be to force our people into a way of life that some of them are not willing or are not ready to adopt.[17]

A sympathetic article covering this important national conference appeared in a national publication, *The New Leader,* written by W. V. Eckardt. Eckardt charged that proposed federal legislation would " 'quickly result in the end of our last holdings on this continent and destroy our dignity and distinction as the first inhabitants of this rich land.' " Eckardt criticized the pro-termination legislators for constructing their offensive in the rhetoric of "freeing" the Indians, a tactic designed to assuage public conscience and hide the fact that "practically every one of the . . . pending bills are, in one way or another, concerned with securing some profitable piece of real estate for non-Indian interests." Contrary to the rhetoric of "emancipating" the Indians, he argued, America's 450,000 Indian citizens were already in possession of every legal freedom, and the pending legislation threatened to remove the "right to live as Indians if they choose to stay with their tribes." He pointed out that this was both a moral and legal right, "guaranteed by solemn treaties, agreements and statutes . . . which were signed by the United States and the once sovereign and equal tribal governments." This piece provided one of the strongest antitermination rationales available in the mass media, one that reflected the discourses that were circulating within Native America and the pro-Indian organizations but that were rarely expressed so candidly to the national public.[18]

The youthful medium of television did not receive much consideration as a site for arousing national pro-Indian sentiment during the early termination period; termination discourses were more likely to be played out in the more established media outlets of newspaper and magazine publishing. However, a localized 1952 Iowa broadcast provided insights into the potential of television to allow Indian people to be heard beyond the reservation. That year, an Iowa television station (woi) broadcast an unusual public affairs program, *The Whole Town's Talking,* which focused on Iowa's Sac and Fox (Mesquakie) Indians, one of the ten tribal groups that would be named in termination bill HCR 108 the following year.[19] The program featured live coverage of a tribal council meeting moderated by Chairman George Young Bear. In a radical ideological break with 1950s televisual depictions of documentary subjects, a tribal elder in the crowd turned to address the television audience with words of welcome: "My dear friends, this is indeed an honor and a pleasure to appear before you this evening, because this is the first time we have appeared before you, in public." The council discussed issues such as the future of the reservation schools, the ambiguous status of Indian citizenship, and the failure of the government to honor treaties and promises. Those treaties "must have ripped somewhere along the line," one tribal elder said, because "if the government had done what they started out to do, today's Indians under sixty years of age would be self-supporting." One elder gave a long and impassioned speech in the Mesquakie language, which remained untranslated. Of special concern were issues of land ownership, taxation, and productive use.

This local broadcast was remarkable in several ways. It was an extremely early television documentary to address the complexities and contradictions of Native American communities facing the threat of termination of federal services. It did so by turning its microphones over to tribal leaders, providing *no* substantial explanation, summary, or closure from an authoritative white narrator or cultural mediator; the indigenous sentiments expressed during the community meeting were allowed to stand on their own. In its framing and in its rhetoric, the broadcast validated the indigenous culture, yet it also, albeit ambivalently, emphasized the perceived inevitability of assimilation and termination. Because of the limited geographical range of its broadcast, this groundbreaking public affairs documentary had little to no effect on the national public. However, it set an important precedent for what might be done at a national level.

Although print journalism had a history of presenting editorial opinions and engaging readers in national political issues, the potential of the youthful medium of television had yet to be tapped in the early 1950s, particularly during the FCC television "freeze" (1948–52), when most programming was regional in nature and neither stations, broadcast signals, nor set ownership had penetrated into a broad national market. Many television historians have noted that as television signals and set ownership exploded across middle America in the mid-1950s, the potential of the medium to create a mediated national culture, presenting a synthetic model of putatively classless utopian (or "normative" American middle-class) lifestyle and values, became more clearly manifested. Yet the medium's potential to deploy discourses of "American" nationhood during this period (especially during the intense period of cold war patriotism) was countered by the more subtle and subversive use of the medium to deploy discourses of Native American nationhood—that is, to coalesce the disparate Indian tribes across America into a sense of supra-tribal national unity in opposition to their common oppressors, while at the same time maintaining their sense of individual tribal sovereignty. Television could provide what appeared to be a more direct, unmediated representation of Native voices and cultures than could print journalism, and those working on behalf of Native American perspectives learned to use the distinctive potential of television image management to engage a national audience.

As the new medium of television became more widespread, the pro-Indian interest groups soon turned their promotional machinery to the national networks. In late 1953, the all-Indian NCAI began a series of ill-fated negotiations with Fred Friendly, producer of CBS television's *See It Now*, to try to arrange coverage of their national convention. Because of the magnitude of such a public relations effort, the NCAI asked the more media-savvy AAIA to help with the project. Correspondence indicates that, although initially interested in a less political Indian story, Friendly was annoyed by the aggressive efforts of AAIA's staff to refocus the proposed broadcast. AAIA Director Alexander Lesser reported that Friendly seemed to be wary that "he was dealing with a 'public relations outfit'": "We tried to show Friendly that the economic, social, educational and health problems of the Navajos are not 'the' problem of today; that it is rather the Federal renunciation of responsibilities to tackle these concrete problems which constitutes the overriding threat to the Indians. . . . It is not a question of schools or hospitals, etc; it is a question of the existence of Indian tribal communities, the overall Federal guarantee of their rights to exist, and . . . federal responsibility to see that the backwardness, educationally and economically, is overcome." Acknowledging that the negotiations failed, Lesser noted that the AAIA staff agreed "that the idea of a timely show on . . . the united fight of Indians against the new Federal policy is a top idea. If CBS does not use it . . . , we think someone ought to use it."[20] Apparently, neither

CBS nor a competing network picked up such a story at that time; it would be five years before NBC's *The American Stranger* tackled the subject. In spite of efforts by interest groups to acquire public affairs time on the two major networks (NBC and CBS) for serious discussion of the political and cultural issues that were being hotly debated in the halls of Congress and on Indian reservations across the nation, television coverage of American Indian issues in the mid-fifties was limited and irregular.[21]

At the same time, this period witnessed the most public political debates on termination in the national print media to date, debates that eventually sparked more extensive television coverage. In 1956, a few feature articles appeared in widely read national magazines such as *Harper's* and *Atlantic Monthly* that were highly critical of the termination movement and became the topic of intermedia debate. Early in 1957, a controversial series in the *Minneapolis Tribune* on socioeconomic conditions in urban Midwestern Indian communities, bluntly critical of the inability of federal, state, and local bureaucracies to provide adequate and timely social services, received a huge public response and national syndication.[22] These stirrings of pro-Indian activism received some anxious commentary and attacks from the conservative press in 1957 and 1958. For instance, the patronizing *Saturday Evening Post* celebrated the government's relocation of individual Indians from "bleak and dreary" reservations ("concentration camps") to the "delights and opportunities" of urban areas ("civilization"), because in their new situation "they save their money, go to church, and maintain decorum regularly." A paternalistic *Reader's Digest* story chided the Indians for their lack of appreciation of all that "we" Americans had done for them, trivializing the process of Indian land claims and constructing the Indians yet again as thieves and villains: "The Indians are on the warpath—not for scalps but for money; in the place of tomahawks they are using law books. The white man took their lands without just compensation, they say. Now they intend to get paid for it.... Ridiculous, you think?... Until [action is taken to stop this], the Indians and their lawyers will continue to collect big wampum from the American taxpayer." The racist tone of these articles enraged Native Americans and pro-Indian interest groups, arousing many of them to prepare public media responses. Pro-Indian interest groups were deluged with requests from tribes about how to respond. To "arm [tribes] with the facts," the NCAI sent a mailing to all Indian tribes, exhorting increased use of media channels (local newspapers, radio and television stations) to increase public awareness and to "correct the misinformation and erroneous impressions that have been created by the [*Reader's Digest*] article . . . so [the public] will know what the facts are."[23]

The first major national broadcast coverage of Native American issues was achieved with the May 26, 1957, episode of NBC's ninety-minute reality series, *Wide Wide World,* entitled "The American Indian: Between Two Worlds." The premise of the series was to exploit live broadcast technology simultaneously from a number of diverse locations, linking the country through television. In this episode, television crews were stationed at seven locations in Oklahoma, New Mexico, Arizona, and Illinois. The entire show was carefully scripted, including interview responses.[24]

The rhetoric of the program emphasized the social and cultural disjunction of the dual cultures that Native Americans faced, portraying them as liminal figures "between two worlds": "One, the modern world of twentieth century America; the other, the timeless world of tradition and proud heritage." For example, with conscious irony, the producers juxtaposed traditional Zuni Pueblo life against "the *new* world"—a laboratory in the Atomic City of Los Alamos: "a different kind of reservation—a white man's reservation . . . not far from the Zuni Pueblo but centuries apart in time." After observing the magnificent advances in science and technology that had converged at this site, viewers were treated to the first television views of the "secret" laboratories where workers, some of them Pueblo Indians, were engaged in nuclear research. In a similar theme, *Wide Wide World* also took the viewer to Tulsa, the site of the Arrows to Atoms Celebration of the state's fiftieth anniversary, for interviews with wealthy art collectors, oil magnates, and sports figures of Indian descent, as well as to a Pima Tribal Council meeting and a Chicago community center for relocated Indians. The program repeatedly emphasized the trope of the American Indian trapped "between two worlds."

Wide Wide World repeatedly constructed Native American culture as an ancient, historical artifact in conflict with the modern world. It problematized the need for individual Indians to join the modern world "on their own terms," to "make the leap" across the centuries. The narration emphasized that these adjustments would impose "great personal, psychological and emotional" stress on individuals, yet indicated that the benefits of "adjustment" were worthy and admirable goals. The documentary remained firmly apolitical on the surface, never mentioning or even implying the existence of controversial termination policies nor dealing with concrete social and policy issues such as education or health. Furthermore, in its attention to life on a number of reservations, the program assiduously failed to mention the existence of the BIA or the relationship between the federal government and Native American people. Rather, it was a documentary of celebration, applauding the Atomic Age as the pinnacle of human progress and constructing utopian America as a melting pot to which Native Americans were adding their own distinct flavor.

Coverage of Indian issues in the national media increased greatly during 1958, as pro-Indian interest groups such as the AAIA tapped into increasing public attention and arranged for more appearances on network public affairs programs. One report on NBC's *Today* featured AAIA's non-Indian president Oliver LaFarge attacking federal practices in Indian land management. Through arranged sales of Indian land by the BIA to benefit white cattle ranchers, LaFarge claimed, "the uneducated, inarticulate peoples of the Plains states were being steadily impoverished." Choosing to respond to LaFarge's political call to arms rather than his paternalistic comments, a representative of the Kiowa/Comanche and Apache tribes wrote to LaFarge in response: "This morning on NBC TODAY I saw you and heard your speech on the problems of American Indians. All that I can say is May God Richly Bless You and all of the members of the Association on American Indian Affairs. Everything you said is true[;] conditions among our Indians is bad . . . worse than it ever has been in the history of the past years. . . . The Indian Bureau is paid to help our Indians, yet they fight us all the time. I wonder who they are working for." [25] Such responses from members of tribal groups encouraged pro-Indian organizations to push onward with their antitermination publicity efforts.

The most politically significant interpretation of the termination crisis to appear on national television was an hour-long NBC documentary, *The American Stranger,* which was broadcast live in mid-November 1958. Researched, written, and narrated by NBC journalist Robert McCormick with the cooperation of various Indian tribes, interest groups, and individuals, this documentary baldly attacked federal termination policies and focused on the contemporary social and economic conditions of the Blackfeet and Flathead reservations of Montana, the Menominee of Wisconsin, and the "landless Indians" in an urban ghetto called Hill 57 in Great Falls, Montana.[26]

The American Stranger's narration harshly indicted the federal government's bureaucratic efforts to coerce the Indians into selling their land and their rights to prized natural resources. McCormick demonstrated what he claimed to be the results of such unscrupulous practices: the loss of cultural and economic resources that accompanied the dispossession of land. McCormick claimed that, in addition to breaking up the tribal land base to which numerous Native cultures were economically and spiritually connected, this federal movement stripped individual Indians of their tribal culture and forced them to embrace "American" and "democratic" values of private ownership and the capitalist work ethic.

Unlike previous documentaries such as the observational *Whole Town's Talking* and the apolitical and celebratory *Wide Wide World,* this broadcast directly confronted both the politics of Indian affairs and the socioeconomic conditions of Indian communities through the mediating presence of a polemical white journalist-advocate, McCormick, who positioned himself implicitly as an ethnographer: listening to, learning from, and, ultimately, speaking "on behalf of" the tribal subjects he represented to and interpreted for the (white) television audience. The first half of the documentary is dominated by the voices and authority of white, male, antitermination liberals representing three major imperialist institutions: the U.S. Congress, the Catholic Church, and the news media. Their antitermination rhetoric, coming from within the realm of accepted political debate in American politics, is marked as distinctively partisan (Democratic) and liberal, though not too radical to be supported by agents of the Catholic Church.

The first half of the broadcast privileges the spoken word over the visual, with only a few montages of land, natural resources, and economic development on the Menominee and Flathead reservations providing a scenic respite from the talking heads of Congressman Lee Metcalf, Father Cornelius Byrne, and McCormick himself. The politics of white America are visually constructed around the *talk* of white men in suits and ties, situated in interior (office) spaces, constricted by walls and windows. In contrast, Indian country and its people and cultures are visually constructed through a trope of vast openness and a foregrounding of the natural world. Even the interviews with tribal leaders are shot outdoors rather than in offices, and McCormick sheds his coat and tie in favor of a casual ethnic shirt for these interviews.

The other primary component in the film's construction of Native America is the focus on the poverty in some American Indian communities, poverty in ironic juxtaposition with the wealth of the land and surrounding natural resources. The rhetorical strategy of *The American Stranger* combines an appeal to intellect with strong emotional bait. The Montana segment frequently focuses on Indian children, with comments such as: "The Blackfeet are desperately poor, and getting poorer. The Indian Bureau has not as yet seen fit to do more than ask the tribe to audit its books. No audit will alter the fact that, for many children in the Heart Butte school, the hot lunches they get are often their only meals. Nor will an audit supply them with shoes and warm clothing for the bitter Montana winter that's just about upon them." Supported by striking close-up shots of schoolchildren hungrily eating their lunches, and later by a visit to pediatric polio victims, this tactic was presumably to gain the sympathy and support of viewers not swayed by the strident political rhetoric. Between the mental attention demanded by the first half and the shameless emotional manipulation of the second, this documentary strategically targeted both the hearts and the minds of the television audience.

The documentary includes a powerful essay about the conditions of poverty on Hill 57, Great Falls' urban Indian ghetto. Here, more than in earlier visual essays, the voice-over narration frames a montage in which stark cinematic images and rousing music predominate. Viewers are never privileged to "meet" any of the residents of this community (who are only photographed from a distance), and the material aspects of the culture dominate the human. However, the cinematic cuts, between shots of shacks framed by the rusted carcasses of junked cars and shots of similarly rusted and overturned toy cars and tricycles of the children who play in a muddy ditch, represent what may be the climactic dramatic moment of the documentary. If the polemical arguments of the first half presented the cause — current federal policies and practices, compounded by a history of genocide and oppression — then this scene presents the ultimate effect. These are the landless, dislocated Indians of the 1950s — dispossessed of their land, their tribe, their culture — who have ended up in urban shanty towns across the West such as Hill 57. This is the dystopian, nightmarish vision of life for Native Americans alienated from kin, community, and sacred land.

Yet, like *The Whole Town's Talking, The American Stranger* also created a space that allowed and encouraged tribal leaders to speak for themselves. Midway through the second half, McCormick lends some of the authority of the documentary to Blackfeet leaders. At a Blackfoot cattle ranch, McCormick interviews tribal administrator Meade Swingley regarding issues of water rights, farming, and taxation of Indian land. Swingley tells of his personal struggle with the U.S. government over the ownership and use of his land. The show next presents another outdoor interview, with Tribal Secretary Iliff McKay regarding government restrictions on oil and gas development by Indians. The momentum of Native voices grows with the coverage of a Blackfoot Tribal Council meeting chaired by Tribal Chairman Walter Wetzel, in which the council of eleven men discusses their ongoing conflict with federal, state, and county governments over the source of funds to provide assistance and social services to their needy tribal members. The discussion highlights the bureaucratic stumbling blocks involved in the use and allocation of tribal funds held by the government.

Following the meeting is a joint interview with Wetzel and McKay outdoors on the steps of the council house. Dressed in traditional non-Indian business clothing (but without ties), these tribal leaders are presented to the audience as well-educated, articulate members of both the tribal world and the white world, enhancing their credibility with non-Indian audiences through their gentle, pedagogical demeanor. During the course of this informative segment, McKay provides a stunning two-minute monologue that interprets the economic history of the Blackfoot relationship with non-Indians since the 1880s. He clarifies the ideological conflict over land ownership: "[When] the so-called allotment system began, . . . the entire reservation was divided up into individual land allotments. Each individual was given a per-capita share in the ownership of the reservation. Well, that was something that was entirely new to Indians. They didn't—it was something they didn't comprehend. They didn't understand that land could be owned and could be traded, could be sold and could be put up as collateral and the like. When a person stops to think about that, that's only been 51 years ago, that this land concept came into being." McKay claims the government adopted a "policy of inaction" that effectively encouraged Indians to dispose of their land, since it became their only collateral: "So, in order to live, in order to get an existence, they have to dispose of their land to get some immediate cash to live on." In contrast to the stumbling verbal style of the congressman interviewed earlier, McKay comes across as a wise statesman whose political and cultural concerns are credible and deserve immediate attention.

This persuasive expression of Blackfoot tribal leaders' perspectives on history and their concerns about their relationship with the government is followed by an extraordinary scene in which three Indian elders (Juniper Old Person, Theodore Last Star, and Charlie Revis), in traditional Blackfoot clothing and hairstyle, express *their* views about the economic realities of the federal machinations of termination. However, two of these elders speak in the Blackfoot language, without translation. This unconventional documentary tactic provides the ultimate affirmation that in spite of a shared national U.S. citizenship, these tribal members maintain a distinct culture and language. The refusal to provide translation by the filmmakers was in fact a strong but subtle statement against assimilation, against the inevitability of a melting-pot approach to language, culture, or nationhood.

In the following weeks and months, this NBC broadcast generated a great deal of national political controversy, arousing the unprecedented indignation of the national viewing audience and mobilizing many viewers into political and humanitarian action, which ranged from calls and letters (to the Department of the Interior, the White House, congressional leaders, interest groups, the network, and the tribes) to the organization of charitable relief efforts for the impoverished Blackfeet. The irate Department of the Interior responded defensively to a massive letter-writing campaign from the general public, grassroots civic organizations, Indian tribes, and professional Indian lobbies, which expressed concern over government practices and praised NBC's coverage. The controversy became a newsworthy topic in itself, with coverage on national television network news as well as in the press across the nation. The broadcast became the focus of congressional subcommittee hearings and was used as a tool in grassroots activism on behalf of Native American causes. Many accounts credit the television show for mobilizing the national support needed to effect eventual changes in federal policies and practices regarding Native Americans.[27]

Why and how, we might ask, did this one particular show—and not any other—so arouse the interest of the public in Native American cultural politics? There are many possible explanations. Textually, the broadcast used all available cinematic techniques in the direct service of political goals. *The American Stranger* might be likened to the most powerful propaganda in its command of the poetic potential of cinematic aesthetics put to the service of a cultural and political argument. The second half of the documentary, in particular, exhibits masterful cinematographic techniques and a rousing musical score to grab the viewers and engage them in the real-life dramas being presented. The speaking "characters" are all sympathetic, likable, and compelling; the "villains" are alluded to but remain faceless through lack of direct representation (a major criticism of the broadcast by federal agencies). The silent "characters," mostly children in poverty, aroused intense nurturing emotions in many viewers and were perhaps the single most important factor inciting viewers to humanitarian action. The political rhetoric of *The American Stranger* was direct, hard-hitting, and persuasive, and in tandem with the manipulative visual and emotional rhetoric, constructed a strong argument for immediate political and humanitarian action on the part of the viewers.

The controversy surrounding *The American Stranger* represents a conjuncture of ideological and political discourses surrounding "the Indian problem": those of legislators hoping to "free" and assimilate Native Americans, the paternalistic BIA wanting to trim its budget, Indian tribal leaders seeking self-determination, Catholic missionaries supporting tribal rights, corporate interests seeking to exploit natural resources on tribal land, and national Indian lobbying groups attempting to shape government Indian policy, among others. The broadcast was the first time Native American political and social issues, as articulated by tribal members themselves who were critical of government policies, found a voice on national television. The ultimate effective power of this television documentary was its ability to coalesce the altruistic forces of American society—the Church and its followers, liberal Democrats, and "friends of the Indians," in collaboration with tribal allies—in political action against the massive, colonizing bureaucracy (represented at its worst by the BIA) as well as in humanitarian action. It provides an early example of television's ability to constitute, at least temporarily, a new power formation through the coalescence of various localized interests into a national forum. *The American Stranger* not only challenged political ethics and policies, it also exposed deeper cultural and ideological differences—issues of race, ethnicity, and nationhood—which would not be easily resolved through changes in policy or legislation.

The American Stranger, and the controversy that crystallized around it, marked the height of the termination era. Interior Secretary Fred Seaton, already uneasy with the complications and controversies aroused by the termination plans, had made some policy statements during the 1958 campaign season that softened the BIA's formerly aggressive stance on termination.[28] With the public interest in Indian Affairs aroused by *The American Stranger* and the strong public sentiment against termination, many congressional bills quietly died, and the implementation by the BIA of new termination actions was gradually curbed. According to Deloria and Lytle, "This admission of failure . . . proved embarrassing to the administration but was a welcome respite to the frightened tribes." However, the federal policy of termination was not

formally repudiated until President Richard Nixon requested that Congress repeal HCR 108 in 1970.[29]

The early 1960s brought some changes in media constructions of Native
Americans: slightly more news and documentary coverage, more self-reflex-
ivity on the part of the networks about their role in perpetuating media stereotypes, and some attempts at revisionist histories of the West that would address those media-reinforced myths. However, the most significant change was
an increased Native American participation in the political and media processes surrounding Indian affairs issues. Stephen Cornell notes that during this
period, "Indians have not only demanded a voice in decision making, but they
have *appropriated* such a voice for themselves, forcing the surrounding society
to respond once again to their actions and agendas." It was during this decade
that a new generation of American Indian activists lay siege to the national
news media, manipulating it to serve their interests and to create a mass-
mediated political spectacle in front of America's television audience. This
new Indian media activism, the seeds of which were sown with *The American
Stranger* in the late 1950s, surged in the early 1960s with "fish-ins" in the Pacific
Northwest, the nineteen-month occupation of Alcatraz Island in 1969–70, and
other similar political protests, and culminated in the spring of 1973 with the
three-month-long television news coverage when American Indian Movement
activists seized Wounded Knee. This period also witnessed the development
of what Cornell calls a "fiercely nationalistic Indian news media," which includes tribal publications and broadcast stations, Native American filmmakers
and producers, and a national Indian news media (both print and broadcast)
directed toward a Native American audience, both tribal and urban, which
serves as the voice of Native American political activism today.[30]

Chief Leonard George, a native Canadian tribal leader, was recently quoted
as claiming, "In hindsight, we can easily say that the native people of North
America were oppressed by three major forces. These were the government,
religion and Hollywood. . . ."[31] I would extend the concept of Hollywood and
its fictionalized media representations to include the journalistic constructions of Native Americans I have elaborated above. This symbolic colonization
has been carried out through a long history of representations and misrep-
resentations of American Indian culture, primarily through stereotyping, in
classical and popular literature, academic scholarship, and the mass media.
Many writers have charted the place of Native Americans historically in the
American popular imagination, in literature and films and fictional television

programs.[32] Nonfictional media representations and discourses, such as those discussed in this essay, also constitute a significant part of these discursive traditions.

In conclusion, I would like to interrogate the political effectivity of 1950s media discourses toward empowering Native Americans. David Spurr conceptualizes colonial discourse as crisis-ridden, unstable, and fragmented; in spite of its obvious ideological function of "serving the forces of order," he suggests that such discourse actually reflects "stress fractures under the burden of colonial authority": "Colonial discourse does not simply reproduce an ideology. . . . It is a way of creating and responding to reality that is infinitely adaptable in its function of preserving the basic structures of power."[33] Throughout the media discourses of the 1950s, such ambiguities, ambivalence, and contradictions are evident with regard to defining the complex meanings of "American Indian" as variously a racial, ethnic, social, or political construct, as well as the problem of confronting the historical specificities of genocide and imperialism with regard to several hundred distinct tribal and cultural bodies. The crisis in hegemony that was augmented by these discourses of late colonialism, I suggest, created cracks and fissures in the structures of power and provided for occasional, irregular, and inconsistent spaces for Native Americans to gain access to the eyes and ears of a national audience, if not to the control of the apparatus of mainstream media itself.

Notes

1   A study that takes on the task of trying to understand a moment in social and political history by applying contemporary tools and insights faces the challenge of explicating multiple sets of terms, each loaded with cultural and political implications. The activist social movements of the past few decades have radically challenged the terminological structures of naming that have been deeply intertwined with systems of racial and cultural imperialism, patriarchal gender structures, and capitalist class structures. Historians are faced with the question of under what conditions to use the often racist or objectionable terms that were current in the specific sociohistorical period, and under what conditions to use terms that reflect more contemporary political usage, particularly by those peoples whose identities are implicated in such terms.

In this essay I have chosen to maintain, in historical context, the 1950s usage of the terms *American Indian* and *Indian,* which were loose labels for a generic classification of the members of the hundreds of independent indigenous tribes existing in the United States at that time. It is important to note that there was no official grouping of these tribes; each tribe considered itself sovereign and had entered into separate processes of negotiation and recognition with the U.S. government. The existence of a generic label grouping members of all tribes into some sort of racial designation was known and generally accepted by tribal peoples as the way they were perceived by the dominant, non-"Indian" society, as an external category—and was in fact frequently used by tribal peoples in this way, since no equivalent term existed internal to the loose collectivity of tribes. Politically today, the use of this term is equivalent to the historically contextualized use of the term *Negro* as a racial classification for people who were later referred to as black, Afro-American, and (most recently) African American.

Since the 1970s, the use of the classificatory term *Native American* has gained favor among some people, though it is not without controversy (even among indigenous peoples), and this term is generally perceived as interchangeable with *American Indian*. However, when considered in tandem with the concept of *Native America*, which has developed among more radical scholars in the past two decades as a term for the nationally unified, politically consolidated body of tribes, the term Native American can be understood to represent a shift in conceptualization from a generic classification of individuals, based upon some vague racial characteristics, to a politicized concept of a unified supratribal nationhood. I have chosen to use these terms when discussing the issues in a critical and analytical way, signaling a shift from past to contemporary discursive constructions through my alternating use of terms. I apologize for any confusion this may cause the reader.

Similarly, common public usage has generally dichotomized social classifications into a white/nonwhite bifurcation, which is obviously problematic. In this article, I have grappled with how to concisely label those Americans who did not share membership in a Native tribe or culture. While acknowledging the inadequacies of such a label (and the problems with labeling in general), I have chosen to refer to the dominant power bloc as white (which, in the 1950s, it most decidedly was), and to the general public as non-Indian.

2 Joan Wallach Scott, *Gender and the Politics of History* (New York: Columbia University Press, 1988), 6.

3 In such a context, "master narrative" takes on a multiplicity of connotations—a narrative both dominant and dominating. See Toni Morrison's *Playing in the Dark* (New York: Vintage, 1993); Jimmie Durham, "Cowboys and . . . : Notes on Art, Literature, and American Indians in the Modern American Mind," in *The State of Native America*, ed. M. Annette Jaimes (Boston: South End Press, 1992), 423–438; Robert Berkhofer, *The White Man's Indian* (New York: Knopf, 1978); and Brian Dippie, *The Vanishing American* (Lawrence: University of Kansas Press, 1982).

4   Ward Churchill, *Fantasies of the Master Race* (Monroe, ME: Common Courage Press, 1992), 131–132.

5   A number of reports and hearings in the late 1940s, from a coalition of both conservative and liberal forces, recommended the unilateral termination of federal assistance to Indians, though for different reasons. However, as termination legislation developed in the early 1950s, it became increasingly clear to liberal "friends of the Indians" that government interests would be served over those of tribes, and many liberals who originally supported early termination talk backed off at this time.

6   Address by Emmons to the National Congress of American Indians annual convention, Omaha, Nebraska, 19 November 1954, National Anthropological Archive, Smithsonian Institution (archive hereafter cited as NCAI Papers). Donald Fixico, *Termination and Relocation: Federal Indian Policy, 1945–1960* (Albuquerque: University of New Mexico Press, 1986), 93–100.

7   Arthur V. Watkins, "Termination of Federal Supervision: The Removal of Restrictions over Indian Property and Person," *Annals of the American Academy of Political and Social Sciences* 311 (May 1957): 47–55.

8   "HCR 108," in *Documents of U.S. Indian Policy*, ed. Francis P. Prucha (Lincoln: University of Nebraska Press, 1990), 233.

9   Stephen Cornell, *The Return of the Native* (New York: Oxford University Press, 1988), 7.

10 A type of imperialist practice that deserves more critical inquiry is what might be called altruistic imperialism. Generally cloaked in either humanitarian Christian rhetoric or in the social action mode of liberal humanism, such imperialist practices easily disguise themselves in the American culture of charity. With regard to American Indians, these practices have been institutionally represented by the Church and liberal white "friends of the Indians" organizations: a continuum of "do-gooders" ranging from proselytizing missionary organizations to activist movements working to effect policy changes. Many of these agents of empire have generally been caught in a paradoxical bind in relation to Native America; the more politicized have served as some of the most effective legal advocates for Indian rights, yet they often constructed a hierarchy of condescension in which Indians were shaped as victims, in need of help and protection. Most altruistic practices do not radically challenge the structure of patriarchal imperialism, but attempt merely to soften its effect. As to the implicit dangers of the ambivalence of such an agency, M. Annette Jaimes has stated, "A great deal of damage can be carried out under the cloak of benevolence. 'Friends of the Indian' have furthered the control of American Indians by whites. . . . Racism also hides beneath benevolence" (Jaimes, introduction to Churchill, *Fantasies*, 3).

11 The primary information on media coverage of Native American issues that forms the basis for this paper was gathered from newspaper and magazine coverage in the

popular press, from the archived records of the Association on American Indian Affairs (Seeley Mudd Manuscript Library, Princeton University; hereafter cited as AAIA Papers) and the National Congress of American Indians (National Anthropological Archive, Smithsonian Institution), and from the extensive archival materials on historical television programming in the Center for Film and Theater Research of the State Historical Society of Wisconsin, Madison, including the corporate papers of the National Broadcasting Corporation.

12   Quote from Vine Deloria Jr. and Clifford M. Lytle, *American Indians, American Justice* (Austin: University of Texas Press, 1983), ix. The AAIA started a film committee in 1949 to monitor Hollywood's fictional representations of American Indians and an advisory team to counsel Hollywood producers about ways to construct more "authentic" and less stereotypical representations on-screen. This committee worked to establish formal relations with the Motion Picture Association of America and the Society of Independent Producers.

13   For example, see "Indians on Their Own," Bluefield (West Virginia) *Telegraph,* 11 October 1953; " 'Freeing' Indians Is a Complex Task," *Minneapolis Star,* 22 October 1953.

14   Most of the newspapers that regularly expressed an interest in Native issues were those city dailies and/or community weeklies in areas near Indian reservations or in a region with substantial Native population — areas in which issues of Indian Affairs would be of interest to the general readership. Other newspapers seemed to be self-selected, based upon the politics or special interest of the editor; some editors ran many editorials and articles about Native issues that were picked up from a wire service. As a result, the penetration of newspaper coverage across the nation was irregular, though most densely focused in the West.

15   A UPI wire story reported that the NCAI had "voiced strong opposition to proposed withdrawal of federal services for Indians" and had urged no passage of legislation affecting Indians "without full consultation and discussion with tribes and states involved" ("Indians Rap Proposed End of U.S. Aid," Dallas *Times Herald,* 11 December 1953).

16   Douglas McKay, "Resources Return to the People," *Nation's Business,* January 1954; *The Shannon County News* (Pine Ridge, South Dakota) 16, no. 2 (1 October 1953).

17   "A Declaration of Indian Rights," dated 10 March 1954 (NCAI Papers); italics added.

18   W. V. Eckardt, " 'Terminating' the Indians," *The New Leader,* 26 April 1954.

19   A videotape of this program is available in the Smithsonian's Human Studies Film Archives.

20   Correspondence dated November 1953 (NCAI Papers); dated December 1953 (AAIA Papers).

21   The majority of the information on television coverage has been pieced together from a variety of references in the AAIA and NCAI Papers: correspondence, memos,

program listings, scripts, transcripts, and so on. The difficulty of reconstructing television coverage from this period is compounded by the fact that most television programming was live, and very few programs were kinescoped so as to remain for archival study. Records indicate a 1954 senatorial debate on Dumont Television entitled *Should the American Indian Be Given Full Citizenship Responsibility?* A 1954 CBS program, *Longines Chronoscope,* was devoted to a discussion of Indian Affairs. CBS ran *The Hopi Way* as part of its Adventure series; a 16mm print is housed with the AAIA Papers at Princeton University. NBC also produced several short news stories.

22 Dorothy Van de Mark, "The Raid on the Reservations," *Harper's,* March 1956, 48–53; Ruth Mulvey Harmer, "Uprooting the Indians," *Atlantic Monthly,* March 1956, 54–57. Peterson letter dated 7 June 1957 (NCAI Papers). Carl Rowan articles in *Minneapolis Tribune,* February 1957 (clippings in McCormick Papers). "Broken Arrow," *Time,* 4 March 1957, 48–49.

23 "Indian Reservations May Some Day Run Out of Indians," *Saturday Evening Post* 230 (23 November 1957): 10. James Daniel, "He's Giving the Indians a Chance," *Reader's Digest* 70 (March 1957): 164–167; Blake Clark, "Must We Buy America from the Indians All Over Again?" *Reader's Digest* 72 (March 1958): 45. Peterson letter dated 12 March 1957 and NCAI *Information Letter* 4, no. 2 (10 May 1958), NCAI Papers.

24 Script for *Wide Wide World,* broadcast 26 May 1957 (NBC Papers).

25 Various correspondence from April 1958 in AAIA Papers; script of *Today* broadcast dated 23 April 1958 (NBC Papers). Letter dated 23 April 1958 from Robert Goomb of Mountain View, Oklahoma (AAIA Papers).

26 Information about *The American Stranger* controversy has been gathered from the following archival records: the papers of Robert K. McCormick and NBC (State Historical Society of Wisconsin); the Department of the Interior and Bureau of Indian Affairs (National Archives); the central files from the Eisenhower White House (Eisenhower Presidential Library, Abilene, Kansas); the Blackfeet Tribe (the papers of tribal secretary Iliff McKay, Browning, Montana); the NCAI and AAIA Papers; Congressman Lee Metcalf of Montana; Senators Mike Mansfield and James Murray of Montana (Mansfield Library, University of Montana, Missoula); the grassroots activist group Friends of Hill 57; and Catholic activists Sister Providencia Tolan (Sisters of Providence Archives and Cheney Cowles Museum, Spokane, Washington) and Father Cornelius Byrne (Gonzaga University, Spokane, Washington). These collections include hundreds of viewer letters, in addition to official correspondence and documents. A kinescope of the broadcast is available at the State Historical Society of Wisconsin's archives.

27 Script of NBC's *Huntley-Brinkley Show* (4 December 1958) in NBC Papers. Newspaper articles dating from 5 December 1958 to 17 May 1959 from various news-

papers, particularly the Great Falls (Montana) *Tribune,* in AAIA Papers. See also J. P. Shanley, "Television," *America,* 6 December 1958; "McCormick Cited for *American Stranger,*" *Christian Century,* 17 December 1958. In the December 1958 tribal newspaper *Char-Koosta,* "Editorially Speaking" by Salish-Kootenai Tribal Chairman Walt McDonald noted: "Many of the Indian people and non-Indian people appreciated the fact that Robert McCormick (NBC) came out in our state and made the picture of the Flathead and principally the Blackfeet Reservations. The BIA in their 31 page rebuttal has merits also, but we old boys who have lived with the Indian question also have some comments."

28   Seaton's September 18, 1958, radio broadcast from Flagstaff, Arizona, after a two-day tour of the Navajo reservation was to become a statement of a major shift in policy by the Interior Department, in spite of the ongoing congressional termination actions. Press release (undated) from U.S. Department of the Interior Information Service (McCormick Papers).

29   Deloria and Lytle, 20.

30   Cornell, 5–6, 138–139. Cornell also notes the formation of the American Indian Press Association in 1970, a news service functioning as a critical source of news for and about Indians nationwide which supplied packets to more than 150 Indian newspapers. The Native American Public Broadcasting Consortium in Lincoln, Nebraska, coordinates the distribution of nonfiction films by many Native American filmmakers. A Native American radio network, MIGIZI, is headquartered in Minneapolis and syndicates a weekly half-hour radio news/feature program to over forty Indian-oriented radio stations nationwide, and other locally produced radio and television programs are distributed through tribal communications offices.

31   Quoted in Doreen Jensen and Cheryl Brooks, eds., *In Celebration of Our Survival: The First Nations of British Columbia* (Vancouver: University of British Columbia Press, 1991), 165. I am grateful to Mary Jane Miller for this quote.

32   See Gretchen Bataille and Charles Silet, eds., *The Pretend Indians* (Ames: Iowa State University Press, 1980); J. Fred MacDonald, *Who Shot the Sheriff: The Rise and Fall of the Television Western* (New York: Praeger, 1987); and works by Dippie, Durham, and Berkhofer cited earlier.

33   David Spurr, *The Rhetoric of Empire: Colonial Discourses in Journalism, Travel Writing, and Imperial Administration* (Durham, NC: Duke University Press, 1993), 7, 11.

EXTRA-SPECIAL EFFECTS

Televisual Representation and the Claims

of "the Black Experience"

Phillip Brian Harper

The Complex Effects of Televisual Representation

Let me begin with two propositions that I think can serve as generally accept-able premises for the analysis that follows. The first is that the representation of black people on U.S. network television has been a highly contested phe-nomenon since at least the days of *Amos 'n' Andy;* the second, which has rami-fications for the significance of the first, is that "representation" is an extremely complex affair, the intricacies of which we have only begun to theorize in the context of African American cultural studies.[1]

It is, I think, safe to say that one of the reasons the televisual representa-tion of black people has for so long served as a focus of debate is that it is seen as having effects that extend beyond the domain of signs as such and into the realm of African Americans' material well-being, which comprises, among other factors, the social relations through which black people's status in this country is conditioned. The standard of simulacral realism that has informed popular demands for greater representation of blacks on TV is rooted in the assumption that such representation would improve the objective conditions characterizing daily life for the mass of African Americans living within the scope of television's influence.

For anyone engaged in critical cultural studies, the suggestion that representation conditions or shapes "reality" is hardly novel. We cannot hope, however, to construct an effective critique of the racial politics of popular culture until this rather elementary proposition is more fully elaborated to account for some of the specific *ways* that such conditioning occurs, which, since representation is itself a complex phenomenon, will most likely be complex as well, often counterintuitive at the least, and very possibly contradictory. Those contradictions are apt to emerge, it seems to me, not just as we consider various televisual productions either across different historical periods or within the same time frame, but even in the context of a single production; and they are likely to indicate not merely the complexity of any given show or series per se but also the highly overdetermined nature of the historical context in which that show or series is produced. To get just a slight sense of such contextual overdetermination for the 1960s and early 1970s — on which period I want to focus in particular — let us examine not a television show itself, but some commentary *about* television that will elucidate some of the claims that I have already made.

One commentator illuminates especially well the issues at stake in the debate about blacks in television that took place during the period in question. As a regular columnist for the *Saturday Review,* Robert Lewis Shayon reliably chronicled the technological, institutional, and generic developments that occurred in broadcasting from the early 1960s through the 1970s. More than this, though, he also incisively analyzed the social significance of such developments and offered thoughtful critiques of various aspects of industry practice. In particular, Shayon was a consistent critic of the treatment of blacks on television, and he had a clear idea of why changes in that treatment were necessary. In November 1962, for example, Shayon extolled television's yet unrealized capacity to "communicat[e] . . . the Negro image to millions of homes," suggesting that the broad dissemination of that "image" would help improve blacks' social standing in the world beyond the television screen.[2] Three months later, in February 1963, Shayon elaborated this idea in a flat-out declaration: "If Negroes were seen more frequently on television — and in featured roles comparable to those played by white actors — their real-life employment picture might be favorably affected. Television's power to change mass habits and attitudes appears to be significant. An improvement in the Negro image on television might be a very important step toward real integration."[3]

The middle of the decade saw Shayon still holding to this notion of television's potential effect on lived social relations. In October 1966, he opined that "a sharing of power in the real world can flow from entertainment images of mutual accommodation" and that "[t]elevision's fantasy world does more than provide entertainment: it structures a belief in what is possible in the real world."[4] Through the end of the civil rights movement up to the dawn of the Black Power era, then, Robert Lewis Shayon maintained the conviction to which I refer above: that television can have a substantive effect on the social context in which it operates and that, as regards black people specifically, an improvement in their social status can result from their mere depiction in mainstream television programming. Such depictions would thus instantiate what, at the beginning of this essay, I call "simulacral realism," derived from the theorizations of, among others, Jean Baudrillard, who has conceived the simulacrum as a representation that usurps the supposed primacy of the "real" object conventionally understood to serve as its "original."[5] Inasmuch as televisual depictions are imagined to have a powerful socially constitutive effect — in Shayon's terms, actually setting the stage for the realization in the "real" world of the scenarios presented on the screen — they closely approximate to the simulacral function that Baudrillard has elucidated. I will have more to say about the standard of simulacral realism later. First, though, it is important to note another aspect of Shayon's commentary that is highly significant for our consideration here.

At the same time that Shayon argued the progressive social impact that would be made by televisual images of "mutual accommodation" (and we should remember that it is by no means certain that such images necessarily *do* have a progressive effect),[6] he also identified another potential result of increased representation of blacks on television, thus indicating the profound complexity of the issues under discussion. In the same November 1962 column cited above, in which he called for the widespread "communication" of the "Negro image," Shayon commented on the just-released findings of the Committee on Integration of the New York Society for Ethical Culture. Having monitored the programming of the three major TV networks from 8:00 A.M. to midnight over a two-week period, the Committee found that only about 22 percent of it featured any appearances by blacks at all, and that a plurality of that 22 percent presented blacks only as singers, dancers, or musicians. Although this data was clearly pertinent to a consideration of the broad social significance of blacks' televisual representation, Shayon also deployed it to address a more specific concern: "the employment of Negro actors" and blacks' general potential for material success within the industry.

Indeed, in his discussion, after reporting the Committee's findings regarding the preponderance of musical acts among black television performers, Shayon immediately raises the topic of these performers' financial welfare, noting that "it would be instructive to know how many performers had permanency of employment. The Negro singer or dancer on television is a transient, an itinerant, with no chance of earning his living exclusively in either the black and white or the color tube." Shayon goes on to remark that "people appearing as themselves" on news broadcasts, informational programs, and educational documentaries—which constituted the category of programming with the second highest frequency of appearances by blacks, according to the Committee's study—"are again merely passing through—usually without benefit of any fee."

This observation is cogent and suggestive. It is absolutely true, for one thing, that a primary, though often elided, stake in televisual representation—in 1962 no less than today—is money and, particularly, the financial interests of those corporate entities with monetary investment in the programming. These interests, it almost goes without saying, are only rarely, if ever, congruent with the concerns about "image" that we normally associate with the critique of the treatment of blacks on television. Thus, for Shayon to raise the question of the *performer's* financial position—leaving aside the historically, socially, and culturally fraught issue of pay *rate,* the astronomic scale of which for post-1960s entertainment "superstars" is a topic for a whole other extensive discussion—is for him to enact a crucial shift in analytical perspective whereby not only is financial interest granted its proper position in the discussion of industry politics, but the status of the "exploited worker," to use that crude and evidently problematic term, is granted its proper centrality with respect to that interest. Shayon's sophisticated understanding of the complex issue of equity in the business is indicated in his continued discussion in the column I am citing, which considers the effect on black television performers' financial success of various rapid developments in the burgeoning field—among them the advent of corporate sponsorship for programs and the establishment of talent unions and with them regularized pay scales.

More pertinent for our consideration here, however—indicating as it does the potentially complex effect of televisual representation — is the link Shayon draws between the relatively small financial take for blacks in television and their relatively frequent TV appearances "as themselves," for this link suggests a similar and converse connection between blacks' financial success and their television appearances specifically as persons *other than* themselves. In other words, although Shayon's advocacy for "[a]n improvement in the Negro image on television," which I cited earlier, implies that such an improvement will bring about certain presumably positive social developments — racial integration, for instance, and the erosion of stereotypes about black people among whites who would otherwise not become familiar with them — his rhetoric here indicates that more immediate material gain by blacks in the field depends not upon the televisual dissemination of an exemplary image of singular black integrity, but rather on black performers' projection of *multiplicitous* images that do not coincide with their "real-life" identities.

This fact is readily explicable, of course; it is a function of the difference between the incomes enjoyed by actors in regular fictional series, on the one hand, and by musicians, dancers, and persons appearing on "factual programs," on the other, whereby the former make significantly more money than the latter. My specific concern, however, is not the objective intelligibility of this income differential, but rather its association specifically with acting in regular fictional series, in which its activity seems actually to *implicate* it as a factor in social stratification within a segment of the black populace. Televisual representation of African Americans thus potentially has at least a dual effect, according to Shayon's logic: The mere appearance of black performers on television can further the *integration* of blacks generally throughout the society as a whole; on the other hand, their *acting* in fictional series also specifically entails a process of social *differentiation* within the black populace. This dual effect of blacks' televisual representation may help to explain the vexed nature of discussion about it among African Americans themselves during the period under consideration.

The Dual Interests of the Black Performer

A particularly economical way of discerning this complexity is to consider comments made not by journalistic observers or "average people" — though I will turn to such comments shortly — but rather by actual black performers, whose remarks often indicate what we might call the divided interest that they

Bill Cosby and Robert Culp in
I Spy. Photo courtesy of
Photofest.

experience with respect to the representation of blacks on TV. A prime person-age with whom to begin our consideration is Bill Cosby, not only because of the "superstardom" he achieved during the 1980s and early 1990s through the success of his NBC series, *The Cosby Show*, but also because of his "pioneer" status in the television industry; he was, after all, the first African American to star in a dramatic series on network television, appearing alongside Robert Culp in the show *I Spy*, which debuted on NBC in 1965. Among the spate of print publicity that accompanied that debut was a feature in *Ebony* magazine in which Cosby made a statement that simultaneously indicated his belief in the unique contribution that the show could make to improved U.S. race rela-tions and his sense of solidarity with other blacks involved in the civil rights struggle: "Negroes like Martin Luther King and Dick Gregory; Negro groups like the Deacons and the Muslims—all are dedicated to the cause of civil rights, but they do their jobs in their own way. My way is to show white people that Negroes are human beings with the same aspirations and abilities that whites have."[7]

At the same time, however, the unabashed statements Cosby made (and has continued to make) about his primary career objective suggest the possible mitigation of that solidarity by means of the very status with which he had been conferred in the industry context. A 1965 *Saturday Evening Post* profile

Diahann Carroll and Marc
Copage in a publicity still from
Julia. Photo courtesy of
Photofest.

provided a summary of the stand-up comedy experience that preceded Cosby's being hired for *I Spy*, and indicated his plans for the future:

> If he clicks in the show [which, at the time of the article's publication, was just beginning its first season], Cosby hopes to phase permanently out of nightclub humor into TV heroics, for one simple reason—money. And he plans to retire from all strenuous activity within 10 years, when he expects to have saved a cool million dollars. "That doesn't mean I don't care about the show," he says. "I'd be upset if I looked like a dodo on that TV screen. But I've got no great artistic ambitions. What show business mainly means to me is cash. . . ."[8]

This sentiment was repeated in a *TV Guide* interview from the following month, in which Cosby bluntly asserted, "Money is of the utmost importance to me"; he mused further, "If this series goes five years, I will be only 33 and rich."[9]

Similar dual references to the capacity of African Americans' televisual representation to improve U.S. social conditions generally and to the specific benefit enjoyed by the performers engaged in such representation were manifested in the press reports attending the emergence, three years after *I Spy*, of *Julia,* the notorious NBC series starring Diahann Carroll as a young black war widow raising her son in a racially integrated setting.[10] In one of numerous pieces in which Carroll angrily defended the series against charges that it did not deal realistically with the exigencies of contemporary black life, she invoked the notion of simulacral realism that I discuss above, asserting television's socially constitutive function by insisting that "The plusses for *Julia* are so obvious that they almost don't bear discussion. Those who are liberal—who already have Negro friends—are in the minority. TV reaches the whole country, offering everybody constant contact with this woman and her child."[11] Two paragraphs later, however, having noted producer Hal Kanter's suggestion that *Julia* could further—precisely by *depicting*—blacks' integration into "the mainstream of American life," the same article observes that

> Diahann [*sic*] has made a life for herself that is considerably better than the mainstream. She rents a handsome three-bedroom furnished house in Beverly Hills; it came complete with gardens, swimming pool and a grey Bentley. That is in keeping with Diahann's tastes. . . .
>
> . . . Diahann's clothes are by Donald Brooks and Scaasi. In restaurants she asks the wine steward for Lafite-Rothschild '55. . . .

The text is accompanied by a photograph of Carroll posed in front of her Bentley on the lot of the 20th Century–Fox studios.

Despite the clear dualism of their relation to the medium, there is no duplicity at work in either Cosby's or Carroll's characterization of their activities within the television industry; on the contrary, in a 1970 interview with *TV Guide* that Shayon quoted in his *Saturday Review* column, Carroll stated forthrightly that she was doing *Julia* for "money and power [because] money is power in this country, and power means freedom . . . to do what I want to do."[12] What is clear, however, is that the power to which Carroll refers, and, particularly, the financial success through which it is achieved, set her apart from the majority of U.S. citizens generally, and certainly from African Americans, as the beneficiary of a process of social differentiation that can only be conceived in terms of class, in the dual sense of that word. Moreover, it is precisely intraracial distinctions of class that become particularly problematic in considerations of the televisual representation of black people as both the medium and debate about it develop through the 1960s and early 1970s.

Two Kinds of Realism and Their Social Implications

I have already elaborated the concept of simulacral realism that both Diahann Carroll and Robert Lewis Shayon evidently embrace, according to which television propounds scenarios that might subsequently (and consequently) be realized throughout the larger social field, regardless of whether they actually preexist there.[13] At the same time, however, many of the critiques issued by the late 1960s and early 1970s implied a demand, not for simulacral realism, but rather for a properly *mimetic* realism — typically referenced in terms of "relevance" in the pertinent discussions[14] — whereby television would "reflect" the social reality on which it was implicitly modeled. Insofar as they diverge, these differing demands for simulacral and mimetic realism might be taken to indicate distinct concerns with the soundness of society generally, in the case of the former, and the psychological well-being of blacks specifically, in the case of the latter. The degree to which televisual mimetic "reflection" has been conceived as a prime factor in black people's sense of psychic identity is indicated in the rhetoric of a 1970 commentary by African American writer John Oliver Killens. Killens, a novelist and critic whose work of the period was informed by the nationalist politics of the contemporaneous Black Arts movement,[15] noted that, through the mid-1960s, a black person could "stare at television and go to an occasional movie and go through the routine from day to day, month to month, and year to year and hardly (if ever) see himself reflected in the cultural media. It was as if he had no real existence, as if he were a figment of his own imagination, or, at best, if he had an existence it wasn't worth reflecting or reflection."[16] Killens goes on to admit that, at the point at which he is writing, "progress *has* been made, in that there are more actors employed in the medium."[17] This development, however, which represents the industry's progress toward meeting Shayon's 1962 demand on behalf of black performers' financial interests, is not sufficient in Killens's view, in which a preliminary demand for television's reflection of individual black subjectivity — measured in the mere *quantity* of images of African Americans appearing on TV — must give way to a call for its reflection of authentic African American social experience, evidenced in the specific *quality* of the images presented on the screen.

By the time Killens's article appeared, *Julia* had been joined on the tube by a notable few other programs that featured black performers, including *The Bill Cosby Show,* in which Cosby, in a transition from the now defunct *I Spy,* portrayed a high school basketball coach; *The Leslie Uggams Show,* an hour-long variety program; and *Room 222,* a classroom "comedy-drama," to which I want to give sustained attention shortly. The problem with all of these programs, according to popular critiques, was that they weren't really "Black shows." As one black man interviewed by John Killens put it, "They're just shows with Black people acting like they White" or, to cite another of Killens's interviewees, "White folks masquerading in Black skin."[18] In his own summation, Killens indicates his allegiance to the principle of mimetic realism that I have already outlined, charging that "the television establishment is attempting to give to the world the image of an integrated society in all facets of American life . . . , which is all well and good except that it is a colossal lie, because America is not an integrated society. It is a segregated society."[19] And, although in this formulation Killens associates television's failure to mirror faithfully the conditions in which black people live their daily lives with its presentation of an integrated society that has no basis in "fact," later on in his piece he offers a slightly different account of what, really, is wrong with the televisual picture. Commenting specifically on *Room 222,* Killens asserts that "[t]he black folk here are full of understanding and wisdom, sympathetic all the way. No basic problems between the races. All men are brothers, right? An undramatic, middle-classish situation that hardly has anything to do with the Black experience."[20]

In this rendering, the inauthenticity of televisual representation of black life is expressly identified with its presentation of a specifically "middle-class" situation in which "the Black experience" apparently cannot inhere, by definition. This fact indicates an interesting feature of Killens's critical position regarding television's treatment of blacks, whereby, on the one hand, concern for black performers' financial success and professional advancement—we might call it their social mobility—is simultaneously registered and bracketed (through Killens's fleeting recognition that "progress *has* been made . . . there are more actors employed in the medium"), while, on the other hand, the call for authenticity is manifested precisely in the demand that the black characters *portrayed* in the medium demonstrate no such socioeconomic advantage.

Paradoxically, therefore, the insistence that television faithfully represent a set of social conditions conceived by Killens and others as composing a singular and unitary phenomenon known as "*the* Black experience" runs smack up against a simultaneous demand that it both recognize and help constitute the diversity of African American society. The tension inherent in this situation was vividly expressed in the debut of *The Leslie Uggams Show,* in which Uggams exhorted her presumably white audience to recognize that "not all black people look alike. I'm not Diahann Carroll. I'm not Julia." At that moment, Marc Copage, the young boy who played Corey, Julia's son in Diahann Carroll's series, ran onto the stage toward Uggams, arms outstretched, calling "Mama, mama!"[21] The shock of this gag inheres, I think, in its simultaneous chastisement about the conceptualization of black people in a monolithic stereotype and its exposure of profound anxieties about the political ramifications of actually instantiating difference among African American subjects. Thus, if *Room 222* upsets John Killens, I would suggest that, the ostensible import of his protest notwithstanding, this is precisely because it works to negotiate an intraracial social difference that is seen as potentially disruptive to the political solidarity of the African American community.

Room 222 and the Differentiation of Black Society

Room 222 ran on ABC-TV from September 17, 1969, through January 11, 1974. Generally a critical success, it won the Emmy Award for Outstanding New Series of the 1969–70 season. In that same season, Karen Valentine and Michael Constantine won Emmys for their supporting performances in the series.[22] But neither of these white actors was the primary focus of *Room 222*. As *The Complete Encyclopedia of Television Programs* indicates, the series was conceived as a "comedy-drama" presenting "life in an integrated urban high school as seen through the eyes of Pete Dixon, a black American history instructor, whose classes are held in Room 222."[23] This description is telling, for whereas its emphasis on the racially integrated character of the fictional Walt Whitman High School duly identifies *Room 222*'s widely noted thematic hook, its observation that series story lines unfold "through the eyes of Pete Dixon" suggests that, interracialist negotiations notwithstanding, black subjectivity in particular constitutes the program's analytical focus. Indeed, the show's abiding orientation along the perspectives of Pete (Lloyd Haynes) and his intermittent "love interest," black guidance counselor Liz McIntyre (Denise Nicholas), rather than authorizing an exploration of interracial relations, founded a persistent engagement with the problem of forging a specifically African American collectivity across potentially divisive intraracial differences. Moreover, Pete's and Liz's solid middle-class positioning allowed for such differences to be figured principally in terms of a social-class stratification that always implicitly informed the show's narrative developments.

In his criticism of the show that I cite above, John Killens implies that it does

The cast of *Room 222*. Clockwise from top left: Denise Nicholas, Karen Valentine, Lloyd Haynes, Michael Constantine. Photo courtesy of Photofest.

not satisfactorily present or otherwise address race-based dissension among the characters who populate the halls of Walt Whitman High. Although it is true that few of the story lines from *Room 222*'s five-year run treat race relations directly or explicitly,[24] the show was characterized from the beginning by drily oblique statements about racial politics, the ambiguity of which I think actually evidences the show's canny awareness of the impossibility of its otherwise speaking to the issue except through platitudes and well-meaning clichés. This ambiguity on racial issues became clear in the first episode, in which Karen Valentine's character, student teacher Alice Johnson, apologetically introduces herself to Pete Dixon, saying, "I know I have a lot of the middle-class hang-ups. I went to a segregated school." Pete replies evenly, "It's ok — so did I."[25] A similar exchange takes place in the episode on which I want to focus now.

First broadcast on November 2, 1973, during *Room 222*'s final season on the air, "Pete's Protegé" depicts the trials of another young, white student teacher, a man this time, whose eagerness to be friends with the students actually hinders his effectiveness as an instructor. The episode starts off with an exchange between student teacher Arthur Billings and Pete that once again manifests a refined ambiguity on issues of race relations. With the students already gathered for class at the beginning of the school day, Arthur is bustling about the room distributing papers when Pete enters, conspicuously equipped with a very professional-looking briefcase. Arthur returns Pete's "Good morning" by eagerly announcing, "I already passed out the test papers so you wouldn't have to take up class time." Pete responds with characteristic cool irony—"Well, that's no way to get the students to love you"—which Arthur meets by ingenuously hoping out loud to "get along with all my classes the way I do with this one." Just then, the school bell rings, signaling the beginning of the class period, and Pete indicates to Arthur that they'd "better get started," adding drily, "I wouldn't want to waste that time you saved me." At this, Arthur good-naturedly moves to take his seat at the rear of the classroom, at the same time unself-consciously tossing off a lame witticism: "I'll go sit in the back of the bus." This near-throwaway line in an otherwise unremarkable scene immediately sets up a superficial dramatic tension as Arthur, turned just slightly away from Pete in preparation to leave the front of the room, suddenly realizes what he has said, his face registering this new awareness before the camera. Pete, standing over his desk just to Arthur's right, looks up from the paperwork he has been perusing and eyes the student teacher with mock wariness as Arthur turns to address him again: "Hey, uh . . . I didn't mean, uh. . . ." Then comes what, in the wry world of *Room 222,* constitutes an effective punch line—Pete's response, delivered in a tone of utter flatness: "Arthur, you've been student-teaching with me long enough to know better." Arthur, evidently uncertain about the meaning of this remark, ends the exchange by intoning hesitantly, "Thanks, Pete," and awkwardly ambles away from Pete's desk, as Pete looks on in smirking amusement.

Now, I have claimed that such scenes evidence the show's canniness about the dubious project of making definitive statements about racial politics on prime-time television. I can certainly see, however, that the noncommittal quips by Pete Dixon might be interpreted as ineffectual efforts to gloss over the profound difficulty of race relations—and, especially, of racial integration—during the contemporary era. Even if we read the statements in this way, however, we would have to recognize that such "glossing over" can really only constitute the show's repression of racial concerns into a sort of "political unconscious" that will necessarily inform the working through of the surface-level plot for any given episode. In other words, I am suggesting that the cool shrugging off of raciopolitical concerns that the show regularly enacts actually signals its profound engagement with racially inflected social difference at a subtextual level, but also that its containment of such concerns within conceptual parameters subjectively constituted by Pete Dixon indicates that their import will become manifest specifically with respect to *intra-* rather than *inter*racial considerations. Thus I propose that, contrary to what its superficial aspect might suggest, *Room 222* is not primarily about racial *integration* at all; rather, it always represents an allegorical narrative about social *differentiation* among black subjects, and, in particular, thematizes the articulation of different black subjects into various socioeconomic class positions.[26]

Let me approach the matter from a different direction for a moment, to buttress my claim that *Room 222* is not first and foremost about integration. In doing this, it will be helpful to consider a bit of advance ad copy for another ABC series that premiered in the same season as *Room 222*. The premise of *The Brady Bunch* involved a man and a woman, each widowed and raising three children—he boys, she girls—who marry and thus consolidate their fragmented households into one big happy family, weekly overcoming the obstacles to that consolidation inherent in their children's gender difference. Thus, as the network put it in its preseason publicity campaign, *The Brady Bunch* dealt with "the most difficult integration of them all, that of the sexes." [27]

If we conceive of integration in this unique way, identifying it as the consolidation—however difficult and problematic—of disparate elements into a single, undifferentiated social entity that on U.S. network television has always been represented as the nuclear family, then we must recognize *Room 222*'s singular disengagement from the networks' integrative mission. That singularity is emphasized if we refer to the programming schedules from the time of *Room 222*'s run, which evidence a contrast between its function and that of the other ABC shows receiving prime-time airplay. Throughout its broadcast history, *Room 222* was juxtaposed in ABC's schedule with programs that depicted variations on the consolidated nuclear family within a specifically domestic context. The show was always preceded in the schedule by one or a combination of the following programs: *The Courtship of Eddie's Father,* with Bill Bixby; *Make Room for Granddaddy,* with Danny Thomas; *The Partridge Family,* with Shirley Jones, David Cassidy, and Susan Dey; *The Odd Couple,* with Tony Randall and Jack Klugman; and the aforementioned *Brady Bunch,* with Florence Henderson and Robert Reed. The classroom series was followed in the schedule, most notably, by *The Odd Couple* and *Adam's Rib,* an adaptation of the Hepburn and Tracy movie that again depicted the difficult reconciliation of the genders within the domestic context, with Ken Howard and Blythe Danner in the starring roles.[28]

Unlike all of these shows, *Room 222* was emphatically not set in the context of the traditional nuclear family (indeed, to my knowledge, it never depicted a single functional nuclear family in all of its five-year run); nor did it set up relations among its characters that could be construed as metaphorically figuring familial ties. Thus, however harmoniously unified the Walt Whitman High School community might have appeared, *Room 222*'s disengagement from the familial vocabulary that is the predominant televisual mode for indicating stable social synthesis suggests that the latter was not its major concern. On the other hand, however, *Room 222*'s classroom setting offered an ideal configuration through which to enact a social *division* that always implicated black subjects specifically, due precisely to the show's focus on Pete Dixon rather than on the various white characters.

Although Pete, and Liz McIntyre, too, is a solidly middle-class professional figure, there is, as Cleveland Amory put it in an early review, a "menace in *Room 222*" as well: "Student Jason Allen (Heshimu) for example, could have stepped out of 'The Blackboard Jungle.'" [29] Indeed, particularly in the early seasons, Jason presented a strong antidote to Pete's and Liz's upright middle-classness; a product of the Los Angeles slums, Jason was portrayed as an angry outsider, deeply suspicious and given to thievery. Over the years, his character mellowed quite a bit, but he still provided the perfect foil to Pete's professionalism by clearly representing socioeconomic disadvantage. The means of this representation was partially explained by John Wasserman, in his 1969 profile of Denise Nicholas entitled "The Girl in 'Room 222'": "Black people, like whites, have different vocabularies and speaking styles for different situations. There are accents, phrasing and sounds for one's peers and friends. There are other noises [*sic*] for outsiders. . . . It is a subtle point, and one which is generally ignored in integrated theater." [30] Wasserman implicitly praises *Room 222* specifically for *not* ignoring this point, but he might have gone even further because, even *within* a given racial group there exist different modes of speech corresponding to, among other things, differences in socioeconomic class, and these, also, were represented in the series. Thus, even as Jason Allen became a respectable member of the Walt Whitman High School community, his dialectal speech (which, like that of the other students, was also marked by the youth slang of the period) set him apart from the professional class represented by Mr. Dixon and Miss McIntyre. In the episode I am considering here, this is evidenced in Jason's brief commentary (the dialectal cadences of which I can only imperfectly suggest in print) regarding the erection of a statue of Walt Whitman in front of the school: "Man, it must be a real groove to have you a statue put up in front of a big buildin'."

Thus, Jason implicitly represents one of the various social classes into which the black community can be differentiated, in contrast to that represented by the black faculty at the school. With the difference between professionals like Pete and less advantaged students like Jason always operative as a subtext to the main action of *Room 222*, the explicit differentiation of the black community into various subcategories can be played out as the division between teacher and student that is regularly the ostensible subject of series episodes. In "Pete's Protegé," Pete has to correct student teacher Arthur Billings's too-close bonding with his students, thus reinforcing the necessary division upon which the community is founded. Having had to take over Pete's class when Pete was out sick, Arthur found himself confronted by a roomful of unruly students whose respect he could not gain precisely because he had identified with them too closely as a "friend," rather than as an authority figure. In response, he has harshly criticized the work of a slow—and, notably, *white*—student whom Pete had been tutoring privately, undermining what little self-confidence the boy had begun to achieve. Upon learning of this development after returning to school, Pete angrily confronts Arthur with his error, exasperatedly insisting, "A teacher can make mistakes. He can have his good days and he can have his bad days. But the one thing that he's *got* to do is stimulate his students! The one thing he *cannot* do is discourage them." When Arthur responds with a dejected, "I know that," Pete demands, "Then why did you tell Leo what you did? Now he wants to quit his tutoring; he doesn't think it makes any difference anymore." After establishing that, although Leo's report is indeed of relatively poor quality, it nonetheless represents the best work that the boy has done, Pete offers an analysis of Arthur's action: "You know, I think that you took it out on him because of what the kids did to you, and you knew he would take it from you." In implicit defense of his reaction to the students' betrayal of him, Arthur protests, "I've been nothing but a friend to those kids, all of them—a real friend! I've played ball with them, I've eaten with them. . . ." Pete, now occupying the screen together with Arthur after having confronted him in a staccato shot–reverse shot series, offers a closing response that further solidifies the teachers' common status as distinct from that of the students, symbolically restoring order to the classroom venue: "That's fine! Don't stop doing that; but you're not a student anymore! . . . You can't be one of the class and in charge of it at the same time, it's too confusing."

Pete's invocation of "confusion" is apt, of course, but it serves just as well in relation to an undifferentiated black collectivity as it does with respect to an undisciplined high school classroom, suggesting the show's engagement in the process of distinguishing Pete's subject position from that of his black students, on more levels that one. As far as the show's critics are concerned, what is *most* confusing and ill defined is the show's exact stance on the politics of interracial relations. But that confusion, as I think I have begun to demonstrate, is evidence not necessarily of any fundamental weakness in the program itself, but rather of its problematic situation at the intersection of demands for televisual fidelity to a unitary "black experience" and the increasingly evident illusoriness of such a social phenomenon. To attempt to represent the latter in 1969 was to engage an extremely complex set of exigencies within African American cultural politics, hence the controversy caused by *Room 222* among many black critics. What that controversy most strongly suggests, however, is that the means of the show's engagement with those exigencies are prime objects for study and analysis — just as the mere fact of it is something to be remarked — amidst the difficult demands of the contemporary context, as what is too easily summed up as "the black experience" becomes increasingly conflicted and dis-integrated.

Notes

This essay originally appeared in Phillip Brian Harper's *Are We Not Men? Masculine Anxiety and the Problem of African-American Identity,* and is reprinted here by permission of Oxford University Press.

1   This is not to say, of course, that a great deal of work has not already been done on televisual representations of African Americans, much of it focusing on specific individual programs. On *Amos 'n' Andy,* see Thomas Cripps, "*Amos 'n' Andy* and the Debate over American Racial Integration," *American History/American Television: Interpreting the Video Past,* ed. John E. O'Connor (New York: Ungar, 1983), 33–54. For an extended consideration of the show's broadcast history in both radio and television, see Melvin Patrick Ely, *The Adventures of Amos 'n' Andy: A Social History of an American Phenomenon* (New York: Free Press, 1991).

2   Robert Lewis Shayon, "Living Color on Television," *Saturday Review,* 24 November 1962, 25.

3   Robert Lewis Shayon, "Living Color on Television — 2," *Saturday Review,* 9 February 1963, 57.

4   Robert Lewis Shayon, "Can TV Overcome?" *Saturday Review,* 29 October 1966, 24.

5   See Jean Baudrillard, *Simulations,* trans. Paul Foss, Paul Patton, and Philip Beitch-
     man (New York: Semiotext[e], 1983).

6   Consider, for instance, the study on *The Cosby Show* of the 1980s and 1990s, which
     indicated that white viewers accustomed to the evident affluence of Bill Cosby's
     television family took it to suggest the decreasing necessity of further activism on
     behalf of African Americans' equitable social treatment. See Sut Jhally and Justin
     Lewis, *Enlightened Racism:* The Cosby Show, *Audiences, and the Myth of the Ameri-
     can Dream* (Boulder, CO: Westview Press, 1992).

7   "I Spy: Comedian Bill Cosby Is First Negro Co-star in TV Network Series," *Ebony,*
     September 1965, 66.

8   Stanley Karnow, "Bill Cosby: Variety Is the Life of Spies," *Saturday Evening Post,*
     25 September 1965, 88.

9   Robert de Roos, "The Spy Who Came in for the Gold," *TV Guide,* 23 October
     1965, 15.

10   On the contemporary controversies regarding *Julia's* racial- and gender-political
     significances, see Aniko Bodroghkozy, " 'Is This What You Mean by Color TV?'
     Race, Gender, and Contested Meanings in NBC's *Julia," Private Screenings: Tele-
     vision and the Female Consumer,* ed. Lynn Spigel and Denise Mann (Minneapolis:
     University of Minnesota Press, 1992), 143–167.

11   "Wonderful World of Color," *Time,* 13 December 1968, 70.

12   Robert Lewis Shayon, "Changes," *Saturday Review,* 18 April 1970, 46.

13   It may actually be through the theorization of televisual realism as simulacral that
     we can explain the failure (as putatively exemplified by *The Cosby Show*) of lived
     reality to approximate the social scenarios that popular series seem to envision.
     Following Michel Foucault by positing the simulacrum as that which suspends
     resemblance by "subvert[ing] the hierarchical relation of model to copy," Scott
     Durham reads Pierre Klossowski's *Diana at Her Bath* as a narrativization of the
     simulacrum that—because its temporality reveals the undoing of the narrative
     subject's self-resemblance—exposes its fundamentally utopian, and hence objec-
     tively unrealizable, character. See Durham, "From Magritte to Klossowski: The
     Simulacrum, between Painting and Narrative," *October* 64 (spring 1993): 17–33; 20
     for the quoted passage. For Foucault's theorization of the simulacrum, see his *This
     Is Not a Pipe,* trans. and ed. James Harkness (Berkeley: University of California
     Press, 1983).

14   On television "relevancy," see Erik Barnouw's classic *Tube of Plenty: The Evolution
     of American Television,* 2d rev. ed. (New York: Oxford University Press, 1990), 430–
     440; and Jane Feuer, "MTM Enterprises: An Overview," in *MTM: "Quality Tele-
     vision",* ed. Jane Feuer, Paul Kerr, and Tise Vahimagi (London: British Film Insti-
     tute, 1984), 1–31; especially 1–4.

15   On this black nationalist aesthetic, see my "Nationalism and Social Division in

Black Arts Poetry of the 1960s," *Critical Inquiry* 19, no. 2 (winter 1993): 234–255; reprinted in *Identities,* ed. Henry Louis Gates Jr. and Kwame Anthony Appiah (Chicago: University of Chicago Press, 1995).

16   John Oliver Killens, "Our Struggle Is Not to Be White Men in Black Skin," *TV Guide,* 25 July 1970, 6.

17   Ibid., 8.

18   Ibid., 7, 8.

19   Ibid., 8.

20   Ibid., 9.

21   John Garabedian, "Unseasonable," *Newsweek,* 6 October 1969, 113–114.

22   Craig T. Norback, Peter G. Norback, and the Editors of *TV Guide* magazine, *TV Guide Almanac* (New York: Ballantine, 1980), 303–304.

23   Vincent Terrace, *The Complete Encyclopedia of Television Programs 1947–1979,* 2d ed., rev., vol. 2 (South Brunswick: A. S. Barnes & Co., 1979), 847.

24   These story lines are summarized in Joel Eisner and David Krinsky, *Television Comedy Series: An Episode Guide to 153 TV Sitcoms in Syndication* (Jefferson, NC: McFarland and Company, 1984), 711–719.

25   Quoted in Cleveland Amory, Review of *Room 222,* *TV Guide,* 25 October 1969, 52.

26   Indeed, it is all the more possible to conceive racial-group politics in *Room 222* as undergoing a type of *repression* when we consider that jokes — such as those Pete Dixon makes in response to racially charged situations — constitute a primary affective indicator of the repressive process in Freud's foundational theorization of it. See Sigmund Freud, "Repression" (1915), in *General Psychological Theory,* ed. and introduced by Philip Rieff (New York: Collier/Macmillan, 1963), 104–115; especially 108 and 110–111.

Further, it is the repression enacted in *Room 222* that actually founds its allegorical character — its status as a text through which another, more or less related one, may be discerned and read, according to the preliminary formulation offered by Craig Owens (see "The Allegorical Impulse: Toward a Theory of Postmodernism," parts 1 and 2 [1980], *Beyond Recognition: Representation, Power, and Culture* [Berkeley: University of California Press, 1992], 52–69 and 70–87; 54 for the current citation). As Owens indicates, the very logic of psychoanalysis, which presupposes that the significance of past (and characteristically repressed) occurrences can be identified through the interpretation of a subject's present symptoms, renders allegory crucial to its project (53).

In Owens's extensive theorization of its function in the postmodern context, allegory is presented as a fundamentally deconstructive (and *self*-deconstructive) phenomenon that, in Paul de Man's formulation, "persists in performing what it has shown to be impossible to do" (cited in Owens, 79). For instance, Owens suggests that, to function as a critique of the museum site as "dumping ground," as

Owens claims they do, the "combine paintings" of Robert Rauschenberg "must also declare themselves to be part of the dumping ground they describe. They thus relapse into the 'error' they denounce, and this is what allows us to identify them as allegorical" (78). Regarding *Room 222*, we might identify as the pertinent "error" the insistent raciopolitical commentary that constitutes the show's discernible burden while at the same time serving as the object of its critique. Notably, it is precisely in such a (self-)deconstructive moment that *Room 222*'s allegorical character merges with its potential simulacral function because, as Scott Durham indicates, the simulacrum enacts a similar self-subversion, constituting as it does "a figure that suspends and reverses the authority that calls it into being" (21).

Such self-deconstruction as apparently operates in *Room 222* does not, it must be emphasized, *negate* the raciopolitical commentary manifested therein; it is precisely that commentary that I propose we take seriously and that, after all, constitutes a primary object of my analysis here. Rather, the contradictions that characterize the program are intrinsic to the cultural text per se and, in this case, do no more than indicate the as yet underappreciated complexity of representational processes in relation to racial-identity politics.

27   "Premières: Old Wrinkles," *Time*, 3 October 1969, 84.

28   Larry James Gianakos, *Television Drama Series Programming: A Comprehensive Chronicle, 1959–1975* (Metuchen, NJ: Scarecrow Press, 1978).

29   Amory, 52.

30   John L. Wasserman, "The Girl in 'Room 222,'" *TV Guide*, 20 September 1969, 26.

NARROWCASTING IN DIASPORA

Middle Eastern Television in Los Angeles

Hamid Naficy

Diaspora Television as a Genre

Middle Eastern television programs aired in Los Angeles are a constitutive part of the dynamic and multifaceted popular cultures in diaspora produced and consumed by immigrant, exilic, and displaced communities in Southern California. These programs are also part of new developments in mass media institutions and practices worldwide that have resulted in the emergence of so-called minority and ethnic television and video.

Multinational and transnational media conglomerates and television networks from RCA to NHK and newsgathering organizations from Associated Press (AP) to Agence-France Presse (AFP) to Cable News Network (CNN) have created and dominated a model of broadcasting that might be called "centralized global broadcasting." At the same time, massive worldwide political, economic, and social restructurings and displacements along with rapid technological advances have ushered in a new model of television that could be termed "decentralized global narrowcasting." This latter category, which in the United States is often called "minority television," is neither homogenous nor all-encompassing; it includes television produced by various peoples and communities in the U.S. with varying relationships to both their homelands and host land. As a result, this essay divides narrowcasting into three categories of television: ethnic, transnational, and exilic. Although these categories are flexible, permeable, at times simultaneous, and can merge under certain circumstances, there are distinguishing features that set them apart.

Ethnic television refers to television programs primarily produced in the host country (in this case, the U.S.) by long established indigenous minorities. Black Entertainment Television (BET) is an exemplar of this category, most of whose programming centers on the lives and experiences of African Americans in the United States. The homeland for many of these programs is understood to be here in the U.S., not someplace else. If ethnic television's programs inscribe struggles, they are usually intracultural (within the U.S.) not intercultural (between the U.S. and geographic other cultures).

Transnational television consists primarily of media imported into the U.S. or of programs produced by U.S. and multinational or transnational media concerns. Many Korean, Japanese, and Chinese programs fit this category because they are imported from their respective home countries. As such, these programs locate their homeland outside the United States and they typically minimize the drama of acculturation and resistance. This theory is corroborated by a study conducted by SRI-Gallup Organization for the International Channel Network, which noted that the Channel's Chinese, Korean, and Japanese viewers "by far prefer programming produced in their native homeland over programming produced locally within the U.S."[1]

In some cases, reliance on imports gives a foreign government, friendly to the U.S. administration, direct access to American homes, thus raising legal and political issues about "unwarranted" use of American airwaves for propaganda purposes.[2] The Korean-language broadcasts, for example, are produced by Korean Broadcasting Service in South Korea, a government-controlled body, and imported and distributed for broadcast in the United States by the government-owned Korean Television Enterprises. In addition to supplying many self-promoting programs, the South Korean government provides "unlimited financial and technical support"[3] that allows Korean-language television in Los Angeles to enjoy a degree of stability and security that producers of diaspora television can only dream about. As a result of such outside assistance, Korean producers of both radio and television programs have been able to block-book prime-time hours on multiethnic stations in Los Angeles, pushing out other ethnic competitors.

Spanish-language national networks in the United States (Univision, Telemundo, and Galavision) are primarily transnational and only partly ethnic, for they are produced primarily by U.S. or foreign multinational and transnational corporations that import much of their programming from Mexico, Venezuela, and Brazil.[4] These programs, which are often modeled after proven U.S. or Latin American shows, adequately address neither problems of acculturation nor issues of diversity and specificity of the various Latin American, Central American, and Chicano populations living in the United States. Instead, they appear to reinforce, on the one hand, the assimilation and Americanization of Latino populations[5] and, on the other hand, the "Cubanization" of Spanish-language programming.[6]

Diaspora television is made in the host country by liminars and exiles as a response to and in tandem with their own transitional and/or provisional status. Television programs produced by Iranians, Arabs, and Armenians and some of the programs of the Jewish Television Network (JTN) fall within this classification. These programs are often produced by small-time individual producers, not media conglomerates of the home or host societies. Thus, they tend to encode and foreground not only the collective but also individual struggles for authenticity, legitimacy, and identity.

Even though ethnic television networks, particularly BET and JTN, are primarily focused on the cultural concerns and personalities of segments of the U.S. population, they also reach mainstream audiences because their programs are delivered in English. As such, ethnic television is a form of "broadcasting." Transnational and diaspora television, on the other hand, are examples of "narrowcasting" because they are aired in foreign languages, which limits their reach considerably.

Diaspora TV, to which Middle Eastern programs primarily belong, is an example of the decentralized global narrowcasting model. The programs are produced in diaspora, usually by local, independent, minority entrepreneurs for consumption by a small, cohesive population which, because of its diaspora status, is cosmopolitan, multicultural, and multilingual. Such decentralized narrowcasting is thus simultaneously local and global, concerned with both present and past.

Taken together, these programs form a new televisual genre of diaspora or exile TV. This is a ritual genre in that it helps the communities in diaspora negotiate between the two states of exile: the rule-bound structures of the home and host societies (*societas*) and the formlessness of liminality in which many rules and structures are suspended (*communitas*). The ritual diaspora TV genre introduces a sense of order in the life of its viewers by producing a series of systematic patterns of narration, signification, and consumption that set up continually fulfilled or postponed expectations. I have elaborated on these generic issues elsewhere.[7]

An examination of these programs reveals Middle Eastern societies — both at home and in diaspora — that are diverse and complex in terms of nationality, language, ethnicity, religion, culture, and politics. These societies do not fit into easy dichotomies such as East versus West, colonizer versus colonized, Israeli versus Arab, and Shi'i versus Sunni. In fact, diversity is a key determinant of narrowcasting that both distinguishes these programs from one another and reveals the dense intermingling of Middle Eastern societies and cultures. At the same time, these programs express certain commonalities that stem from not only historical and cultural affinities of Middle Eastern people but also the production and transmission of these programs in diaspora.

Production, Transmission, Consumption

Los Angeles is perhaps the most ethnically diversified broadcast market in the world. KSCI-TV (channel 18), an independent station, provides around-the-clock programming in some sixteen languages that is either produced in the U.S. by ethnic, transnational, and exile groups or imported from their home countries. KMEX-TV (channel 34) and KVEA-TV (channel 52), which belong to Univision and Telemundo national networks, respectively, offer Spanish-language programming only. The independent stations KDOC-TV (channel 56), KWHY-TV (channel 22), and KRCA-TV (channel 62) also provide many hours of programming in Spanish as well as in other languages. Black Entertainment Television and Jewish Television Network are available from national cable companies with outlets in Los Angeles. Rounding out this televisual menu, local cable companies air locally produced minority programs on either a lease-access or public-access basis.

KSCI-TV claims to provide the most diverse ethnic and linguistic menu of any station in the country.[8] It broadcasts the bulk of the Middle Eastern programs; the rest are aired by cable carriers and public-access outlets. Table 1 lists all of the Middle Eastern programs aired in 1992 in Los Angeles by broadcast, cable, and access channels. The overwhelming majority of these programs are produced in Los Angeles; Iranians produce the largest number and the most diverse menu of programs (22 hours per week), followed by Jewish/Israelis (7 hours), Armenians (5 hours), Arabs (3 hours), and Assyrians (2 hours).

Table 1 Middle Eastern TV Programs Aired in Los Angeles, 1992*

Program Title	Language	Frequency	Length (in min.)	Broadcast Channel
Arabic Programs				
Arab-American TV	Arabic/English	Weekly	60	KSCI-TV
Alwatan (My country)	Arabic	Weekly	60	KSCI-TV
Islam	English/Arabic	Weekly	30	KSCI-TV
The Good News	Arabic	Weekly	30	KSCI-TV
Armenian Programs				
Armenian Teletime	Armenian	Weekly	60	KSCI-TV
Horizon American TV	Armenian	Weekly	60	KSCI-TV
Tele-U.S. Armenians	Armenian	Weekly	180	Public access**
Assyrian Programs				
Bet Naharin (Assyria)	Assyrian	Weekly	60	Cable
Assyrian-American Civic Television	Assyrian	Weekly	60	Cable
Iranian Programs				
Aftab (Sunshine)	Persian	Weekly	120	Cable
Cheshmandaz (Perspective)	Persian	Biweekly	30	KSCI-TV
Diyar (Country)	Persian	Weekly	60	Cable
Emshab ba Parviz (Tonight with Parviz)	Persian	Weekly	30	KSCI-TV
Harf va Goft (Words and talk)	Persian	Biweekly	30	KSCI-TV
Iran	Persian	Daily	30	Cable
Iran va Jahan (Iran and the world)	Persian	Weekly	30	KSCI-TV
Iranian	Persian	Weekly	60	KSCI-TV
Jam-e Jam (Bowl of Jamshid)	Persian	Weekly	60	KSCI-TV
Jonbesh-e Iran (Iran's uprising)	Persian	Weekly	60	KSCI-TV
Mardom va Jahan-e Pezeshgi (People and the world of medicine)	Persian	Biweekly	30	KSCI-TV
Melli (National)	Persian	Weekly	60	Cable
Midnight Show	Persian	Weekly	30	KSCI-TV
Mozhdeh (Glad tidings)	Persian	Weekly	30	Public access
Negah (Look)	Persian	Weekly	30	Cable
Pars	Persian	Weekly	60	KSCI-TV
Pezeshg-e Khub-e Khanehvadeh (Family's good physician)	Persian	Weekly	30	KSCI-TV
Shahr-e Farang (Peep show)	Persian	Weekly	60	Cable
Sima-ye Ashena (Familiar face)	Persian	Biweekly	30	KSCI-TV
Sima-ye Azadi (Face of freedom)	Persian	Weekly	60	KSCI-TV
Sobh-e Ruz-e Jom'eh (Friday morning)	Persian	Weekly	30	KSCI-TV
Sokhani ba Ravanpezeshg (A talk with psychiatrist)	Persian	Weekly	30	KSCI-TV
You and the World of Medicine	English	Triweekly	30	KSCI-TV

Table 1 Continued

Program Title	Language	Frequency	Length (in min.)	Broadcast Channel
Israeli-Jewish Programs ***				
Jewish Television Network News	English/Hebrew	Triweekly	30	Cable
The Diane Glazer Show	English	Weekly	30	Cable
Community Affairs	English	Weekly	30	Cable
Jerusalem on Line	English	Weekly	30	Cable
Beyond the Headlines	English	Weekly	30	Cable
Judy's Kitchen	English	Weekly	30	Cable
A Conversation with Robert Clary	English	Weekly	30	Cable
The Goldbergs	English	Weekly	30	Cable
JTN Specials	English	Weekly	30	Cable
Twenty 2 Forty	English	Weekly	30	KSCI-TV
Israel Today	Hebrew	Weekly	30	KSCI-TV
The Phil Blazer Show	English	Weekly	30	KSCI-TV

Source: Compiled by the author.

Notes:

* Reflecting their exilic and diaspora status, there is considerable flux in the fate of these programs. This table, therefore, only reflects their status in the latter half of 1992.

** The coverage of cable companies and public-access channels is limited to only a small geographic segment of Los Angeles. To cover the entire area, multiple copies of programs must be aired by a number of cable companies. As a result, not all Middle Eastern shows are available in all areas. On the other hand, the signal of broadcast channels such as KSCI-TV can reach the entire area.

*** With the exception of *Israel Today* and *The Phil Blazer Show,* all of the Israeli-Jewish programs are syndicated as a package by the Jewish Television Network.

Transmission by KSCI-TV and cable carriers is on a lease-access basis, whereby TV producers lease time from the station to air their programs. The cost varies from $600 to $2,500 per hour depending on transmission time and channel. Public-access programs are generally aired free of charge. Some of the Middle Eastern programs originating from Los Angeles are syndicated via tape (e.g., Jewish Television Network and *Iranian*) and others are transmitted by satellite via the International Channel Network (e.g., *Arab-American TV, Emshab ba Parviz,* and *Aftab*) to cities across the United States with large Middle Eastern populations.

The emergence in the early 1990s of the International Channel Network, run by the parent company of KSCI-TV in Los Angeles and reaching over 13 million households nationwide, has far-reaching potentials for minority programmers. Ethnic and diaspora broadcasters can reach their compatriots in other cities in the United States and aid in creating a kind of national minority identity and an ethnic economy. This wider reach of nonmainstream programming by satellite also creates the possibility for national advertisers such as IBM, AT&T, Toyota, Bank of America, Crest Toothpaste, and Metropolitan Life to target minority niche markets. According to the studies commissioned by the International Channel Network, the ethnic communities that it serves are upscale, with a "higher level of disposable income than the U.S. population as a whole."[9] The International Channel Network (whose motto is "We speak your language") carries Middle Eastern programs that are Los Angeles originated and aired and also programs that are not aired there, such as *Arabic Drama, Arabic News, Pakistani Serial, Ariana* (Afghanistan TV), and *Hineni* and *Shalom Show* (both in Hebrew).[10] There are many other large cities with Middle Eastern populations (e.g., Chicago, Detroit, Houston, New York, San Francisco, and Washington, D.C.) that support at least one local Middle Eastern program, usually broadcast in Arabic or Persian.

There are no reliable, up-to-date statistics on the number of viewers for Middle Eastern TV shows. None of the standard rating services such as Nielsen and Arbitron gauge the preferences of ethnic audiences except those for the Spanish-language programs. As a result, it is practically impossible to know with any degree of certainty how many people watch the Middle Eastern TV programs and what they like or do not like about them. The statistics compiled by KSCI-TV on its Middle Eastern audiences in 1987 are unreliable because they seem to be based largely on population figures and not on actual viewership. They are, however, important because they form the basis on which the station determined its lease-access and advertising rates (see Table 2). These figures must no doubt be different today due to the tremendous surge of Middle Eastern populations into Southern California that doubled during the 1980s, from 144,100 to 300,000, making Los Angeles the "largest and most diverse center of Middle Easterners in the United States and in the Western world."[11] The popular press's account of the Middle Eastern populations, however, vastly differs from these figures, which are based on the 1990 census data.[12] Complicating the determination of audiences are such factors as generational differences, sub-ethnicity, interethnicity, and cross-viewing of Middle Eastern programs.

By and large, Middle Eastern programs target the entire family as their primary audience, a fact reflected in the "magazine format" of most of the programs, which tries to present something for every family member. The engine of the diaspora TV genre, this format consists of news, music, interviews,

Table 2   KSCI-TV's Middle Eastern Viewership, 1987

Nationality/Language	Weekly Households	Weekly Viewers
Arabic	42,486	132,756
Armenian	46,350	148,000
Iranian/Persian	69,327	235,710
Israeli/Hebrew	27,750	88,800

Source: Compiled from KSCI-TV data.

satirical skits, soap opera serials, cartoons, and advertisements. Some families plan their day around their favorite shows, such as *Arab-American TV*.[13] The programs may target the entire family, but they are often successful only in reaching either the older generations or the recent immigrants. Youngsters and second- or third-generation immigrants are usually left out or only given a nod in the programs. Communities that support a large number of programs, however, are able also to sustain specialized programs. For example, *Diyar tv* targets younger Iranians by specializing in pop music. The entire program is devoted to interviews with Iranian pop stars in exile, their music videos, and ads about entertainers.

Politics, Commerce, Religion

Under normal conditions, society's established structures tend to differentiate and regulate the roles and status of its members. In the liminality of exile, however, many traditional structures of the self and of group identity come under severe questioning or dissolve entirely. This situation encourages the forging of new or the reconfiguration of old identities and politics. Exilic liminality, therefore, is a period of profound change, one that can breed radicalism and extremism of all kinds. For a variety of reasons, the Middle Eastern diaspora TV in Los Angeles tends to fall into a conservative form of political and cultural radicalism that is marked by a type of long-distance nationalism and chauvinism driven by longing, nostalgia, fetishization of the homeland, and a burning desire for return.

Chief among the reasons for political conservatism is the U.S. capitalist system and the commercial TV structure within which diasporic TV must operate. The majority of Middle Eastern TV programs are commercially driven, and program producers generate their income by selling time to businesses for spot advertisements, which are usually for ethnic products and services or government-sponsored "ads" for national ideologies. The average income from ads placed in a single program amounts to several thousand dollars.[14]

The ratio of ads to program matter varies tremendously. Israeli-Jewish programs, particularly those of the JTN, carry the fewest ads, and Iranian and Armenian programs contain the most (although not all Iranian programs carry ads).[15] Although JTN, which packages nearly ten shows a week, carries very few ads for consumer products, it heavily promotes tourism to Israel in its programs and in its ads for El Al Israel Airlines. It also continually urges its viewers to subscribe and donate funds to the network. From time to time, a list containing donors' names is displayed on the screen.

In the case of certain communities such as Iranians, the amount of money spent on television production, transmission, and advertising is large enough to create a thriving ethnic economy that helps not only to consolidate a shared ethnic identity but also to facilitate exchange of information and business transactions among community members. However, despite such a collective economic power, as independent producers unattached to established broadcast networks, Middle Eastern programmers must seek additional funding to augment their income. Some Jewish and Arabic television programs solicit subscription fees from their viewers. Even producers of commercially driven shows that carry many ads, such as several Iranian shows and *Arab-American Television,* buttress their income by sponsoring music concerts and entertainment banquets (*haflahs*) that generate both additional profits and programs. Another strategy, with less desirable side effects, is the producers' practice of accepting money for on-air interviewing of celebrities and newsmakers, a practice in which some Iranian and Armenian producers are known to engage. Others are reputed to accept money from their governments at home or from opposition political factions abroad. Such assertions are difficult to substantiate and, at any rate, they shift dramatically over time.

The negative end result of such a tight imbrication of commerce and politics is both the commercialization of the news and the politicization of the entertainment shows. This and other factors force the producers into chauvinistic, partisanal politics, which in the case of Iranians has meant a shrill and doctrinaire anti-Islamist and pro-royalist discourse, and in the case of Armenian programmers, a vehement anti-Turkish and anti-Azeri stance. Such politicization is evident in the preponderance of newscasts that report and music videos that depict acts of violence at home. These factors may also help explain the general disdain that many Middle Eastern viewers, especially youngsters, express about these programs.

Although most programs tend to hide their political or religious sponsorship or affiliation, some do not. These programs tend to be less conservative in outlook, some promoting radical change. Less dependent on market forces, they are either semicommercial or essentially noncommercial, in that they do not carry ads for consumer products. For example, for quite some time, *Horizon Armenian TV,* whose producer is the Armenian National Committee Media Network that promotes Armenian revolutionary aspirations for a free, independent, united Armenia, was noncommercial and was largely sponsored by contributions from the Armenian community. In the past few years, perhaps in response to the massive restructuring of the former Soviet Union, it has changed to a commercially driven format.

The relationship among money, politics, religion, and diaspora television is particularly complex for Iranians. The religiously oriented program, *Mozhdeh,* produced by the Assembly of God Church, and the politically oriented program, *Sima-ye Azadi,* produced by the Mojahedin-e Khalq, a guerrilla organization stationed in Iraq fighting to overthrow the Islamist government in Iran, do not carry ads for consumer products, but they are propaganda programs for the respective ideologies and practices of their producing organizations. These programs do not hide their ideologies, allowing them to colonize the program entirely. However, another higher-quality program, *Aftab,* much of whose contents come from Iranian government sources, engages in a discourse of subterfuge by emphasizing Iranian culture and downplaying Islamist politics.

The only program that promotes Islam as a religion and a way of life in the U.S. is *Islam.* Produced since 1985 by Islamic Information Service in Southern California, the program appears to have three chief aims: to counteract the negative stereotype of Islam and of Muslims in the U.S.; to help non-Muslims learn more about Islam; and to help Muslim children in the U.S. feel better about their faith.[16] *Islam* features lessons and testimonials about various tenets of Islam as well as interviews and discussions with religious scholars and historians about various theological, jurisprudential, and political questions. Although not openly sectarian, the program appears to favor Sunni Islam, which is dominant in the Middle East. The program also urges viewers to contribute financially to Islamic causes and to vote for legislation favorable to Islamic causes and Islamic values and to Muslim politics worldwide. *Islam* does not carry ads for consumer products, but it promotes a Tape of the Month Club through which viewers may purchase copies of past programs. The program is financially supported by contributions the producer collects from the community.

Nationality, Nationalism, Language

Language is one of the chief markers of nationality and of national identity. Contemporary immigrants in the West have formed what might be called postmodern diasporas, communities created by voluntary or involuntary movements of people who are pushed or pulled across ethnic and national boundaries in response to rapidly changing political, economic, and social orders brought on by the dismantling of the party states, the resurgence of radical forms of Islam, and the globalization of multinational capital. However, although physically separated from their "habitus," these postmodern diasporas have not neglected their indigenous cultures and languages; instead, using electronic media, they have worked actively to celebrate and sustain them. Videos from the homeland and television programs made in the diaspora are powerful vehicles in this process. However, using indigenous languages to establish difference between the cultures of the Middle Eastern countries and the U.S. tends to highlight national languages at the expense of regional or local languages and dialects of the homeland.

For example, until 1992 nearly all Iranian programs were in Persian, the national language of Iran. No regularly scheduled Iranian program has been aired in Kurdish or Turkish, which are regional languages of significant populations in Iran (and perhaps in Los Angeles as well). Thus, Iranian programs have tended to use language nationalistically. Although nationalism demands linguistic purity, professional communication permits its violation in the interest of assimilation. Thus, the first regularly scheduled Iranian program to be aired entirely in English is a medical show, *You and the World of Medicine,* in which physicians advise viewers about various illnesses, their diagnoses, and modes of treatment.

Arabic programs, on the other hand, seem to have favored a kind of pan-Arabism driven by Egyptian Arabic. Pan-Arabism is particularly strong in the case of *Arab-American TV,* which attempts to appeal to all religions and cultures of the Arab Middle East. Ironically, linguistic pan-Arabism seems to be informed less by a genuine desire for collective identity among disparate Arabs in diaspora than by the desire to counteract the generally negative stereotypes of Arabs in the U.S. by presenting a united front. However, the TV shows that form the resulting pan-Arabist cultural artifact tend to suppress regional differences and the specificities of Arabic cultures, and in the end they may serve to feed the offensive stereotypes.

A number of programs are bilingual, broadcasting in various proportions of Arabic, Hebrew, and English. For example, with the exception of its short local news section, which is in English, *Arab-American TV* is presented entirely in Arabic. This strategy seems to fulfill the different generational needs of its viewers. Elder members who are understood to be more attached to the "old country," the Arabic language, and the politics of their homelands are served their program segments in Arabic. Younger viewers, on the other hand, who are presumably more focused on their lives in the host country, are served local news (chiefly entertainment news) in English.

Of the Israeli-Jewish programs, *Israel Today* is entirely in Hebrew. The overwhelming majority of the JTN program package is in English. However, the use of English does not work to suppress Jewish ethnic identity. In fact, the majority of the news on the English-language *Jewish Television Network News* is about events of interest from either inside Israel or various Jewish diasporas in the world. Likewise, although the entertainment shows such as *A Conversation with Robert Clary* are in English, they tend to highlight famous American Jewish entertainers and celebrities. Such programming presumes that, for Jewish Americans, it is not the language of the broadcasts that constructs ethnicity so much as their cultural and political contents. Perhaps for these viewers other forms of artistic expression such as cinema, literature, poetry, and jokes are better able to link language to nationality and ethnicity. One effect of using the English language and national celebrities is that Jewish programs, with the exception of *Israel Today* and *The Phil Blazer Show*, locate themselves in the present United States. Jewish programmers seem to be less ambivalent about their politics of location and about identifying themselves as American because, unlike most other Middle Easterners in this country, they are relatively confident of their social acceptance and their economic and political power in mainstream America.

All Assyrian programs, whether produced by Iranian or Iraqi nationals, are in Assyrian, and they tend to work toward preserving and propagating the religious, historical, and cultural values and beliefs of Assyrians in their worldwide diaspora. All Armenian shows are primarily in Armenian, with *Armenian*

Teletime in Lebanese Armenian and *Horizon* in Eastern Armenian; English-language materials form part of both broadcasts. Armenian *Tele-U.S. Armenians* programs contain many films, newscasts, and television materials in the original language imported from (formerly Soviet) Armenia.

Ethnicity, Subethnicity, Interethnicity

Middle Eastern populations in Los Angeles are ethnoreligiously very diverse, a diversity that up to now has remained largely repressed by the desire to create a strong national identity in diaspora. For example, although many Iranian Baha'is, Armenians, Jews, and Muslims are involved in making Iranian TV programs, there is no program that espouses openly the religious beliefs, cultures, or languages of any one of these four groups. Instead, programs foreground a kind of essentialist Iranianness. Caught in the liminality of exile in a host society that has been generally hostile to them, Iranians have stressed consolidation of nationality from a distance. Internal differences may be expressed behind this harmonious veneer.

However, the veneer is not completely opaque, for submerged ethnicity ruptures through, often in the form of commercials for subethnic products and businesses or interviews with subethnic figures.[17] *Jam-e Jam* and *Iran va Jahan* are good examples of Jewish submerged ethnicity among Iranian programs, where Jewish businesses are advertised more heavily. Likewise, *Twenty 2 Forty,* an irreverent lifestyle and exercise show packaged by JTN, does not highlight its Jewishness at all, but the presence of Jewish ethnicity is inscribed in the program in such moments as when the host conducts "man-on-street" interviews with passersby about the meaning of the word *kvetch.*

In addition to submerged ethnicity, interethnicity is another operating principle for Middle Eastern programs not only during their production but also at the time of their reception. Because of the long historical intermingling of societies and cultures of the Middle East, there are many things that Middle Easterners in diaspora share, which allow them to enjoy watching programs from different Middle Eastern countries. For example, Iranian Jews may enjoy not only Persian-language programs but also Hebrew- and English-language programs produced by JTN. Palestinian Arabs may appreciate the Hebrew-language program *Israel Today,* and Christian Copts may benefit from *Arab-American TV.* Interethnicity and multilingualism create intertextuality that tends to be liberatory because it allows both the unforeseen juxtaposition and overlapping of cultures and the transgression of boundaries that have divided Middle Eastern peoples. The consumerist-driven postmodernity is neither entirely liberatory nor is it universally celebrated. From certain vantage points, fragmentation and decentering may be considered to be disempowering, but the potential for interculturalism, intertextuality, and transgressive juxtapositions that the postmodern diaspora offers can be regarded as its empowering and redeeming rewards.

Notes

This is a revised version of "Narrowcasting and Nationalism: Middle Eastern Television in Los Angeles," *Afterimage* 20, no. 7 (February 1993): 9–11, and is reprinted here by permission.

1   "Cable TV's Perfect Niche Marketing Vehicle," 1991, 3.

2   David Holley, "South Korean Ownership of TV Firm Admitted," *Los Angeles Times*, 11 February 1986, B-1.

3   Ha-il Kim, "Minority Media Access: Examination of Policies, Technologies, and Multi-Ethnic Television and a Proposal for an Alternative Approach to Media Access" (Ph.D. diss., University of California, Los Angeles, 1992).

4   For example, 50 percent of the programs carried by Univision Television Network, the leader in Spanish-language programming in the United States, which reaches some 60 percent of the Spanish-speaking audience, is produced in the United States, with the balance imported chiefly from Mexico and Venezuela (Claudia Puig, "Univision President Bolts to Rival Telemundo," *Los Angeles Times*, 27 May 1992, D1–2).

5   Victor Valle, "Latino TV Re-Creates U.S. Images," *Los Angeles Times*, 18 August 1988, F-1.

6   In the late 1980s, Mexican Americans in Southern California charged that both Telemundo and Univision were working to reduce the Mexican influence at the networks, despite the fact that 60 percent of the 22 million Latin Americans living in the United States are of Mexican descent (Frank del Olmo, "TV Dispute Sheds Light on the 'Hispanic Myth,'" *Los Angeles Times*, 29 May 1989, B-5).

7   See my *The Making of Exile Cultures: Iranian Television in Los Angeles* (Minneapolis: University of Minnesota Press, 1993).

8   The breakdown of these programs by language on KSCI-TV is as follows (hours/week, week of May 17, 1992): Arabic 3.0, Armenian 5.0, Cambodian 1.5, Mandarin 9.5, French 2.5, Tagalog/English 5.0, German .50, Hungarian .50, Hindi/English 1.0, Persian 15.5, Italian .50, Japanese 14.5, Hebrew 1.0, Korean 22.5, Russian 1.0, and Vietnamese 5.0 (source: KSCI-TV).

9 Quoted from the International Channel Network publicity.

10 According to the International Channel Network literature, by March 1992, the broadcast hours per week devoted to Middle Eastern shows was as follows: Iranian 8.5, Arabic 6.5, Hebrew 4, Armenian 2.

11 Mehdi Bozorgmehr, Claudia Der-Martirosian, and Georges Sabagh, "Middle Easterners: A New Kind of Immigrant," in *Ethnic Los Angeles,* ed. Roger Waldinger and Mehdi Bozorgmehr (New York: Russell Sage Foundation Press, forthcoming).

12 For example, the *Los Angeles Times* estimated that the number of Iranians in Southern California alone has increased from 200,000 in 1984 to 800,000 in 1991 (Charles Perry, "Nouruz: Have a Happy Equinox," *Los Angeles Times,* 19 March 1992, H-1).

13 Brian Clark, "Arab-Americans on the Air," *Aramco World,* 1992, 12–15.

14 In the case of Iranians, for example, producers can expect to earn from advertisements approximately $2,500 for a half-hour show and $5,000 for a one-hour show. From this must be subtracted, of course, the cost of production and airtime rental.

15 Although KSCI-TV has tried to keep ad time in a one-hour program to twenty minutes, some Iranian programs, to the chagrin of viewers and station officials, have frequently carried up to forty-five minutes of ads in a one-hour time slot.

16 From *Islamic Information Service News* 2 (1990).

17 On "submerged ethnicity" in media, see Ella Shohat, "Ethnicities-in-Relations: Toward a Multicultural Reading of American Cinema," in *Unspeakable Images: Ethnicity and the American Cinema,* ed. Lester D. Friedman (Urbana: University of Illinois Press, 1991).

RE-COVERING RACISM

Crack Mothers, Reaganism, and the Network News

Jimmie L. Reeves

White Offenders and Black Delinquents

This paper condenses an argument about the racial dimensions of the Reagan era war on drugs from a book-length study about the struggle over the meaning of cocaine as represented in television news reports from the 1980s.[1] Perhaps the chief finding of the larger study is the disturbing disparity in the journalistic treatment of white "offenders" and black "delinquents." In the early 1980s, when cocaine was primarily associated with white "offenders," the approved purifying solution for the cocaine problem was therapeutic intervention. The signature image of this coverage was of a white, middle-class male in his late twenties voicing the clichés of a cleansing confession during a group therapy session. Like the rebirth rhetoric of Reaganism, then, the drug news of the early 1980s was heavily inflected by the *discourse of recovery.*[2]

However, the journalistic discovery of crack in late 1985 signaled the beginning of a period of frenzied coverage in which the race and class dimensions of the cocaine problem established in the early 1980s would be almost completely inverted: what was once defined as a glamour drug and white transgression became increasingly associated with poor people of color isolated in America's inner cities—the so-called urban underclass. Instead of focusing on therapeutic intervention, the post-crack coverage foregrounds modes of exclusion enforced by the three *P*s of the hard sector of the modern narco-carceral network: police, prosecution, and prison. Rather than activate the discourse of recovery, then, the crack crisis triggered a *discourse of discrimination* that provided journalistic justification for the symbolic criminalization of a generation of black youth. In contrast to the therapeutic confessions of the earlier drug news, the signature image of this discourse was the footage shot with a handheld camera of the police raiding a crack house. This footage exemplifies the convergence of the reportorial with the policing gaze — a perspective that, in the context of the inner city, is perhaps best described as the colonizer's point of view on the colonized.

Despite major disruptions in the journalistic treatment of the anticocaine crusade during the 1980s, one recurring theme provided a degree of continuity to the cocaine narrative. As the news frame shifted from "recovering" white offenders to "arresting" black transgressors after the 1986 crack crisis, issues related to "unsettling developments" in American family life continued to play a central role in the journalistic construction of the cocaine problem. In this coverage, concern about "the family" focused on the contaminated generation that "dropped out" and "turned on" in the 1960s, the families lost by white–male–middle-class transgressors in therapy stories, and the restoration of "family values" through efforts such as Nancy Reagan's antidrug activism.

As part of a broader investigation of these concerns, this paper analyzes how the ideal of the nuclear family inflects the sinister images of maternity projected in news coverage featuring crack mothers. Ultimately, I hope this examination of the journalistic discovery of a new composite "she-devil" provides insights into how the "conservative egalitarianism" of the Reagan coalition used "family values" to renovate long-standing white/black antagonisms deploying what Spiro Agnew might call a "positive polarization" of the electorate along color, rather than class, lines.

Contextualizing the Drug News:
Reaganism and the Packaging of Backlash
Reagan as Auteur?

Rather than approach Ronald Reagan in terms of "leadership" or "charisma," this study conceives of the proper name *Reagan* as performing what Foucault terms the "author function" for a top-heavy economic, electoral, and moral coalition that solidified in the 1970s around the politics of resentment and the worship of mammon.[3] Expansive and multifaceted, Reaganism was the chief expression of a political "war of position" sponsored by entrepreneurial interests during the chaotic economic transformations of the 1970s.[4] The war on drugs was, at root, a Reaganite project that expressed the New Right's basic "law-and-order" response to social problems grounded on economic distress.

To uncover the cynical production and exploitation of drug hysteria during the Reagan era, this study adopts a "bottom-up" perspective of the war on drugs—an oppositional perspective that identifies more with "the policed" than with elite policymakers. From this perspective, the war on drugs is best understood as a classic example of the modern "political spectacle." According to Murray Edelman, such spectacles tend to "perpetuate or intensify the conditions that are defined as the problem, an outcome that typically stems from efforts to cope with a condition by changing the consciousness or behavior of individuals while preserving the institutions that generate consciousness and behavior."[5] This spectacle redefines the failure of the drug control establishment to solve the drug problem with modern disciplinary measures. As a result, the power of the "soft" and "hard" sectors of its carceral networks have been extended, facilitating the implementation of more of the same failed measures: more police raids, more jails, more prisons, more prosecutors, more drug testing, more treatment, more education, more rallies, more surveillance—more disciplining of the body and more regulating of the population. This vicious cycle is especially evident in the dramatic expansions of the national drug control budget, the addiction treatment industry, and the U.S. prison population during the Reagan-Bush administration.

For example, in 1981, only $1.5 billion was devoted to domestic enforcement, international/border control, and demand reduction. Under Reagan's leadership, the drug budget more than quadrupled ($6.6 billion spent in 1989) at a time of drastic cuts in most other government programs. Under Bush, that number nearly doubled again: the 1993 allocation was $12.7 billion, with the lion's share going to domestic enforcement programs.[6] Similarly, a major component of the "soft sector" of the drug control establishment, addiction treatment, was one of the most expansive growth industries in the U.S. service economy during the Reagan era. As Stanton Peele explains: "Private treatment centers have become important operations for many hospitals, and numerous specialty hospitals and chains—like CompCare—devote themselves to the treatment of alcoholism, chemical dependency, obesity, and assorted new maladies like compulsive gambling, compulsive shopping, PMS, and postpartum depression. . . . The number of such centers more than quadrupled and the number of patients treated in them for alcoholism alone quintupled between 1978 and 1984."[7] What Peele condemns as the "diseasing of America" would continue to advance after 1984: in a scathing (though tardy) exposé of the questionable practices of the drug treatment industry, ABC's Sylvia Chase reported that "the number of profit-making psychiatric hospitals" doubled yet again between 1984 and 1991.[8] Finally, as a place of separation, panoptic surveillance, and *in*carceration where the delinquent is detained and delinquency is contained and maintained, the prison is the chief manifestation of the hard sector of the drug control establishment's "correctional" network. During the Reagan era, the U.S. prison population nearly doubled (from 329,821 in 1980 to 627,402 in 1989) as the number of drug arrests nationwide increased from 471,000 in 1980 to 1,247,000 in 1989. By 1990, the United States had the highest incarceration rate in the world (426 per 100,000 compared to 333 per 100,000 in South Africa, its closest competitor). In that same year, when about half the inmates in federal prisons were there for drug offenses, African Americans made up nearly half of the U.S. prison population, and almost 25 percent of young black males in their twenties were either in jail, on parole, or on probation (compared to only 6 percent of white males).[9]

These ballooning numbers speak powerfully of the hypocrisies and inequities of an era in which the ruling bloc embarked on a highly self-conscious program to loosen governmental constraints on the rich and tighten "margins of illegality" on the poor. The war on drugs was central to enabling the incongruities of this cynical political agenda: it succeeded in defining *social problems* that grew from global transformations in late capitalism (deindustrialization, job migration, the vanishing "family wage" of a vanishing manufacturing economy, the flexible exploitation of fragmented labor markets in a burgeoning service economy, the rise of transnational corporations, etc.) as *individual moral problems* that could be resolved by voluntary therapeutic treatment, compulsory drug testing, mandatory prison sentences, and even the penalty of death.

The New Racism?

Part of the panic generated by the "crack crisis" of 1986 was its violation of a racially inflected system of illicit taste distinctions. A pleasurable substance that was once the province of the wealthy had finally "trickled down" to the most subordinate levels of the American socioeconomic racial order. In this violation of taste distinctions, cocaine would not only lose some of its value as a status symbol, but it would become associated with a mode of drug abuse that is more a matter of desperation than recreation. By inverting the established meanings associated with cocaine transgression, the crack crisis coverage and its images of black youth "running wild in the streets" would help fortify and justify the prevailing racial attitudes of the predominantly white Reagan counterrevolution.

These attitudes, which were most explicitly and notoriously voiced in focus groups made up of the infamous "Reagan Democrats" of Michigan's Macomb County, are characterized in the research of a number of scholars as a "new racism." Summarizing this research, Robert M. Entman identifies three components of this backlash mentality: "anti-black affect—a general emotional hostility toward blacks," "resistance to the political demands of blacks," and a "belief that racism is dead and that racial discrimination no longer inhibits black achievement."[10] Entman also observes that the so-called new racism springs in part from the widespread suppression of old racial bigotry that proposed that racial minorities were intellectually and biologically inferior to the white race. As Michael Omi and Howard Winant put it, the New Right has "gained political currency by rearticulating a racial ideology" that "does not display overt racism."[11] To understand this symbolic recovery, the racial ideology of Reaganism must be seen as a response to two competing discourses: the discourse of "special interests" who demand group rather than individual rights, which is associated with the radicalism of the demonized 1960s; and the older discourse of white supremacy, which persists in such far right fringe groups as the Ku Klux Klan, the White American Resistance, the Order, the Posse Commitatus, the Aryan Nations, the Farmers Liberation Army, and the Christian-Patriots Defense League.

In the space between these two discourse systems, Reaganism fostered an emergent racial formation that replaced the Social Darwinism of traditional white supremacy with the cultural Moynihanism of conservative egalitarianism.[12] I coin the term *cultural Moynihanism* to indicate how Reaganist racism appropriated and reaccentuated the mainstream, ethnicity-based theory of the modern sociology of race. According to Omi and Winant, between 1930 and 1965, as the biologistic paradigm of Social Darwinism suffered from its association with Nazi ideology, the ethnicity paradigm came to operate as "the progressive/liberal 'common sense' approach to race [in which] two recurrent themes—assimilationism and cultural pluralism—were defined."[13] The key works of this period were E. Franklin Frazier's *The Negro Family in the*

United States[14] and Gunnar Myrdal's *An American Dilemma: The Negro Problem and Modern Democracy.*[15] Challenging the concept of the "inherent moral degeneracy of the Negro," Frazier developed an antiessentialist environmentalist argument that tied relatively high rates of black illegitimacy to "the social and economic subordination of the Negro" both in the rural South and in the slums of northern cities.[16] Although heavily influenced by Frazier's work, Swedish economist Myrdal provided an account of the American experience and a critique of American democracy that was Eurocentric in outlook, much like Alexis de Tocqueville's inquiry penned a century earlier.

In step with the most progressive thinking of their age, Frazier and Myrdal championed an assimilationism for African Americans that was erroneously based on the analogy of European immigrants. This flaw enables ethnicity theory to account for rites of inclusion that broaden notions of what it means to be "white" in America, but it prevents the theory from fully grasping how the controlling rites of exclusion figure in the same process. As a dangerous "half-truth," ethnicity theory's reliance on this analogy underestimates the importance of the discourse of discrimination in perpetuating the dominant social/cultural/racial/gender order. As Patricia Hill Collins demonstrates, this discourse of discrimination is especially salient to the experience of women of color. Often situated in the curious position of the "outsider within," African American women have long played an important symbolic role in the white imagination. In Collins's words: "As the 'Others' of society who can never really belong, strangers threaten the moral and social order. But they are simultaneously essential for its survival because those individuals who stand at the margins of society clarify its boundaries. African-American women, by not belonging, emphasize the significance of belonging."[17] The "significance of belonging," of sharing in the rights and privileges of being "free and white" in America, then, quite literally has a "dark side," for it is sustained by the ongoing othering, marginalization, and stigmatization of the "nonwhite" category. By treating all contact with the dominant order as the same regardless of context (voluntary immigration, territorial conquest, genocide, or slavery), the ethnicity paradigm obscures historic disparities in the treatment of "white" and "nonwhite" groups. Despite this fatal flaw, Frazier and Myrdal's shared utopian vision provided much of the theoretical justification for civil rights struggles in the 1950s and 1960s.

Unfortunately, the ethnicity paradigm's view of black culture as "pathological" would increasingly take center stage in "the defense of conservative (or 'neoconservative') egalitarianism against what is perceived as the radical assault of 'group rights.'"[18] In 1965, a report written by Daniel Patrick Moynihan was issued by the Office of Policy Planning and Research of the Department of Labor. Titled *The Negro Family: The Case for National Action,* the Moynihan report characterized the black family as a "tangled web of pathology."[19] The Moynihan report was a significant new twist in the ethnicity paradigm, for it blames the victims of a long history of systematic racial oppression, economic exploitation, and social exclusion for their own misery, supposedly caused by their own failure to "assimilate" as individuals into an "accommodative" and increasingly "color blind" society. Since the publication of the Moynihan report, a series of studies operating in or drawing from the ethnicity tradition (most notably, by Moynihan, Nathan Glazer, Ben Wattenberg, Thomas Sowell, and Charles Murray) have provided the New Right with seemingly "objective" research that justifies eliminating affirmative action programs, cutting welfare funding, and prosecuting a brutal war on black youth under the guise of the war on drugs.[20]

In this malicious appropriation of ethnicity theory, the New Right's mercenary intellectuals have redefined the economic turmoil and familial instability accompanying the shift from a manufacturing economy to a service economy as simply the consequences of cultural pathologies driven by individual immorality. In Craig Reinarman and Harry G. Levine's phrasing: "Unemployment, poverty, urban decay, school crises, crime, and all their attendant forms of human troubles were spoken of and acted upon as if they were the result of individual deviance, immorality, or weakness. The aperture of attribution for America's ills was constricted. People in trouble were reconceptualized as people who make trouble; social control replaced social welfare as the organizing principle of state policy."[21] Blithely dismissing over two hundred years of slavery and another one hundred years of legalized racial discrimination, this blame-the-victim mentality struck a responsive chord with millions of white middle- and working-class Americans. In a time of declining expectations, vanishing jobs, and escalating housing and medical costs, the New Right's moral ahistoricism not only released members of the white majority from any sense of responsibility, but it also gave them reason to feel that *they* were "truly victimized." As the anti-affirmative action "black-lash"[22] by powerful African American conservatives like Clarence Pendleton Jr., Thomas Sowell, and Justice Clarence Thomas verifies, the coinage of the new culturalist racism has much more exchange value and much wider investment opportunities than that of old-time biologicist racism. The new racism is more subtle, more respectable, less inflammatory — and more politically robust than its precursors.

This versatility is particularly evident in *The Vanishing Family: Crisis in Black America*, a CBS News special report that aired in January 1985. Narrated by Bill Moyers, the notoriously "liberal" journalist at the center of the New Right's recent attack on PBS, the report both featured and furthered the cultural Moynihanism of conservative egalitarianism. Moyers, like Moynihan, acknowledges that racism was at one time a decisive force limiting the lives of African Americans. But, also like Moynihan, Moyers ultimately denies that racism can explain the contemporary suffering of poor African Americans in the inner city. Describing a black neighborhood in Newark, New Jersey, as "a world turned inside-out," Moyers argues that both the alien value system of this world and the poverty of its inhabitants grow from a moral irresponsibility that is destroying "the" black family.[23] Illustrating his report with men who refuse to support their children and women who feel they can get along fine without husbands, Moyers concludes that there are very few "positive role models" in this neighborhood. Moyers states his negative assessment most clearly in a passage that dehumanizes these transgressors: "There are successful strong black families in America. Families that affirm parental authority and the values of discipline, work, and achievement. But you won't find many who live around here. Still, not every girl in the inner city ends up a teenage mother, not every young man goes into crime. *There are people who have stayed here.* They're out-numbered by the con artists and pushers. It's not an even match, but they stand for morality and authority and give some of these kids a dose of unsentimental love."[24] Like many of the network news reports of the same period, Moyers's dialogue overtly locates "con artists" and "pushers" as a separate category from "people." In the final analysis, for Moyers, the black households he surveils in Newark suffer more from depravity than discrimination: they fail to "affirm parental authority," to value "discipline, work, and achievement," and, most important, to "stand for morality."

The intersection of "family values" with cultural Moynihanism, then, is one site where the backlash politics of race and gender converge. The discursive power of this convergence explains, in part, why cultural Moynihanism also provides a common grounding for both Murray's conservative egalitarianism and Moyers's liberal pluralism. According to Stephanie Coontz, this common grounding has generated what is often called "the new consensus" among conservatives and liberals: what African Americans need "is not government programs but a good dose of sexual restraint, marital commitment, and parental discipline."[25]

Analyzing the Drug News: The Chain of Othering

In the 1980s, a particularly sinister type of maternal discourse would capture the imagination of moral crusaders both inside and outside the news establishment. Standing in stark contrast to the composite Reaganite "she" in need of protection, the crack mother was a composite "she-devil" in need of discipline; like the "emblematic mother" idealized in the New Right's pro-family agenda, the transgressing mother was also reduced to her reproductive identity. The media construction of the crack mother animated a complex set of meanings that often dovetailed with the fetal rights rhetoric of the anti-abortion movement. Like the "murderous mommies" denounced by Operation Rescue, the crack mother was berated in the drug news as an enemy to the innocent life within. In 1989, *The Washington Post* announced "Crack Babies: The Worst Threat Is Mom Herself," a headline that was something of a journalistic credo in the late 1980s.[26]

Policing Pregnancy

The journalistic discovery of and obsession with the crack mother and baby are most properly understood as parts of a larger policing of pregnancy by the medical establishment. Most of the primary locations for the early stories on cocaine and pregnancy are hospital maternity wards. In this news discourse, the maternity ward operates as a surveillance setting where the spectacle of birth allows medical authorities to scrutinize and stigmatize transgressing mothers.

The first such story appeared on September 11, 1985. In it, CBS's Susan Spencer announces the results of a preliminary study showing that the rate of spontaneous abortions among pregnant women using cocaine was three times higher than the average rate. Although the story did feature the remorseful confession of "Linda," a white woman in Chicago who gave birth to a baby who displayed the "jittery" symptoms of cocaine withdrawal, Spencer did not dwell on the sins of the mother. Instead, she structured the package as a general health warning addressed specifically and explicitly to women. Using the second-person singular address, Spencer concludes her report with the direct exhortation: "The message is clear: If you are pregnant and use cocaine—stop."

However, by December 20, 1985, when CBS issued the second network alert about this potential danger, the warning was laced with a righteous indignation that set the tone for the "crack mother" subplot of subsequent coverage. Told by male journalist Terry Drinkwater, the story focuses less on warning women than on the damage done to babies — babies who, according to substitute anchor Charles Kuralt's lead-in, are "victims who aren't even old enough to know better." The shift from warning women to demonizing mothers is captured best in the final moments of the report, when Drinkwater considers the condition of an eighteen-month-old girl whom a male foster parent predicts may grow up to be a "twenty-one-year-old with an IQ of perhaps 50, barely able to dress herself, and probably unable to live alone." In a closing line that is saturated with moral disgust, Drinkwater reports, "The mother told authorities she was just a recreational drug user."

These journalistic horror stories that cast the mother in the role of the monster took on racial overtones in 1986. In keeping with the general paradigm shift in the framing of drug news, the "cocaine mothers" of the 1985 warnings were predominantly white, and the "crack mothers" of the coverage in 1986–88 were predominantly women of color. In this shift, the discourse of the crack mother would resonate with the cultural Moynihanism of the "new racism": the "epidemic" of crack babies became yet another example of the "poverty of values" crippling America's largely black inner cities.

The Other Mothers

The harsh journalistic treatment of crack mothers conforms to a pattern of racial disparity that Rickie Solinger uncovered in her provocative study of the treatment of illegitimacy before *Roe v. Wade.* According to her study, in the 1950s, transgressing mothers-to-be were the subject of "racially distinct" policies and practices. Although all unwed mothers were reduced to their reproductive identities as "breeders," errant white women were viewed as "socially productive" because their babies had value on the adoption market: "White women in this situation were defined as occupying a state of 'shame,' a condition that admitted rehabilitation and redemption. The pathway was prescribed: casework treatment in a maternity home, relinquishment of the baby for adoption, and rededication of the offending woman to the marriage market. . . . White illegitimacy was generally not perceived as a 'cultural' or racial defect, or as a public expense, so the stigma suffered by the white unwed mother was individual and familial."[27] As an "individual" and "familial" defect, unwed motherhood for white transgressors was treated as a symptom of "mental illness" that could be rectified through therapeutic solutions. Like the white cocaine transgressors of the early 1980s news coverage, the white unwed mother was an "offender" whose psyche could be rehabilitated and whose reproductive capacity could be recovered and legitimated.

Black single pregnancy, in contrast, was defined as "socially unproductive," "the product of uncontrolled sexual indulgence, the product, in fact, of an absense of psyche." Where white transgressors suffered from a "shame" that could be eliminated by purifying confession and repentance, the pathology of delinquency was literally inscribed on the body and in the genes of the black unwed mother. Her very life was a punishable offense requiring "punitive, legal sanctions." As Solinger states: "Black women, illegitimately pregnant, were not shamed but simply blamed, blamed for the population explosion, for escalating welfare costs, for the existence of unwanted babies, and blamed for the tenacious grip of poverty on blacks in America. There was no redemption possible for these women, only sterilization, harassment by welfare officials, and public policies that threatened to starve them and their babies."[28] These same oppositions—white/black, shame/blame, offender/delinquent, therapy/pathology, recovery/discrimination, inclusion/exclusion—organized the cocaine coverage of the 1980s.

While the treatment of white unwed pregnancy has changed significantly since the 1950s, the social construction of black illegitimacy as the pathological cause of economic distress persists, a fact that was painfully evident at a pivotal moment during the second presidential debate of the 1992 campaign. In an interchange with an African American woman who wanted to know how the candidates "could honestly find a cure for the economic problems of the common people" if they had no personal experience with poverty, President Bush offered a particularly revealing non sequitur: "Well, listen, you ought to—you ought to be in the White House for a day and hear what I hear and see what I see and read the mail I read and touch the people I touch from time to time. I was in the Lomaxa AME Church. It's a black church just outside of Washington, D.C. And I read in the—in the bulletin about teenage pregnancies, about the difficulties that families are having to meet ends—make ends meet. . . ." Given the identity of the questioner and racial makeup of the congregation, the church bulletin comment is clearly a botched attempt to blame illegitimacy for black economic distress.

Tomorrow's Delinquents

Four days earlier, during the first presidential debate, H. Ross Perot, who claims to have survived an assassination attempt by Black Panthers, was much more coherent and effective in articulating the key features of the "common sense" regarding crack mothers that circulated in the news coverage of the 1980s: the chemical scapegoating of social ills born of economic deprivation; the racially coded framing of certain forms of fertility as "socially unproductive," as "subsidized deviancy"; and, perhaps most disturbing, the stigmatization, not only of the mothers, but also of their "permanently and genetically damaged" progeny. Quoting Perot: "Any time you think you want to legalize drugs, go to a neonatal unit, if you can get in. They are 100 and 200 percent capacity up and down the East Coast. And the reason is crack babies being born. Baby's in the hospital 42 days. Typical cost to you and me is $125,000. Again and again and again the mother disappears in three days and the child becomes a ward of the state because he's permanently and genetically damaged. Just look at those little children and if anybody can think about leave — legalizing drugs, they've lost me. . . ."

The characterizations offered by Perot were not unique to conservative politicians. Even *Rolling Stone,* a publication once associated with the counterculture, claimed that these babies are "like no others, brain damaged in ways yet unknown, oblivious to any affection."[29] Such demonizing claims were taken to their dehumanizing limit by Boston University President John Silber, who apparently believes that crack babies are not even invested with a *soul.* Speaking as "a mere generalist" in an account published in *The Boston Globe,* Silber explored the limits of human redemption by stating that "St. Thomas would have a hard time justifying" priorities that allot insufficient primary health care to children who could go on and live "to the greater glory of God, while spending immense amounts on crack babies who won't ever achieve the intellectual development to have consciousness of God."[30]

Perhaps not surprisingly, this attention to the social havoc wrought by crack babies was not justified by sustained studies of the problem. As pediatricians Barry Zuckerman and Deborah Frank argue, such divinely inspired public policy statements and widespread demonization of crack babies have "evolved in the absense of any credible scientific data regarding the sequelae of prenatal exposure to cocaine beyond the newborn period": "Moreover, this furor over prenatal exposure to cocaine obscures in the public mind any debate regarding society's responsibility for other conditions, such as lack of access to prenatal or pediatric care, malnutrition, measles, or lead poisoning, which jeopardize the development of many impoverished American children, whether substance exposed or not."[31]

There was, indeed, both an "epidemic" of premature and unhealthy babies and a rise in the infant mortality rate in the 1980s. But these health crises had less to do with cocaine than with Reagan's budget cuts and Reaganist doctrines of privatization and deregulation. In 1981 alone, cuts in Medicaid and other public assistance programs stripped more than 1 million poor women and their children of medical benefits. Because of the rising cost of health insurance under deregulation, the number of people without coverage soared during the 1980s, as did the percentage of births to mothers with inadequate prenatal care. Susan Faludi summarizes the research on these drastic changes:

> A 1989 University of California research team reviewed records of more than 146,000 births between 1982 and 1986 in California, and found that babies born to parents with no health insurance — a group whose numbers had grown by 45 percent in those years — were 30 percent more likely to die, be seriously ill at birth, and suffer low birth weight; uninsured black women were more than twice as likely as insured black women to have sickly newborns. A similar 1985 Florida report tracing the dire effects of lost prenatal care concluded, "In the end, it is safer for the baby to be born to a drug-using, anemic, or diabetic mother who visits the doctor throughout her pregnancy than to be born to a normal woman who does not."[32]

Even though it was damaging to many more children than the "cocaine epidemic," the health insurance crisis did not result in a moral panic because it did not correspond to the "poverty of values" view of social and economic problems. In comparison, the crack mother reinforced the "new consensus" that African Americans need "sexual restraint, marital commitment, and parental discipline," providing the basis for an old-fashioned, racially inflected moral panic in both the news media and the political arena.

A story appearing in the October 25, 1988, broadcast of *The NBC Nightly News* is an extreme illustration of the panic idiom at work. Reported by Michelle Gillen, it is the second segment of a two-part investigative series titled "Cocaine Kids." Calling it a "spotlight" report, Tom Brokaw's lead-in draws attention to its surveillance and sets up the we/they rhetoric that structures the story. According to Brokaw, when these cocaine kids "leave the hospital, they don't leave their problems behind."

Overlaying clichéd shots of fragile babies in a maternity ward, Gillen's opening narration also situates the contaminated children as "they": "They are the nation's tiniest drug victims. They are growing into the country's most unwanted children. . . . The babies begin life sick, often premature, suffering withdrawal from the mother's drugs. Their troubles, and ours, are only beginning." After moving from the maternity ward to the streets, where "their mothers often vanish . . . leaving their babies behind for hospitals and overwhelmed foster care systems to cope with," Gillen introduces a genuine specimen of a crack mother whose sexuality and fertility are "out of control." The "mother of two crack babies now in foster care," "Stephanie" is now "back on the streets, back on crack and pregnant again." As a metonymy for the situation of most black mothers, Stephanie's deviancy, according to the logic of Gillen's report, is typical.

In *person*alizing social problems, such reporting often treats the most visible and extreme instances of a phenomenon (the mentally ill homeless, for example) as paradigmatic of the whole problem.[33] But Gillen's report is a moment in an even larger discursive "tradition": the long-standing objectification of women of color as "outsiders within." According to Collins, as projections of white fantasies, desires, and fears, women of color have typically been represented as the Other in the form of four "controlling visions": the mammy, the matriarch, the welfare mother, and the Jezebel.[34] Some as old as slavery, one as fresh as the New Right, these distorted images of black women are the sources from which the hybrid crack mother emerged.

As a composite "she-devil," the crack mother takes the image of the welfare mother, so prominent in the demonology of Reaganism, and fuses it with the sexually aggressive Jezebel. According to Collins, the Jezebel occupies a central position in the "nexus of elite white male images of Black womanhood because efforts to control Black women's sexuality lie at the heart of Black women's oppression."[35] A particularly menacing image of fertility, the crack mother personifies an out-of-control black sexuality that is almost as threatening to the Reaganite imagination as its much older male cousin, the marauding black rapist. Playing on many of the same fears mobilized by the Willie Horton ads, the news discourse of crack mothers like "Stephanie" gave the New Right another racially charged code word to deploy in its holy class war against poor people of color.

But Gillen's investigative report is less about the sins of a monstrous mother than the demonization of her "they-like" offspring. After visiting foster homes and schools burdened by the challenges posed by cocaine kids, Gillen returns to her prophetic opening thesis that "their problems, and ours, are only beginning." "With crack so cheap and accessible in inner-city streets," states Gillen in a stand-up bridge to her closing arguments, "and with the waiting list for drug treatment programs so long, no one is even guessing at how widespread the epidemic of crack babies will be. But the few experts who are paying attention warn that there is a price to be paid—and they say the price will be enormous." In the following shots, back-to-back sound bites given by two experts, Rep. George Miller of the Select Committee on Children and Judge William Gladstone of a Florida juvenile court, provide the elite white male spin on cocaine kids, one that also relies on Gillen's we/they language:

> MILLER: We are going to have these children, who are the most expensive babies ever born in America, are going to overwhelm every social service delivery system that they come in contact with throughout the rest of their lives [*sic*].
>
> GLADSTONE: These kids have enormous, uh, physical problems, mental problems. They will go into a system that is woefully inadequate, woefully underfunded. They'll grow up to be tomorrow's delinquents.

Following these grim predictions, the story ends with a close-up shot of a cuddly black baby crawling on a blanket in a foster home. However, the youngster seems positively evil when Gillen's closing narration concludes, "There are tens of thousands of crack babies on the way. A generation born at risk. A generation which may pose an even greater risk."

Gillen's story bears witness to a historical process that is at least as vicious as the so-called cycle of poverty. Where Spencer's package first broke the cocaine mother story as a medical warning addressed to women and Drinkwater's package developed the warning into a horror story that demonized mothers, Gillen took the next step: demonizing the cocaine kids themselves. This chain of "othering" is precisely how the narco-carceral network sustains itself by reproducing deviance. Conscientious members of the medical community are increasingly troubled by the explosion of research spawned by the crack baby hysteria. According to an editorial by Thomas P. Strandjord and W. Alan Hodson published in the *Journal of the American Medical Association*, this crusading research is "fraught with many methodological errors": "These include sampling bias of the study population, identification and documentation of the actual use of cocaine by mothers (other than by self-reporting), the quantification including time and duration of fetal exposure, other pre-natal factors associated with drug-abusing mothers (nutrition, smoking), and the host of social and environmental factors (poverty, neglect, malnutrition, violence, child abuse, lead poisoning) that could adversely affect a develop-ing infant over the first few years of life."[36] In fact, one of the few studies that attempts to account for some of these intervening factors provides support for a cautious optimism about the long-term developmental consequences of prenatal cocaine exposure. The researchers found no mean developmental dif-ferences at two years of age between children labeled as cocaine babies and a control group made up of children of the same social class.[37]

Other researchers who are also sensitive to the class dimensions of the "crack baby" problem have suggested that the urgency to label such infants as "irremedially damaged" is often motivated by the desire to escape responsi-bility for the welfare of disadvantaged children. For instance, Linda C. Mayes, Richard H. Granger, Marc H. Bornstein, and Barry Zuckerman suggest in a commentary also published in the *Journal of the American Medical Associa-tion* that the rush to judgment about the "extent and permanency of specific effects of intrauterine cocaine exposure on newborns" is "closely tied to a significant social political issue": "Minimally, expectations for such children are lowered. The attribution of irremedial damage makes it more difficult to find services for these children, and such services may be geared to care-takers rather than to challenge children's capacities to remediate effectively. Even more damaging is the difficulty finding adequate homes for such chil-dren since potential foster or adoptive parents are often concerned about assuming the care of cocaine-exposed children because of their perceived im-pairments."[38] Contrary to the chemical and maternal scapegoating of Perot and Gillen, the worst threat to America's cocaine kids, in the long run, may be the label "crack baby" itself. Once attached, the label identifies the child as abnormal and stigmatizes the subject passing through social service and educational systems.[39] In the words of Dr. Claire Coles, "If a child comes to kindergarten with that label, they're dead. They are very likely to fulfill the worst prophesies."[40] Such labels often work as self-fulfilling prophesies in a double sense: they justify intense surveillance and tracking procedures that in-terpret everything as effects caused by the damage done in the womb, and they cause the stigmatized children to behave accordingly, as subjects under intense surveillance (less spontaneous/emotional/outgoing/trusting and more with-drawn/apathetic/introverted/wary than their "normal" peers) — behaviors that are then attributed, not to the surveillance procedures, but to the mother's "deviancy."[41] In large part, the label preordains them to be "tomorrow's delinquents."

The dynamic of a self-fulfilling prophesy was always at the heart of the obsession with crack babies. After the "discovery" of the epidemic, cocaine tended to be blamed for any baby in distress born prematurely to mothers who may or may not have taken the drug but whose unhealthy lifestyles included alcohol, smoking, and drug abuse. As a study published in *The Lancet* found, this prophetic stigmatization was especially apparent in the medical community. According to the study, abstracts on the impact of cocaine use during pregnancy were more likely to be accepted for presentation at the annual meeting of the Society for Pediatric Research if they reported "positive" evidence of impairment—even though rejected papers with "null" or "negative" findings tended to be more methodologically rigorous.[42] Medicine's tendency to follow the demands of its cultural and political contexts is revealed to be even more pernicious in a 1990 issue of the *New England Journal of Medicine*. According to a study by I. J. Chasnoff, H. Landress, and M. Barett, physicians and clinics are more likely to report pregnant black women and women on welfare to law enforcement agencies for using illegal drugs than their white and middle-class counterparts.[43] Like Solinger's study of unwed motherhood, Chasnoff and his colleagues discovered the same noxious disparities in the treatment of white "offenders" and black "delinquents"—disparities that also contaminate television news and its reporting of the 1980s anticocaine crusade.

The Meaning of Family Values

As Coontz observes, at the heart of much of the "hysteria about the 'underclass' and the spread of 'alien' values is what psychologists call projection": "Instead of facing disturbing tendencies in ourselves, we attribute them to something or someone external—drug dealers, unwed mothers, inner-city teens, or satanist cults. But blaming the 'underclass' for drugs, violence, sexual exploitation, materialism, or self-indulgence lets the 'over-class' off the hook. It also ignores the amoral, privatistic retreat from social engagement that has been the hallmark of middle-class response to recent social dilemmas."[44] These projections and evasions provide the master code for deciphering the meaning of "family values" as it is deployed in contemporary political discourse. The subject of much contestation during the 1992 presidential campaign, family values has become a vehicle for constructing a moral veneer on what Coontz terms the "amoral, privatistic retreat from social engagement." As suggested above, the convergence of family values with the cultural Moynihanism of the new racism provides a common grounding for the antiwelfare, anti–affirmative action, antitax, antibusing, and antifeminist backlash of the Reagan coalition. Cynically converting the material advantages of the bourgeois nuclear family into a virtue, the family values of the New Right "lets the 'over-class' off the hook" by recasting (or "projecting") poverty as a moral transgression and self-righteously reversing economic cause with familial effect. In this warped moral universe, women of color are subject to the multiple jeopardies of a sex/gender system that blames mothers for family problems and a race/class system that blames the pathological black family for economic problems. As Collins observes, the "holier-than-Thou" moralism of this standpoint links "gender ideology to explanations of class subordination"—a linkage that diverts attention away from the structured inequalities and upward redistribution of wealth of the Reagan-Bush era by blaming black poverty on bad mothering.[45]

Notes

1   Jimmie L. Reeves and Richard Campbell, *Cracked Coverage: Television News, the Anti-Cocaine Crusade, and the Reagan Legacy* (Durham, NC: Duke University Press, 1994).

2   As Joanne Morreale put it, "Reagan's rebirth rhetoric offered secular salvation, a symbolic resolution of personal and public crises. . . ." See her *A New Beginning: A Textual Frame Analysis of the Political Campaign Film* (Albany: State University of New York Press, 1991), 40.

3   See Michel Foucault, "What Is an Author?" in *Foucault Reader*, ed. Paul Rabinow (New York: Pantheon Books, 1984), 101–120.

4   The view of Reaganism as being engaged in a "war of positions" is informed by Stuart Hall's discussion of Thatcherism, which, in turn, is informed by the writings of Antonio Gramsci. See Stuart Hall, *The Hard Road to Renewal: Thatcherism and the Crisis of the Left* (London: Verso, 1988), 3.

5   Murray Edelman, *Constructing the Political Spectacle* (Chicago: University of Chicago Press, 1988), 25.

6   These numbers are derived from a graphic presented by Martha Falco, "Foreign Drugs, Foreign Wars," *Daedalus* 121, no. 3 (summer 1992): 6.

7   Stanton Peele, *Diseasing of America: Addiction Treatment out of Control* (Boston: Houghton Mifflin, 1989), 126.

8   "To the Last Dime," prod. Stanhope Gould, ABC's *Prime Time Live*, 18 July 1991.

9   Clarence Lusane, *Pipe Dream Blues: Racism and the War on Drugs* (Boston: South End Press, 1991), 44; "Prisoners in 1988," *Bureau of Justice Statistics Bulletin* (Washington, DC: U.S. Department of Justice), April 1989; "Profile of State Prison Inmates 1986," *Special Report, Bureau of Justice Statistics* (Washington, DC: U.S. Department of Justice), January 1988; Sharon LaFraniere, "U.S. Has Most Prisoners per Capita in the World," *The Washington Post*, 5 January 1991, A3; Ron Harris, "Blacks Feel Brunt of Drug War," *Los Angeles Times*, 22 April 1990, A1; "Young Black Men Most Likely to Be Jailed," *Washington Afro-American*, 10 March 1991, A1.

10 Robert M. Entman, "Modern Racism and the Images of Blacks in Local Television News," *Critical Studies in Mass Communication* 7 (December 1990): 332–335. For quantitative studies of the new racism, see the following articles published in *Eliminating Racism: Profiles in Controversy*, ed. P. Katz and D. Taylor (New York: Plenum Press, 1988): L. Bobo, "Group Conflict, Prejudice, and the Paradox in Contemporary Racial Attitudes," 85–114; J. B. McConahay, "Modern Racism, Ambivalence, and the Modern Racism Scale," 91–125; and D. O. Sears, "Symbolic Racism," 53–84. Also see B. M. Roth, "Social Psychology's Racism," *The Public Interest*, no. 96 (winter 1990): 26–36.

11 Michael Omi and Howard Winant, *Racial Formation in the United States: From the 1960s to the 1980s* (New York: Routledge & Kegan Paul, 1986), 125.

12 For a genealogy of modern racism, see Cornel West, *Prophesy Deliverance! An Afro-American Revolutionary Christianity* (Philadelphia: Westminster Press, 1982).

13 Omi and Winant, 14–15.

14 E. Franklin Frazier, *The Negro Family in the United States* (1939; reprint, New York: Dryden Press, 1948).

15 Gunnar Myrdal, *An American Dilemma: The Negro Problem and Modern Democracy*, Twentieth Anniversary ed. (1944; reprint, New York: Harper & Row, 1962).

16 Rickie Solinger, *Wake Up Little Susie: Single Pregnancy and Race before Roe v. Wade* (New York: Routledge, 1992), 60. Also see Frederick Hoffman, *Race Traits and Tendencies* (1896); William Hannibal Thomas, *The American Negro: What He Was, What He Is, and What He May Become* (1902); and A. H. Shannon, *The Negro in Washington: A Study of Race Amalgamation* (1930).

17 Patricia Hill Collins, *Black Feminist Thought: Knowledge, Consciousness, and Politics of Empowerment* (New York: Routledge, 1990), 68.

18 Omi and Winant, 14.

19 U.S. Department of Labor, *The Negro Family: The Case for National Action* (Washington, DC: Government Printing Office, 1965), 5.

20 For a summary of this research, see Alphonso Pinkney, *The Myth of Black Progress* (Cambridge, UK: Cambridge University Press, 1984), 7–17. See also Lee Rainwater

and William Yancey, eds., *The Moynihan Report and the Politics of Controversy* (Cambridge, MA: MIT Press, 1965); Nathan Glazer and Daniel Moynihan, *Beyond the Melting Pot* (Cambridge, MA: MIT Press, 1965); Nathan Glazer, *Affirmative Discrimination: Ethnic Inequality and Public Power* (New York: Basic Books, 1975); Ben J. Wattenberg and Richard Scammon, "Black Progress and Liberal Rhetoric," *Commentary* (April 1973); Thomas Sowell, "Are Quotas Good for Blacks?" *Commentary* (June 1978); Thomas Sowell, *Affirmative Action Reconsidered: Was It Necessary in Academia?* (Washington, DC: American Enterprise Institute for Public Policy Research, 1975).

21   See Craig Reinarman and Harry G. Levine, "The Crack Attack: Politics and Media in America's Latest Drug Scare," in *Images of Issues: Typifying Contemporary Social Problems,* ed. Joel Best (New York: Aldine de Gruyter, 1989), 127.

22   See Mike Davis's discussion of "black-lash" in relation to reactionary African American response to the crack panic in *City of Quartz: Excavating the Future in Los Angeles* (London: Verso, 1990), 289–292.

23   This is derived from Patricia Hill Collins's critique of the Moyers report. See "A Comparison of Two Works on Black Family Life," *Signs* 14, no. 4 (1989): 875–884.

24   Quoted by Herman Gray, "Television, Black Americans, and the American Dream," *Critical Studies in Mass Communication* 6 (December 1989): 381; emphasis added.

25   Stephanie Coontz, *The Way We Were: American Families and the Nostalgia Trap* (New York: Basic Books, 1992), 235. Also see Ken Auletta, *The Underclass* (New York: Random House, 1982), and "Working Seminar on the Family and American Welfare Policy," in *The New Consensus on Family and Welfare: A Community of Self-Reliance* (Washington, DC: American Enterprise Institute, 1987).

26   Douglas J. Baharov, "Crack Babies: The Worst Threat Is Mom Herself," *The Washington Post,* 6 August 1989, Outlook, 1.

27   Solinger, 24–25.

28   Ibid.

29   Ellen Hopkins, "Childhood's End," *Rolling Stone,* 18 October 1990, 66–72, 108, 110.

30   See Richard Saltus, "Silber Attacks Health System," *The Boston Globe,* 30 April 1991, metro/region, 15.

31   Barry Zuckerman and Deborah A. Frank, " 'Crack Kids': Not Broken," *Pediatrics* 89 (February 1992): 337–339.

32   Susan Faludi, *Backlash: The Undeclared War against Women* (New York: Crown Publishers, 1989), 428. Faludi cites Paula Braverman, Geraldine Oliva, Marie Grisham Miller, Randy Reiter, and Susan Egerter, "Adverse Outcomes and Lack of Health Insurance among Newborns in an Eight-County Area of California, 1982–1986," *The New England Journal of Medicine* 321, no. 8 (24 August 1989): 508–514;

Lynn M. Paltrow, "When Becoming Pregnant Is a Crime," *Criminal Justice Ethics* 9, no. 1 (winter–spring 1990): 2–3, 14.

33   See Richard Campbell and Jimmie L. Reeves, "Covering the Homeless: The Joyce Brown Story," *Critical Studies in Mass Communication* 6, no. 1 (March 1989): 21–42.

34   Collins, *Black Feminist Thought,* 68–78.

35   Ibid., 77.

36   Thomas P. Strandjord and W. Alan Hodson, "Neonatology," *Journal of the American Medical Association* 268 (15 July 1992): 377–378.

37   I. J. Chasnoff, D. R. Griffith, C. Frier, and J. Murray, "Cocaine/Polydrug Use in Pregnancy: Two Year Follow-Up," *Pediatrics* 89 (1992): 284–289.

38   Linda C. Mayes, Richard H. Granger, Marc H. Bornstein, and Barry Zuckerman, "The Problem of Prenatal Cocaine Exposure: A Rush to Judgment," *Journal of the American Medical Association* 267 (15 January 1992): 406–407.

39   See Al Dale's report on ABC's *World News Tonight* (2 July 1992), and Dan Rutz, "Crack Babies May Have Better Future than Thought," CNN, 8 August 1992.

40   Quoted by Ellen Goodman, "The Myth of the 'Crack Babies,'" *The Boston Globe,* 12 January 1992, op-ed, 69.

41   Ellen Whitford, "Cocaine Babies Problems Overstated? Emory Team's Conclusions Rock the Boat," *The Atlanta Constitution,* 10 April 1992, H7.

42   G. Koren, K. Graham, H. Shear, and T. Einarson, "Bias against the Null Hypothesis: The Reproductive Hazards of Cocaine," *The Lancet* 2 (1989): 1440–1442.

43   I. J. Chasnoff, H. Landress, and M. Barett, "The Prevalence of Illicit-Drug or Alcohol Use during Pregnancy and Discrepancies in Mandatory Reporting in Pinellas County, Florida," *New England Journal of Medicine* 322 (1990): 1202–1206.

44   Coontz, 270–271.

45   Collins, *Black Feminist Thought,* 74.

"RELIVING THE PAST OVER AND OVER AGAIN"

Race, Gender, and Popular Memory in *Homefront*

and *I'll Fly Away*

Mimi White

Historical Stakes

In the fall of 1991, *Homefront* and *I'll Fly Away* premiered on American network television, two fictional dramatic series set in the recent past — *Homefront* in the immediate post–World War II period and *I'll Fly Away* in the early 1960s.[1] While the programs are distinctive in the periods they address, in their style and tone, and in the ways they negotiate the act of narrating the past, they are also striking in their similarities. Notably, in the course of their narratives, they produce and project a historical consciousness about America's recent past in terms that centrally include attention to issues of gender, race, and class.

Both programs reconstruct periods in U.S. history that are overdetermined in contemporary popular memory as eras of decisive transformation, especially for women and African Americans, ultimately having decisive impact on American society as a whole. During World War II, many women were employed in factory jobs previously considered strictly "men's work," but they lost their positions to returning soldiers after the war, ending up back in the home or in more traditional, low-paying jobs. At the same time, the postwar period ushered in the cold war, the unprecedented militarization of the U.S. industrial core, the baby boom, the rapid expansion of suburbia, and the widespread penetration of commercial television, all of which promoted an

expanding consumer culture. In the U.S. public sphere, the early 1960s are syn-
onymous with the increasing visibility of the civil rights movement, especially
with the work of Freedom Riders, voter registration drives, African Americans
entering historically white colleges, and other activities aimed at exposing and
redressing the segregation characteristic of public life in the American South.

The shows also provide a prominent place for African American characters
in the context of contemporary, mainstream dramatic fiction television programming.[2] Indeed, part of the remarkable nature of both programs lies in
their central inclusion of African American characters. Yet this very observation must be considered symptomatic, signaling the implicit racist presumptions and standards of dominant television practice, such that a few programs
with a black presence stimulate substantial critical interest. What links these
programs, beyond mere "minority presence," is the way in which a direct
interest in the status of African Americans and women, along with distinctive
working-class characters, arises in the context of historical fiction. As a result,
the programs draw together issues of historical representation and popular
memory with questions of gender, race, class, and national identity. History
becomes the locus of an ostensible multicultural investigation that is, by virtue
of the fictional setting, retrospectively inscribed.

In this regard, it is useful to recall Michel de Certeau's understanding of
historical representation as a strategic assertion of unity and interpretive coherence.

> It constantly mends the rents in the fabric that joins past and present. It as-
> sures a "meaning," which surmounts the violence and the divisions of time.
> It creates a theater of references and of common values, which guarantee a
> sense of unity and a "symbolic" communicability to the group. Finally, as
> Michelet once said, it is the work of the living in order to "quiet the dead"
> and to reunite all sorts of separated things and people into the semblance of
> a unity and a presence that constitutes representation itself. . . . *It leads to*
> *an avoidance in the unifying representation of all traces of the division which*
> *organizes its production.* Thus, the text substitutes a representation of a past
> for elucidation of present institutional operation that manufactures the his-
> torian's text. It puts an appearance of the real (past) in place of the praxis
> (present) that produces it, thus developing an actual case of quid pro quo.[3]

From this perspective, it is temporally coincidental, if theoretically unsur-
prising, that these two programs appeared on television concomitant with the

Clarence Thomas–Anita Hill Senate investigation, culminating in Thomas's appointment to the Supreme Court.[4] This was another drama involving male and female African Americans that included important historical dimensions. The hearings directly evoked history as a crucial interpretive frame, with Thomas's references to lynching parties, central questions posed by Hill's detractors about the temporality of events (especially the time lag between the harassment and its public reporting), and larger issues raised about memory and truth. In relation to the dramatic public confrontation of the Thomas-Hill Senate hearings, the historical fictions of *I'll Fly Away* and *Homefront* may have served to elide or occlude contemporary circumstances for African Americans and women in particular, within and without Hollywood.

Both *Homefront* and *I'll Fly Away* are designed to reflect prevailing ideas about "quality television" in the 1990s. They are crafted to attract critical acclaim, with their attention to constructing an appropriate period look, as they integrate African American experiences into the fabric of prime-time flow and popular memory. The programs also succeeded in these terms with substantial popular critical acclaim despite low ratings. Toward the end of the 1991–92 television season, as the networks decided the future of these programs, *TV Guide* launched a campaign to save five quality programs whose ratings made their future uncertain, including *Homefront* and *I'll Fly Away*. This involved a discussion of why each show deserved renewal and included a series of phone numbers that readers could call to indicate support for a particular program's continuation. On a number of occasions, the widely syndicated advice columnist Ann Landers mentioned *Homefront* as her favorite show and urged her readers to watch it. Both programs were renewed for the 1992–93 season. But despite continued critical praise, neither series established sufficient ratings, and both programs were canceled in 1993. In response, PBS announced that it was picking up the existing episodes of *I'll Fly Away* for the 1993–94 schedule, including production of a two-hour movie to wrap up the story for viewers; the movie was first shown in October 1993, just before they started rerunning the series. Prime-time network drama hereby finds new life as a public television series. Although certainly not part of "elite" culture, both programs represent "quality" within middlebrow American popular television culture.

In this context, the introduction of stories that address postwar social concerns is an integral part of their quality appeal. The care with which these programs are produced, visibly carried by the mise-en-scène and narratively expressed in the exploration of popular memory and social experience, can be considered television's representational equivalent of the unity of appearance of the past offered by professional historical writing that displaces intervention and transformation in the present.

In one sense, history provides the possibility for distance, enabling viewers to declare at any given moment, "But that was then; this is now," even as they identify with the fiction from their position in the present or recognize their own experience. Historical fiction can thus serve as a safety net for general social reception, as the programs structurally imply that the problems they address in narrative terms, in particular regarding race and gender, were worse "back then." In this light, such historical dramatizations, indeed the very existence of these programs, propose that the problems have at least been substantially ameliorated in the course of the history between the diegetic past and the viewer's present. As allegedly true fictions, history hereby engages memory, imagination, and experience via a safe distance.

At the same time, setting the programs in the past facilitates—and perhaps even demands—the dramatization of racism and sexism in the name of historical accuracy. Common clichés about women's place in society, and even more aggressive verbal and physical racist attacks on African American characters, are naturalized and integrated as part of the "truth" of the historical past. Thus dramatized, the oppressions of the past become the implicit motive and explanation for the subsequent emergence of the civil rights and women's movements. These tacit explanatory frameworks, based in the temporal structures of historical narrativity, are in turn embedded in more particularized story trajectories which displace and reconstrue these interests in relation to individual, fictional characters. In these ways, the historical perspective in general, combined with the particular histories these programs represent, activates intertwined and contradictory positions regarding the ongoing implications of the issues these programs engage, by virtue of the very historical moments they depict.

The question inevitably arises of whose memory—popular or otherwise—is being deployed, a question for which there is no single, definitive answer. The historical perspective has the capacity to activate individual memory and experience in terms that inflect reception of the programs. The subsequent analysis of the programs is less concerned with deciding their value once and for all, or for all viewers, than it is with seeing how the particular combinations of narrative concerns, cast in historical terms, produce contradictions that may be irresolvable in the final analysis. The specificity of these contradictions has everything to do with the uses of history and memory and the overdetermined place of women and African Americans within the trajectories of prime-time television series.

On the one hand, historical narrative allows for an exploration of the gender and racial discrimination that is a part of U.S. history. This is the "progressive" impulse informing these shows. On the other hand, the historical perspective enables, and perhaps even encourages, the representation of this discrimination, including vivid dramatization of brute racism and sexism. Here, intended or not, so-called truth to history becomes a strategy for enacting racial and gender oppression on dramatic television on a routine basis. Moreover, this enactment cuts at least two ways: it is diegetically situated in the past, fit into the "realism" of historical fiction; at the same time, the dramatic and representational codes the programs deploy directly implicate, indeed constitute, the present of televisual narration. When it comes to the depictions of gender and race oppression, the context of historical fiction cannot totally mitigate the fact that these are contemporary stories and images.

An Algebra of Difference

Both *Homefront* and *I'll Fly Away* include African Americans cast in central narrative roles that are initially defined in conventional terms, as characters who serve the domestic needs of white families. These positions are tacitly sanctioned by recourse to historical accuracy in the biracial world these programs depict, wherein African Americans "naturally" cater to the needs of whites, to whom they are subservient. Yet these characters do not remain background figures who only hover on the edges of the important affairs of the white characters they serve.

On *Homefront,* Abe and Gloria are the domestic help for the show's wealthy industrialist. When their son, Robert, returns from the war to River Run, Ohio, Abe urges him to seek employment at the factory owned by his boss, Mike Sloan, and Robert is hired as a janitor. This fulfills the son's expectations about what he can realistically expect from white American society, but Abe is shocked by Robert's treatment, especially given Robert's status as a war hero and Abe's own long-standing relationship with the Sloans. After Abe is rebuffed by Mike Sloan when he inquires about a better job for his son, he initiates a ploy to get Robert a position on the production line. He taps into a secret "system within the system," exploiting a network of African American service workers who routinely come into contact with powerful white leaders. In response to his efforts, Mike Sloan receives a personal phone call from Eleanor Roosevelt's office regarding Robert's position in the factory. This call serves as Abe's revenge, for Mike Sloan had only laughed when Abe first quoted Eleanor Roosevelt on the subject of employment opportunities for returning soldiers. By deploying the network of black service workers, Abe succeeds in literalizing Roosevelt's public service appeal, much to Mike Sloan's surprise and consternation.

Robert ends up working on the production line, only to face racial harassment from his fellow workers. As a labor union begins to organize, racial tension is initially a major issue and a stumbling block, but is gradually overcome in favor of worker solidarity, at least in the Sloan factory. Racial oppression, in both institutional and individual forms, is raised again and again as a stumbling block for the African American characters, only to be narratively overcome by African American networking, class solidarity, personal commitments, and so forth. The generalizable struggle of African Americans within U.S. history as a group is thus resolved in diverse, nonsystemic and nonsystematic ways, often through utopian fantasy. In this way, racism is dramatized as an ever-looming problem, even though its solution or redress is construed in strictly individual terms. Although Robert gets a job because of Abe's efforts on his behalf, Robert remains unaware of the mechanism; meanwhile, other African Americans who fought in the war are not necessarily similarly rewarded, though a few additional African American characters appear on the factory floor and at union meetings.

Similarly, contradictions emerge with regard to white women in *Homefront.* Anne and her daughter, Linda, both lose well-paying jobs on the production line to war veterans—including Robert and a member of their own family, Hank. Anne takes a job as a drug store clerk; Linda accepts a position as a file clerk in the factory (for much lower pay than she had been making during the war), but also works with the labor organizer to establish a union for the men on the production line who have displaced her. At the same time, her brother Hank is promoted to a position in management, overseeing plant safety. As a union enthusiast, the single, independent white female functions in the narrative as a promoter of solidarity between the white majority among the blue-collar workers, the African Americans who join the union, and the Jewish labor organizer who introduces the union to River Run. Despite Linda's pivotal role as a linchpin enabling mediation among conflicting gender, race, and class interests, her particular family situation implies that class divisions have little systematic relation to everyday life and social conditions.

This implication is made literal in her living situation, because her family resides together: mother, daughter, and two sons—one married, one single. The household exemplifies a conventional (and nostalgic) depiction of a traditional extended family, even though it simultaneously embraces divergent class positions. Hank resides with his family because they need his financial support to maintain the house, the women having lost their well-paying factory jobs to returning soldiers, including Hank. To complicate matters and to provide an additional historical alibi, due to the postwar housing crunch, Hank and his wife cannot find decent affordable housing for themselves. Thus, historical reference combines with dramatic necessity to keep the family together despite conflicts in their class alliances, in an image of domestic life that fulfills idealized evocations of the extended nuclear family as a bastion of support—the very family that has presumably been lost with the increasing pressures of consumer society and the increasing movement of women into the workplace as a result of economic necessity and feminist aspirations.

Hank is only one of a group of three childhood friends from River Run who went off to war. From the start, Hank is set in contrast to his long-time best friend, Charlie Haley. Like Hank, Charlie returns to the town in which he grew up, yet he has no apparent family in town. Moreover, he returns with a British war bride, much to the distress of his fiancée, who awaits him at the train station dressed in a wedding gown; Hank returns to marry his hometown sweetheart. Charlie works on the production line at the Sloan factory, becomes active in the Union, and lives with his wife, Caroline, in a one-room apartment, sharing a bathroom with a war widow, Gina. Gina had married the Sloans' son in Europe—unbeknown to his parents—and returned to Ohio ahead of him. He died on his way back home, leaving his pregnant Jewish Italian wife to fend for herself in the face of suspicious, hostile in-laws. Despite their common status as war brides, the two European women in turn generate further oppositions. Whereas Caroline is quickly shown to be manipulative, untrustworthy, crassly self-interested, and materialistic, Gina is idealized, generous and warmhearted to a fault even though she is abandoned by her wealthy in-laws. (The cold-heartedness of this treatment is exacerbated by the fact that Gina is a concentration camp survivor.) The program thus generates extended networks of relationships among characters who interrelate and intersect in a variety of ways, almost on the model of a planned matrix: the guy who marries the girl back home versus the best friend who returns with a British bride versus the Italian bride who returns unexpectedly without her husband; the industrialist; the upwardly mobile middle-class guy; the traditional working-class stiff; and so on.[5]

In this context, there are specific characters who seemingly embody nascent civil rights and feminist consciousness from the very start. Robert's job situation in the Sloan factory provides the occasion for discussion about what the U.S. owes African American soldiers for their contributions to the war and what they can realistically expect in return. In the course of an argument between Abe and Robert on this issue, Robert offers an initial exposition of a position that will be more fully articulated in the Black Power movement — nearly twenty years later in "real time." By contrast, Abe supports gradual and incremental change within the system, valuing small steps in a larger history of progress for African Americans since the Civil War. Their conflicting opinions offer two distinct and apparently mutually exclusive positions, a binarism that is typical of mainstream media constructions of African American politics: gradual transformation versus revolution; Martin Luther King versus Malcolm X; civil disobedience versus civil unrest; rural Southern Baptist versus urban northern Muslim; or, in a recent varient, Clarence Thomas versus Anita Hill. This takes on the appearance of a structural genre component, polarizing the African American community according to the logic of a choice between two antagonistic positions (a structure that also emerges in *I'll Fly Away*).

In a similar mode, Linda complains vocally and bitterly about how unfair it is that she and her mother are losing their jobs to the men returning from the war. By expressing resentment not only over changes in her earning power, but also for the loss of personal fulfillment that her factory job represented, Linda articulates attitudes about the postwar transition in women's lives that are more fully developed in feminist scholarship and films produced in the late 1970s and 1980s.[6] Much of this historical work proposes that there were few, if any, appropriate channels for expressing these kinds of sentiments in the immediate postwar era (for instance, in the equivalent of a prime-time television program like *Homefront*). The program signals its sensitivity to the oppressions of the past and to possible avenues of redress that presumably exist only in the fiction's future. This future, which the program's viewers occupy, is anticipated in the fiction via the ideas the program puts in its own characters' mouths. The historical past is hereby figured as a terrain of possibility, pregnant with latent futures yet to be realized—quite literally in the case of *Homefront,* with first Gina and then Ann carrying babies.[7]

Yet, while *Homefront* promotes a nascent feminist consciousness in the character of Linda, each of the program's leading female characters conforms to dominant codes of feminine attractiveness, including Linda. For example, her friend Ginger aspires to a successful career in show business. As part of her success, she becomes the "Lemo Tomato Girl," a role that includes singing on the radio, having her image depicted on product billboards, ads, and labels, and being featured in the Lemo calendar in conventional pinup poses. Here the program fully participates in the production of idealized glamour images of women from the 1940s through a process of imitation and reduplication that is far from critical, for it directly associates these images with the desire and fulfillment of at least one of the central female characters. These codes of appearance—including the hairstyles, apparel, and makeup of all the female characters—are in turn an integral part of the nostalgia appeal of the program, participating in the construction of an overall retro look.

Finding a firm interpretive stance among divergent character positions becomes more difficult as the program structures its characters in nearly algebraic configurations of similarity and difference. This difficulty is exacerbated by the apparent impossibility of sustaining certain representations at all, a circumstance that emerges most acutely (but not only) when questions of race and sex are conjoined. In this regard, one notable subplot of the 1992–93 season involved Robert's revelation that he had fallen in love with a white French woman during the war and his subsequent trip to France to find her. They return as a married couple to River Run, where they face ongoing racism and the threat of violence. They enjoy an evening at a jazz club where several men appear to accept Robert's white wife until he realizes that they think he is her pimp. They attend a baseball game where they are heckled and jeered and finally compelled to leave. The repeated, tangible threats—hate mail, phone calls, and rocks thrown through windows—come from unseen members of the white community, none of them program regulars. As the violence escalates, the interracial couple is written out of the show, with the explanation that Robert has decided to pursue his education at Wilberforce Academy across the state.

This sequence of events underscores one of the theoretical limit points of televisual representation and liberal conscience when it comes to African

Americans in history. On the one hand, it is hard to imagine a prime-time television program repeatedly dramatizing overt racism in these terms — however "true to history." It is, somehow, at once too much and too little: excessively repetitious but with insufficient dramatic development for the purposes of series television. On the other hand, to exacerbate the racism by placing it at the center of dramatic development (instead of remaining a tacit social structure), as the program inevitably does, calls for narrative transformation; someone has to die or leave to alleviate the pressure of the dramatic conflict proposed by escalating racist attacks. Yet, the program itself is incapable of resolving the racism in the past, which is the context of its fiction, an alibi that supports the interracial couple's departure from the show. Ironically, this contributes to contemporary blockages in representation by getting rid of one more rare African American character on prime-time television.

The instigation for this sequence, leading up to the characters' departure, is an interracial marriage, a social/sexual configuration that is inevitably multivalent in its interpretive possibilities. In fact, the whole question of sexualized interracial relations was raised much earlier, during the program's first season. When Gina, the Sloans' pregnant and widowed daughter-in-law, is first compelled to leave their home with no financial support, Abe and Gloria invite her to stay with them. In this context, the friendship and support she receives from the whole family, including Robert, is disrupted by the impossibility of a white woman living in the African American community. The program strongly implies that Robert and Gina's relationship is generally (mis)construed as sexual in nature. Ultimately, Robert is severely beaten by the police, leading Gina to resolve to find her own place. The program seems to forget this particular sequence of events when it brings Robert back from France with his white wife to live with him in the African American community. He seems unaware of the problems this may cause, despite the beating he received the previous season. Instead, memory is superseded by a repetition compulsion focused on the dramatic and eroticized charge to be gained by interracial coupling.

The program thus proposes certain progressive impulses by raising the issues of racism, women's oppression, and labor struggles in the course of its narrative, but because of its own logic of truth to history, the program ultimately has to evacuate the characters and plot twists that most directly address these issues. The program thereby marks its own trajectory as historical narrative in terms that are self-effacing or self-negating.[8]

Integration How? Segregation Forever?

Although *I'll Fly Away* differs from *Homefront* in significant ways, it participates in similar narrative logics and processes, especially in the intertwining of multiple stories that variously emphasize race, gender, and class in a historical context. The very premise of the show sets race and gender issues into direct relation, as Forrest Bedford has to hire a new maid himself because his wife has been hospitalized for a nervous breakdown. At the same time, he initiates an affair with a white female lawyer, Christina LeKatzis. Thus, the program sets up its central characters according to a logic of opposition and division. The African American domestic cares for the house and children, while the white professional woman, who verges on "spinster" status in the prefeminist American South, serves as personal/sexual company for the father. Both are introduced to fill a gap left by the absent wife, represented as a well-worn southern female stereotype, the madwoman.

The preponderant narrative development of the program proposes Forrest and Lilly as exemplary characters, each coming to consciousness regarding the question of civil rights. This progress, a demonstration of individual bourgeois enlightenment, is contravened by the program's systematic introduction of narrative situations and characters who represent alternative positions. For example, as Lilly is increasingly engaged by the civil rights movement, the program introduces a cousin who is vocally against the goals and methods of civil rights activism and is fully figured as an Uncle Tom,[9] satisfied with the status quo of a white power structure that he can serve. He justifies his position in terms of the need to support his family, genuinely believing that he is well treated by the whites for whom he works. When Lilly and her father pressure him to reconsider his politics, he writes a letter to the local white paper, explicating his anti–civil rights position in a public forum and instigating a decisive break between Lilly's immediate family and that of her cousin.

Throughout the episode, the cousin's position is presented as a reasonable and realistic articulation of attitudes toward civil rights held by a portion of the African American community in the early 1960s. Yet, as the spokesman for a position that is hardly dominant in the 1990s, the character aids and abets the program's ongoing status quo: the segregated South. Given the presence of such opinions—either in the historical past of the program's fiction or in the historical present of the program's production—how could one expect all segregationist white people to realize the need for change? The character of Lilly's cousin, introduced in the name of historical truth and representational diversity in the African American community, articulates in historical terms an alibi for ongoing segregation, spanning the distance between the represented past and the narrational present.

In a slightly different version of this alibi, Forrest Bedford's transformation vis-à-vis civil rights is repeatedly tied to his sexual affairs by narrative simultaneity, such that his egregious failings in one area are compensated and even excused by his increasingly liberal consciousness and actions in the other. During the second season of the show, his wife dies just before being released from the mental hospital (publicly considered accidental because she was hit by a car, the death is fraught with ambiguity, for there are hints that she may have committed suicide). His relationship with Christina becomes increasingly strained as her expectations of a more public courtship are stifled by Forrest's expressed need to observe a reasonable period of mourning for decorum's sake; his guilt remains undiscussed. At about the same time, Forrest is appointed the U.S. attorney for the region, working under the aegis of the Kennedy Justice Department. In this context, Forrest considers initiating a grand jury investigation of two local Klansmen who killed an African American naval officer in his district, even though he has been urged by Washington to drop the case.[10] In a single episode, Forrest and Christina break up because of his unwillingness to make a public commitment to her, and he simultaneously decides to pursue the civil rights case. Bluntly put, his behavior as an absolute "heel" in the world of sexual relationships is neatly counterbalanced by his "heroic" decision to proceed with a civil rights case that is both personally and professionally risky.

Sexuality and racial identity are more directly brought together in a subplot from the program's second season (1992–93) involving Forrest's son Nathan, a high school senior, and his interest in an African American student in his class, Claudia Bishop. This relationship participates in the binary logic contrasting Nathan with his best friend and wrestling teammate, Paul Slocum, who is from a rural "white trash" family. Slocum justifies his aggressive racism through reference to his class identity: as he explains to Nathan, the only status he has in the world comes from being better than "niggers." While hardly a vocal proponent of civil rights, Nathan's criticism of Slocum's overt racism and his nascent (and largely mute) relationship with Claudia begin to trace the possibility of an alternative attitude for whites in the segregated South.

The introduction of the character of Claudia Bishop is also the context for bringing civil rights activism to the high school, as Claudia and her friends demonstrate for equal access to extracurricular activities. In the course of a sit-in during a basketball game, Nathan looks on as first the athletes then the police beat up the protesters. The attack on the students has the capacity to be both horrifying and titillating, a spectacle for the gaze of (male and female) white characters in the fiction, which fully enacts the powers of the white middle-class male gaze, justified here as dramatically and historically compelling. Nathan's refusal to participate even in verbal epithets leads Paul to abandon him in disgust—thus clarifying for the viewer Nathan's distinctive stand, even as he is immobilized, unable to even speak on behalf of the African Americans save for uttering a single "No" lost in the general crowd noise. Yet his apparent concern is aroused by a particular African American female, underscoring the sexualized nature of his nascent civil rights conscience, which threatens to carry over to the scene where he watches Claudia and her friends being violently assaulted.[11]

At the same time, this sequence of events, and Nathan's relationship to Claudia more generally, functions as a displacement with regard to Nathan's father. The program assiduously avoids any sense of sexual attraction between Forrest and Lilly despite the fact that she is the only adult female in the Bedford household. For most of the series, Forrest's relation with Chris LeKatzis functions as a representational hedge against this possibility. However, the specter of a more socially and culturally familiar scenario—of white men possessing African American women through the combination of white male power and the projected exotic allure of women of color—returns in Nathan's interest in Claudia.[12]

Historical Voices

Because these programs produce fictions that link issues of race, gender, ethnicity, and class in history, they resonate with some of the most pressing questions in contemporary theory regarding multiculturalism and representational practices.[13] Yet, as the more particular analysis suggests, both *Homefront* and *I'll Fly Away* elaborate these concerns in terms of narrative and characterological formulas that may push certain limits and raise certain possibilities, but too often end up negating their most interesting progressive representational practices. The question of history and memory thereby returns with particularly acute pressure: the historical context provides much of the apparent relevance and interest of these programs, especially for women and African Americans, yet it also furnishes the logic whereby the programs evade the very issues that are, presumably, of most intense interest.

In this regard, I want to emphasize that these programs are very insistent about their own historicity. Personal and public memory are directly promoted, especially through narrational devices such as Lilly's voice-over narration in *I'll Fly Away* and period newsreels in *Homefront*. The programs deploy verbal and visual chronicles to signal that their status as *historical narratives* is a crucial part of their singularity and potential appeal. These strategies also evoke popular memory in concrete terms; the pasts made present in the programs are represented as part of a larger, collective set of memories and experiences that the programs simply re-mediate. Although they cannot offer full remediation for the circumstances they enact to achieve their historical dramas, in the process, questions of memory and historical voice are rendered with particular intensity.

Homefront deploys details of everyday life, especially in the form of artifacts such as furniture, hairstyles, and costume, along with plots that draw attention to post–World War II mass culture. References to mass culture, especially baseball and radio, also contribute to the sense of nostalgia and mass popular memory produced by this program. Ginger's involvement in radio and television suggests that the histories of both the postwar era and U.S. broadcast media are closely related, an implication confirmed by period newsreel footage under the end-titles each week. Although popular newsreels are directly cited as historical source documents in the program, they bear no immediate relation to the story, covering a wide range of topics (e.g., the spectacle of a frivolous world-record-breaking stunt, the progress of French military activity in Vietnam, advances in the U.S. automobile industry).

The newsreels simultaneously signal the agency of a formal historical voice and of individual popular memory. For viewers who lived through the period depicted, including older baby boomers, the newsreels may evoke actual memories and experience, establishing a personal relation to the historical world that the newsreels and the program reference. For younger viewers, whose own memory and experience postdate the fiction, the newsreels might stand instead as authentic albeit popular historical documents that help both to ground the authenticity of the program's representation and to extend the vision of the characters' historical milieu. In both cases, the voice of history carried by the newsreels is a highly conventionalized, impersonal, male authority.

In *I'll Fly Away,* the most consistent historical voice comes from the character of the maid, Lilly Harper, who reads from her diary in voice-over. These voice-overs often feature the most sustained verbal performance by the actor/character who delivers them, in a program that is characterized by decidedly laconic and slow-paced drama.[14] Although the diary is a historical fiction, a simulated primary source, it nonetheless has the capacity to lend authenticity to the program as a representative of a privileged historical document of daily life. Lilly's voice represents the private historical counterpart to the national historical events that gradually unfold in the course of the program. This personal historical voice is particularly interesting in the larger context of the show, especially in its mediations of public and private, white and black, male and female, and silence and vocality.

The conjunctions and disjunctions between Lilly's diary entries and the episodes they frame offer one delineation of the place of African Americans in history, especially when it comes to their everyday lives. Lilly's most explicit personal expressions take place at the formal margins of the program, often with only an indirect connection to the causal dramatic events that compose each episode. The voice-over thereby opens a measurable gap between the white family, which is more definitively at the center of the narrative, and Lilly, who hovers on the periphery. Among other things, this marginality suggests that the central program diegesis is *not* her point of view, visually or narratively, but that of the (white, male) world that she must negotiate.

This suggestion is reinforced in a number of ways. As an African American domestic, Lilly is allowed to speak freely only within highly constrained places and contexts. For example, she is chastised by Forrest for sharing voting rights literature with other maids when they are watching white children in their care at the park. Because of such constraints, her diary emerges as the privileged place of self-expression and self-revelation, where she recounts stories, dreams, ideas, and memories that are not necessarily integral to the dramatized events of a particular episode. The program uses these entries to build up a distinctive sense of her character on the margins of the central narrative events.[15]

Although Lilly and Forrest are both characterized by a certain spareness of speech, they are not equal. Most obviously, Forrest participates in the a priori privileges of his race, gender, and class. He is a lawyer, a state attorney who argues courtroom cases; his professional success hinges on the ability to speak forcefully and persuasively. Yet, especially in his personal life, he is characterized as pensive and laconic. His silences in this context serve a range of functions, suggesting his inability to understand or articulate certain issues, even a profound thinking process through which transformative consciousness can be seen at work. His silences permeate the show with an ambiguity that both prevents him, at least initially, from being understood as simply a liberal, and saves him from overtly articulating the racism and bigotry of many of his peers. This willful ambiguity enables Forrest to be read as a "complex" character who is open to change. All of the impetus for his transformation comes in the public sphere, in relation to legal cases he witnesses or argues, rather than from any direct interaction with Lilly, even as she increasingly participates in civil rights activism. Silence becomes one way in which the program offers a mediating space among a variety of positions for the contemporary viewer, including suggesting the difficulty of simply speaking in a historical voice.

Media History and Mediated Memory

I do not mean to submit these programs to a form of double jeopardy when it comes to their respective treatments of history, where nothing they do — good intentions notwithstanding — can ever measure up to some hypothetical "good representation" or can adequately capture the truth of the past, especially when it comes to the experiences of African Americans and women. Rather, I have read through the overdeterminations of the programs as historical fictions in the context of dramatic series/serial television, to specify the difficulty of even defining an acceptable status for these images and stories, a problem that has everything to do with history, including the history of television representation. In the process, what emerges are self-contradictions and ambiguities of interpretation produced by the programs' respective engagement with historical fiction offering a diffused sense of historical identifications and memories, public and private.

Questions of historical "voice" are further complicated by the programs' reliance on popular culture and media as integral aspects of the history they deploy. The historical record that grounds these programs is drawn from the popular media; these stories and images have already circulated in the public arena in a variety of forms. This includes the popular revival of Rosie the Riveter images from World War II as a symbol of women's strength, as well as other intermediating works of popular fiction that viewers may know (e.g., *To Kill a Mockingbird* and *The Long Walk Home*). In this theoretical vein, it is not accidental that on *Homefront*, the character who is interested in a show business career starts out aiming for Hollywood but instead ends up on local radio in Ohio and later on the first local television station, tracing postwar transformations in the American mass media.

Public histories and personal memories intersect in narratives and images that can be readily reproduced, especially on television. In this light, the striking absence of popular media within the fictional world of *I'll Fly Away* may constitute a form of excessive nostalgia, as the pace of life in the Bedford household without radio or television harkens back to an even earlier period, before the civil rights activism of the late 1950s. This absence is supplemented by the show in its restagings of civil rights actions that were shown on television, such as Freedom Marches and sit-in protests. History serves simultaneously as the alibi and the product of these programs, crisscrossing personal memory with public history and historical fiction.

In the fall of 1993, before it began airing reruns of *I'll Fly Away,* PBS broadcast the original made-for-TV movie it had produced to conclude the series. The movie contains, in exacerbated forms, many of the contradictions already noted. The episode is set in the characters' future; it opens as Lilly's grandson comes to spend the weekend with her. He ends up hearing about her family's participation in the civil rights movement. Lilly is the expressed narrator, directly recounting the story as a lesson for her grandson to concretize his relation to an African American struggle that involved ordinary people in everyday circumstances. The story Lilly tells not only chronicles the "heroism" in the past but also unwittingly repeats the self-negating logic described in relation to *Homefront.* Her story involves her father's public confrontation with racism that ended with her family's leaving town to ensure their own safety; with her own departure from the Bedford home, the fictional context for the series comes to an end.

The crux of the story concerns the nephew of one of Lilly's close friends, a young man from Detroit who comes to visit for the summer. In a loose adaptation of the Emmett Till incident, he approaches a white woman in a manner considered unacceptable in the South and is lynched as a result. Lilly's father witnesses his abduction by two white men, and he is helpless to do anything but stand by and beg for mercy on behalf of the Detroit youth. With Forrest Bedford's support and assistance, he ultimately decides to identify the whites and to testify against them in a trial, forcing Lilly and her family to leave town to avoid retribution by the white community.

A number of things are striking about this episode in relation to the series as a whole. For one, throughout the series, Lilly was centrally involved in civil rights activism while her father stood by on the sidelines, fairly supportive but at times somewhat disapproving (especially given her responsibility as a single mother). Yet, the film construes her father's decision to testify as the heroism of civil rights involvement. At the same time, the film casts Forrest as an aggressive supporter of the civil rights cause, coming to Lilly's house in the middle of the night, at her request, upon learning of the lynching; he praises her father's willingness to come forward and promises protection. When the program was a weekly series, he seemed largely oblivious to Lilly's participation in civil rights activities, except to discourage her from sharing voting rights pamphlets with other maids in the neighborhood. His gradual progression toward civil rights involvement, largely focused on litigation, had little to do with activity in the immediate African American community. The program's original construal of civil rights activities, and Lilly's and Forrest's discrepant relations to them, was one of its strengths; it stressed the centrality of local African American involvement at the heart of civil rights activism. All of this is displaced or rewritten in the final movie, which shifts the burden of activism from Lilly and other African American women in the community to the patriarchal figures of Forrest and Lilly's father. The final episode "forgets" its own fictional past by situating patriarchy, especially southern white patriarchy, squarely at the center of the narrative of civil rights progress.

This causality is depicted in a series of scenes late in the film that continually reframe the historical place of African American women and destabilize the authority of the character who is supposedly telling the story. Lilly's departure from the Bedford home is dramatized in her parting scenes with John Morgan, the youngest child,[16] who is in bed when Lilly wakes him to say goodbye. At first he is hurt by her apparently unwarranted departure and refuses to offer words or signs of affection. When she leaves the house with Forrest, who is driving her home, John Morgan comes running out in his pajamas to express his love and cries in her arms. While they are in the foreground, Forrest, in soft focus, watches their tender interaction centered in the background. Thus, in this emotionally overdetermined scene, her departure occurs under the watchful eye of white authority.

The next scene returns to Lilly and her grandson in the present. He thanks her for the story, proudly proclaiming, "You were all heroes," and Lilly bestows on him her scrapbook documenting his family's involvement in the civil rights movement. This scene celebrates both the value of the African American family and an oral and popular culture that enables a sense of continuity with one's heritage, providing what is probably the most decisive moment of affirmation of the link between African American activism and the family offered by the episode. In the subsequent scene, Lilly returns to the town where the events took place, apparently for the first time in thirty years. She drops in on Forrest and as they visit, she catches up on his family and learns that John Morgan has died. Forrest thanks Lilly for helping to open his eyes in the past, enabling him to see things from a new perspective, an avowal that is quite startling to regular viewers of the series. Fully nostalgic, he places his actions decisively in the past, declaring, "We fought the good fight, didn't we." "We still are," Lilly responds, pulling the issues toward the present. However, she then repeats her grandson's words, but transfers them to Forrest. "I want you to know that I and a lot of other people considered you a hero. And still do." Her grandson's statement about ordinary African Americans engaged in heroic activities to promote civil rights is thereby redirected to the program's representative of the good conscience of white patriarchy.

The last scene finally reveals Lilly's life since her days as the Bedford maid. She is introduced to a large audience as author Lilly Harper and stands to read from her latest novel.[17] Her novel, she explains, is about a young black woman in the rural South during the civil rights movement. As she begins to read from the novel, titled *I'll Fly Away,* her voice-over narration replaces the soundtrack, and she talks about her realization that the key to the future lies in "reliving the past over and over again." Thus, the program gives Lilly the last word, doubly inscribed in the form of her novel—much of which viewers presumably have witnessed—and also in the familiar personal voice-over that terminates the episode and the series. But this voice is already positioned in the shadow of Forrest Bedford, who unambiguously represents the progress of the South (and, by extension, the U.S. at large) and the heroism of civil rights activism in the final episode. The ambiguities that left Lilly decentered in relation to white patriarchal southern society and thereby autonomous as an African American woman have been supplanted by the more conventional narrative of white male heroism.

Homefront and *I'll Fly Away* negotiate issues related to social progress in the recent past. The prime-time series "relive the past over and over again," in terms that are too often self-negating in relation to both the past and the present, especially when it comes to questions of race and gender. Thus, the final episode of *I'll Fly Away* heralds the end of new production for the program in the present by removing the character of Lilly Harper from the aegis of the white household. Between this moment in the fiction's past and the fictional present, she has evidently become a successful author. Yet, the conventions of dramatic television cannot sustain the authority this position confers. Rather, in historical television fictions, the African American woman may have the last word as an author only if her story, like that of Lilly Harper, follows the logic of *I'll Fly Away*.

Notes

1   *Homefront* (Latham/Lechowick with Lorimar, ABC, 1991–93) is a serial melodrama, with multiple characters involved in a number of parallel, ongoing stories, set in River Run, Ohio. Program regulars include the wealthy owner of the town's factory and his wife (Mike and Ruth Sloan); a widow with three grown children (Anne, Linda, Hank, and Jeff); a Jewish, New York labor organizer (Al); and an African American couple (Abe and Gloria) who work as domestics for the industrialist, along with their son (Robert), a war hero.

   I'll Fly Away (Brand/Falsey with Lorimar, NBC, 1991–93) is a semi-serial dramatic show set in a small town in the South during the escalating civil rights activism around 1960. The central white family is headed by an attorney, Forrest Bedford (portrayed by Sam Waterston), whose wife has been hospitalized for mental illness. There are three children—John Morgan, Nathan, and Francie—and as the program opens, the father is in the process of hiring a new domestic, Lilly, who will take care of the children and the house during the day. Lilly is a single mother who lives with her father and her young daughter, Adlaine.

2   In this context, I am distinguishing dramatic fiction from situation comedy, crime/police dramas, and music videos, television genres wherein African American presence was more apparent, and at times even prominent, throughout the 1980s.

3   Michel de Certeau, *Heterologies,* trans. Brian Massumi (Minneapolis: University of Minnesota Press, 1986), 205; emphasis added.

4   For discussion of the Thomas-Hill encounter see Toni Morrison, ed., *Race-ing Justice, En-gendering Power: Essays on Anita Hill, Clarence Thomas, and the Construction of Social Reality* (New York: Pantheon, 1992); Nancy Fraser, "Sex, Lies, and the Public Sphere: Some Reflections on the Confirmation of Clarence Thomas," *Critical Inquiry* 18 (1992): 595–612.

5   The self-consciously extreme microcosmic nature of the community created on the program, as if to hit every imaginable demographic in advance and cover every race/class/gender identity, was first suggested to me by Mark Williams.

6   Mimi White, "Rehearsing Feminism: Women/History in *The Life and Times of Rosie the Riveter* and *Swing Shift*," *Wide Angle* 7, no. 3 (1985): 34–43.

7   The implications here also extend to *I'll Fly Away*, when a high school student has to deal with an unwanted pregnancy and a boyfriend who does not want to marry her.

8   The death of Hank's wife during a period of union-management strife and Hank's departure from the program at the end of the first season similarly represent self-negating trajectories in the context of dramatic development focused on questions of class.

9   For a discussion of common black stereotypes in popular media, see Donald Bogle, *Toms, Coons, Mulattoes, Mammies, and Bucks: An Interpretive History of Blacks in American Films* (New York: Continuum, 1989).

10 The two men had previously been tried for murder and exonerated; Forrest is planning to reopen the case based on civil rights legislation.

    This plot development obviously echoes the two Rodney King trials in Los Angeles in 1992 and 1993. The King trials involved four policemen who were videotaped beating King after a high-speed car chase. They were initially acquitted in 1992, provoking riots in a number of cities in the U.S., and were retried in 1993 on the grounds of denying King his civil rights through excessive use of force. The program episodes initially aired during the second season of *I'll Fly Away*, between the two trials.

11 It is perhaps coincidental, but nonetheless suggestive, that the actress portraying the African American high school student, Nbushe Wright, played the female lead in *Zebrahead* (1992), a film about an interracial romance in a Detroit high school.

12 This is especially the case insofar as the program provided another context in which Nathan could have developed a sympathetic interest in African Americans. In the first season, the coach allowed an African American to join the wrestling team, despite the widespread segregation of extracurricular activities that triggered the protest the following season. Although he is allowed to compete with the team, he is kept rigidly separate in all other contexts: he eats separately, rides in the back of the bus, is not allowed in many locker rooms to change, and so forth.

13 I am thinking in particular of the work in Russell Ferguson, Martha Gever, Trinh T. Minh-ha, and Cornel West, eds., *Out There: Marginalization and Contemporary Culture* (New York and Cambridge, MA: New Museum of Contemporary Art/MIT Press, 1990). Of related interest are Gina Dent, ed. *Black Popular Culture* (Seattle: Bay Press 1992); Simon Durning, ed., *The Cultural Studies Reader* (New York: Routledge, 1993); and Lawrence Grossberg, Cary Nelson, and Paula Treichler, eds., *Cultural Studies* (New York: Routledge, 1992).

14 This has not escaped the notice of some popular critics. One reviewer notes, "The show's two-hour pilot moves as slowly as, well, molasses in January" (Richard Zog-

lin, "The Way We [Maybe] Were," *Time,* 30 September 1991, 78). Other critics use phrases such as "deliberate pace," and producers have said their intention was to produce a "quiet" show.

15   There is one episode in which the diary figures prominently, when Lilly discovers that Francie has read part of her diary.

16   Her "good-byes" to the older children are literally shunted to the margins, referred to, but occurring off-screen, confirming the sense that the intimacy between white charges and African American maids is best figured in relation to young children.

17   This development is not wholly surprising. Lilly is seen successfully pursuing a high school diploma in the course of the series and her name resonates with Harper Lee, author of *To Kill a Mockingbird,* a novel and a film that are obviously evoked by *I'll Fly Away.*

KING TV

Sasha Torres

Rodney King Live

It is news to no one that the beating of Rodney King, the Simi Valley trial of his attackers, the "disturbances" that followed the state verdicts, and the officers' federal trial and its verdicts were organized by national ideologies of television as well as national ideologies of race. That this fact is self-evident may explain why so little, relatively speaking, of what has been written in the popular and academic presses about this sequence of events has addressed with any specificity the intersection of those ideologies.[1] No one likes to be obvious.

Perhaps I'll be risking just that, but here goes: In this essay, I want to try to think the televisual apparatus's deployment of racial images through a set of texts located at the nexes of "fictional" and "nonfictional" TV; of "live" and recorded TV; of quotidian television and "special event" (such as catastrophe coverage and the season premiere); and of black and white production, audience, and image. These texts are George Halliday's videotape of the beating of Rodney King; CNN's April 29, 1992 coverage of the reaction to the Simi Valley verdict; and the 1992 season premieres of two established, prime-time network series, *L.A. Law* and *Doogie Howser, M.D.*[2] I'm interested in the relation of these texts — which we might call King TV — to each other; thus, I want to sever them from their local situations within series, or network or cable scheduling as we more conventionally think of it. For my purposes, these season premieres have as much to do with each other, or with a badly focused homemade videotape, as they do with any other installment of their respective series. By reading these texts outside of the programming flows in which they were originally embedded, I'm following the lead of Herman Gray's provocative reading of *The Cosby Show* against the Bill Moyers documentary *The Crisis in Black America* in his article "Television, Black Americans, and the American Dream."[3] With Gray, I'm interested in stitching together the scraps of U.S. TV's representations of race and race relations and reading the genuinely crazy quilt that results.

I will argue here that the most important ideology of television at work in and around King TV is the discursive stance Jane Feuer and others have theorized as "liveness."[4] In a groundbreaking 1983 article, Feuer situates liveness as the promise of presence and immediacy offered by video technology, with its capacity to record and transmit images simultaneously (a capacity that film, which needs to be developed in order to signify, lacks). Arguing against accounts of television that suggest that liveness constitutes an essence or *ontology* of the medium, Feuer rather situates liveness as television's governing *ideology,* whose importance is marked by its omnipresence: "as television in fact becomes less and less a 'live' medium in the sense of an equivalence between time of event and time of transmission, the medium in its own practices seems to insist more and more upon an ideology of the live, the immediate, the direct, the spontaneous, the real. This is true of both program formats and metadiscourse (references to the 'Golden Age' of live television, 'Live from New York, it's Saturday Night,' the many local spots glorifying 'instant' camera news coverage, 'live' coverage of the Olympics, etc.)."[5] For Feuer, liveness works to equate TV's discourse with "the real": "[f]rom an opposition between live and recorded broadcasts," she writes, "we expand to an equation of 'the live' with 'the real.' Live television is *not* recorded; live television is *alive;* television is living, real, not dead."[6] Further, she suggests, through a reading of ABC's *Good Morning America,* that liveness often organizes and unifies the profound fragmentation that characterizes television's address (broken up, as it is, into innumerable segments of advertising, programming, self-promotion, etc.). Moreover, the function of liveness in unifying *textual* fragmentation is recapitulated in its project of unifying *national* fragmentation: the live presence of the anchor on *Good Morning America* serves not only to buffer the "extreme" fragmentation of the show's text, but also to produce and reproduce what Feuer calls "its ideological problematic of family unity and national unity-in-diversity."[7]

The Halliday video

As an ideology of television, liveness has been crucial to the work of King TV. In relation to the Halliday video, liveness figured crucially in the Simi Valley trial as that which prompted the prosecution's failure to produce a reading of the video to counter that advanced by the defense. As Judith Butler has pointed out in "Endangered/Endangering: Schematic Racism and White Paranoia," "what the trial and its horrific conclusions teach us is that there is no simple recourse to the visible, to visual evidence, that it still and always calls to be read, that it is already a reading, and that in order to establish the injury on the basis of visible evidence, an aggressive reading of the evidence is necessary."[8] The generalized misapprehension of the power of the visible that Butler correctly identifies here was, I suggest, further overdetermined in this case by the ideology of liveness: the prosecution's faith in the video's liveness, and its consequent overconfidence in the video's presumedly privileged relation to the real persuaded them that they could rely on the self-evidence of visuality.

In national coverage of the rebellion itself, at a moment in which the codes of liveness crossed with those of catastrophe coverage, liveness served first to signal the scale of these events, to alert the TV audience to their importance for the life of the nation. For although, as Feuer suggests, liveness permeates television's address and can be found everywhere on TV virtually at all times, liveness also serves, during crisis or catastrophe, as a marker of the exceptional event: in the commonplace televisual attention-getter, "We go live to the scene," the scene we go live to is, definitionally, a place where something unusual is happening. And when the medium, in another attention-getting ploy, remarks upon its own liveness, with a graphic that says "live" in the corner of the screen, it's specifying its discourse as different from the more usual fare of recorded programming interspersed by live announcements, or, in news programming, by the direct address of the anchorperson.[9] On U.S.

television, events that justify this kind of interruption of the standard programming schedule are generally understood to be national crises. Indeed, this
exceptional liveness both designates and constitutes such events in the U.S.,
events such as, for example, the Thomas-Hill hearings, the *Challenger* disaster,
the Waco standoff, and the World Trade Center and Oklahoma City bombings.
As Feuer's notion of "unity-in-diversity" suggests, liveness produces a national
gaze largely by recirculating the materials and positions of the local; consider
cnn's use of local Los Angeles station ktla's video feed on the first night of
the uprising, for example, or L.A. Congresswoman Maxine Waters's omnipresence on "national" television in the wake of the Simi Valley verdict.

In addition to designating events in Los Angeles as worthy of national attention, the liveness of the rebellion coverage also served particular functions
within the television industry, occurring as it did at an historical moment
in which the boundaries of liveness, fictionality, and the real were being actively reorganized, as television news organizations considered the limitations
and advantages of using amateur tapes and network entertainment divisions
searched for more ways to exploit the profit potential of "home video." tv
news used its live coverage of the rebellion to reclaim for itself the functions of
immediacy and presence that Halliday's video, and other amateur videos like
it, threatened to usurp. If the very rawness of Halliday's tape had established
its "authenticity" and if Halliday's fortuitous presence at the scene served as a
powerful if implicit indictment of tv news's claims to timely ubiquity, then tv
news reactivated and reappropriated the prestige function of liveness with its
coverage of the verdict's aftermath. tv news effected this recovery in two ways:
by insisting, at least in the hours immediately following the verdict, on its utter
counterintuitiveness, and thus shoring up the ideology of liveness as common
sense; and by narrating the production of its own images as an example par
excellence of daredevil news gathering, remarking ceaselessly on the potential
dangers to their personnel "on the scene."

In reclaiming liveness for itself, tv news coverage of the rebellion reasserted
its own authority in a particularly pernicious way. Because much of the live
coverage of the rebellion was shot from helicopters, live television fulfilled
its function of promoting national unity-in-diversity by aligning the view afforded by its cameras with the perspective of the police who regularly patrol
South Central in similar helicopters.[10] This gaze policing Los Angeles in flames
was only occasionally interrupted by a view originating on the ground. These
choices, which were of course not merely "practical" but rhetorical and politi-

cal as well, determined what liveness made visible—primarily massive "property damage," which was, after all, President Bush's first concern[11]—and what liveness persistently refused to see, such as the racial and ethnic diversity of the "looters" and the fact that many of them were looting and distributing basic necessities like diapers and food.[12]

Liveness increasingly generates its own fictional recyclings, which work through and reimagine both the contemporary nation and its history. Many examples of this representational nexus might be adduced: the situation of the Gulf war within the narrative of *Major Dad,* the Thomas-Hill episodes of *Designing Women* and *Murphy Brown,* the reconstruction of the sixties by *China Beach.* Though many arguments have been made about the tendency of television to cannibalize its own images and stories, most of this work has focused on strategies of "recombination" among fictional forms.[13] In the rest of this essay, I consider the recirculation of nonfictional liveness in King TV's fictional texts, interrogating the effects of this intertextual interface and arguing that we can discern in these intertextual conversations a struggle among televisual forms and genres to represent the nation, its truths and its contradictions. Fictional forms such as the sitcom and the prime-time drama produce their own relevance to national life by appropriating and recirculating liveness. In the process, they must inscribe its limits.

L.A. Law and Televisual Justice

The 1992 premiere of *L.A. Law*'s penultimate season cannibalizes liveness and its purported access to the "real," in hopes that the immediacy of liveness will provide some sense of urgency to its own plots and thus spur flagging viewer interest in the series. This appropriation of "real life" is of course nothing new for the series: it pioneered the "ripped-from-the-headlines" aesthetic that has become standard television fare in the years since its 1986 premiere. And the series had taken up the question of Rodney King's beating in an episode from the 1991–92 season, in which Jonathan Rollins defends a black man who led police on a high-speed chase by claiming that his client's repeated exposure to the video on television had plausibly made him fear for his life at the hands of the LAPD.

The 1992 premiere stages its appropriation of liveness by worrying the questions posed by the verdict and its aftermath both explicitly and implicitly; I'll return in a moment to the ways in which this episode stages explicitly the interface of its characters with the concrete practices of the uprising, persistently placing white bodies as the victims par excellence of urban violence. First, though, I want to discuss a subplot that more obliquely takes up the intersections of race, representation, and the law. Arnie Becker, the sleazy divorce attorney who has wanted for several seasons now to move into the practice of entertainment law, is thrown a placating bone by his partners: he is representing an amusement park employee named Champion who has been fired from his job of dressing up as Homer Simpson because he became ill, took off the Homer-head of his costume, and vomited where park visitors could see him.[14] He has been fired, in other words, for "breaking the illusion" associated with his character, and he is suing Familyland in an attempt to get his job back.

The explicit function of this subplot is comic relief: we are treated to lots of Homer-style humor and asked to entertain the spectacle of this case, which is completely ridiculous. The plot also alludes nostalgically to many earlier *L.A. Law* plots from other seasons, and thus reminds audiences of the series' better days. But it also serves as a site in which a number of issues central to *California v. Powell* may be posed, transmuted, and resolved. The Familyland case against Champion hinges, for example, on a videotape, taken by a park visitor, of Champion collapsing and vomiting. Against Arnie's objections, Familyland's attorney introduces the tape, and claims, in a parody of the prosecution in the Simi Valley case, that this evidence establishes unproblematically Champion's transgression. And Arnie's closing argument mimics the LAPD officers' defense perfectly: "Ladies and gentlemen, this case is about perception. Let's also talk about reality. Fifteen seconds of tape is hardly representative of Mr. Champion's nineteen years at Familyland. What occurred before that camcorder was turned on, or after it was turned off? What are we missing here?" The substitution of Champion for Koons, Powell, Wind, and Briseno is crucial to the larger work of this episode, because of how this substitution situates embodiment and especially physical pain. *L.A. Law* perfectly extends the logic of the officers' defense, which hinged on the displacement of Rodney King's body, of Rodney King's pain, by the potential for the officers' pain: they had to beat him to prevent him from beating them.[15] Arnie's case neatly sidesteps even the necessity for such substitution by making Champion's "crime" self-evidently victimless and self-evidently the result of his body's own pain. And simultaneous with its replacement of the black body in pain with the white one, the episode dramatically lowers the stakes. The only thing Arnie is defending, after all, is the right of incompetent white masculinity (i.e., Champion) to represent itself as larger-than-life incompetent white masculinity (i.e., Homer Simpson): more interesting, more entertaining perhaps, but still recognizable. Because Arnie is not, for example, defending the right of incompetent white masculinity to police and brutalize the bodies of people of color, the ideological move here is to reenact the logic of the Simi Valley trial in a context in which the outcome hardly matters — even, it seems, to the participants, for Champion himself disappears from the courtroom during Arnie's summation.

In the episode's more explicit engagements with the uprising, outcomes clearly matter; the question to be asked, of course, is to whom they matter, and how, and why. Here again, *L.A. Law* borrows the strategy of the officers' defense by fixating obsessively on the threat people of color pose to white bodies. Three of the episode's subplots bear this out. In the first, Assistant District Attorney Zoey Clemmons comes home from the hospital to recover from a gunshot wound sustained in connection to a case in which her boss, a black woman, asked her to perjure herself. The scene I'm most interested in occurs after Zoey and Tommy Mullaney, Zoey's ex-husband and McKenzie, Brackman associate, have a fight and Zoey, still debilitated by her injury, leaves Tommy's apartment to brave the riot, claiming, "I know what it's like to get shot; I know what it's like to be dead." Later, she returns with Chinese take-out to find Tommy watching a "live" broadcast of a Tom Bradley news conference in which Bradley is discussing the deployment of the National Guard. Tommy turns off the television and Zoey explains why she's come back: "I was sitting in my apartment listening to the helicopters and the sirens and the gunshots, and the more I listened, the more afraid I got. And so I decided that the best way to combat my fears is just to live my normal life." At this point, Zoey confesses to Tommy that she "deserved to get shot" as punishment for her perjury and that she was "really disappointed" not to have had the classically mass-mediated near-death experiences — "seeing auras, leaving [one's] body" — because she felt "like I hadn't earned the privilege." With this, she turns to Tommy and asks, "Do you want to see my scar?" When he assents, she stands, opens her dress and takes the bandage off her chest. Tommy kisses the wound as a sultry saxophone — the feature of the *L.A. Law* soundtrack that serves as the series' most durable signifier of an imminent sexual encounter — becomes audible. Tommy and Zoey exchange a meaningful look. They kiss.

The civic drama of the rebellions is here reoriented in relation to Zoey's role in another municipal theatrical; many of the elements — deceit, corruption, gunshots — are the same, and in both scenarios, the question to be adjudicated is how Zoey will live her "normal life." More to the point, the pathos of her guilt leaves no room for those for whom "helicopters, sirens, gunshots" constitute precisely the stuff of "normal life" under the regime of the same LAPD on whose behalf Zoey, as district attorney, must work. From the broadcast of the Bradley news conference to the closing kiss, this scene moves ever inward: from civil unrest, to civic corruption, to the traumatized white body, to the healing powers of bourgeois white heterosexuality.

But if bourgeois white heterosexuality is situated in the Tommy-Zoey subplot as that which heals or redeems the traumatic encounter between the white body and urban unrest, the second subplot, involving Douglas Brackman, establishes bourgeois heterosexuality as urban unrest's first casualty. In this plot, Douglas stops at a liquor store on the way to his wedding (in a link with the Tommy-Zoey subplot, Douglas is getting remarried to his ex-wife, Sheila) to buy some champagne. As he enters the store, we hear a TV in the background broadcasting local news of the looting: "What seems to have begun as loosely organized protests against that not-guilty verdict has in some cases . . ." The voice of the oblivious Douglas at this point dominates the soundtrack, drowning out the television. He approaches the Asian shopkeeper, asking, "Is this the best champagne you carry?" But the merchant has eyes only for the TV, which promises to "go now to our aerial reporter live from South Central." Seeing that the looting is spreading to his own neighborhood, he says, "Oh, trouble, big trouble," as Douglas tries to get his attention: "Say, could you put this in a box? . . . I'm running late. I'd appreciate you picking up the pace." At this point, the merchant disappears behind the counter, as Douglas calls to him, "And while you're back there, a bow would be nice." The merchant returns with a shotgun, and Douglas, misunderstanding the man's intention to protect him from the "trouble" that is, in the merchant's words, "too close for comfort," tries to appease him: "Forget the bow. I was way out of line." The shopkeeper's instruction — "Leave now. Hurry" — is punctuated by the sound of breaking glass, as a barely differentiated mass of black and Latino bodies surges past the impeccably tuxedoed Douglas (his may be the only white body on the premises).

Here the menace lurking at the margins of Zoey's attack is thoroughly literalized. It's tempting to read Douglas's presence here as punishment for the insufferable way he treats the owner of the store — as punishment, in other words, for his snobbishness and his entitlement, just as Zoey may have been shot as "punishment" for her perjury. But such a reading would be undermined by the further development of this subplot: later in the episode, after he has been

Liquor store under siege. Douglas. Undifferentiated bodies of color.

picked up by the LAPD for, ironically enough, looting, Douglas is faced with the necessity of warding off the aggressive sexual advances of a black man while he's being held by police. Here *L.A. Law* refigures the scary mobility of Rodney King's sexuality, the scary mobility marked densely by King's purportedly inexplicable behavior upon getting out of his car after the chase: "shaking his behind" at the assembled officers.[16] For Douglas, faced with the much more legible version of King's behavior that *L.A. Law* imagines, class privilege serves as the last line of defense: after spitting on his assailant, who recoils, he yells, at him and any other potential attackers within earshot, "I'm supposed to be at the Bel Air Hotel, with my wife, having room service. I love room service. The next miscreant that so much as looks at me is a dead man." Douglas's outburst is ostensibly played for laughs, and its "humor" thus serves as an alibi for its astounding classism. In other words, this moment suggests self-ironically, but suggests nonetheless, that class privilege, rather than generating urban unrest, should be clung to as a bastion against "miscreants."

This question of punishment culminates in the final subplot I'll discuss. Stuart Markowitz is driving to Douglas's ill-fated wedding in his gold Lincoln Town Car. Impatient, honking at the other drivers, he turns off a crowded surface street onto a side road and finds himself in a black and Latino working-class neighborhood in which a menacing group of men of color obstructs his passage. They attack his car, break the windows, drag Stuart from the car, and beat him with bricks and baseball bats. Most of the shots of the beating — many of which work more or less self-consciously to reframe the images of Halliday's video in lurid color and better focus — are taken from two alternating angles: high-angle shots that allude to the helicopter's-eye-view of liveness in general and to the footage of the Reginald Denny beating in particular, and medium close-ups, mostly of blows connecting with Stuart's body, shot from ground level.

Stuart's beating, edited to
evoke both the King and Denny
beatings

After witnessing the horrors of this scene, it's hard to remember Stuart's impatience and the contrast between his enormous luxury car and the neighborhood he was driving through. And after listening to Ann Kelsey (Stuart's wife) ask Leland McKenzie at the hospital, "Why would somebody do this to such a gentle soul?" our amnesia is further reinforced. In the closing scene of this subplot, we learn that Stuart is suffering from that classic TV trauma, "massive brain damage." When he recovers consciousness, looks at Ann, and calls her "Mom," *L.A. Law* delivers its crowning blow, deploying melodramatic codes to ensure that, in this episode at least, the spectacle of Stuart's impairment within the family will effectively displace our memory of his breathtakingly entitled sense that he might superimpose himself anywhere on the city's geography, at any time, without risk.

Each of these three subplots engages questions of agency, of punishment, of white guilt. And each of these plots situates those questions in relation to others about how the nature and status of white bourgeois heterosexuality—the default mode of adult sexuality in mass-mediated culture—might be altered or perverted via its contact with its racial, sexual, and class others. In the bizarre sexual iconography of Zoey's encounter with Tommy, for example, the scar she reveals to him stands in for the nipple that can't be shown within the codes of network "standards," thus establishing a circuit in which the heterosexual rendezvous, inaugurated and enabled by Zoey's to-be-looked-at-ness, seems to require that the body that is revealed must also be damaged. In addition, Douglas's scene of public heterosexualization—his marriage—is deferred by his encounter with the urban sublime. In case we missed this point, the episode provides an explicit scene in which the specter of interracial homosexual rape follows directly from this deferral. Finally, Stuart's reduction, by urban violence, from loving husband to helpless child aligns bourgeois marriage with incest. White bodies and white middle-class sexuality constitute, for *L.A. Law*, the rebellion's most important victims.

In *L.A. Law*'s imagination of the uprising, there are no black or Latino victims, and there is no black or Latino leadership. Indeed, this episode represents repeatedly the corruption or irrelevance of African American public officials. It highlights Tom Bradley's dissociated mumbling about calling in the National Guard, and it is at pains to remind us of the black district attorney who is indirectly responsible for Zoey's brush with death. This tendency finds its fullest expression in Jonathan Rollins's sham bid to represent South Central on L.A.'s City Council, when, as he tells Leland sheepishly, "Everyone knows I live in Brentwood, just have a post office box in South Central." Even when Jonathan finally drives to "the riot zone" and dispenses with his African American campaign manager, who imagines this trip as nothing more than a photo opportunity, his redemption is assured only by his staying to help a *white* property owner in a futile effort to douse his burning building with a garden hose.

Liveness, which is everywhere in this episode, authorizes this revisionist representation of the uprising. The presence and content of live broadcasts within this narrative are constantly adduced as evidence of the crisis state in which these white Angelenos find themselves. Rather than interrogating the universalizing gaze of liveness, *L.A. Law* does its best to collate that gaze with its own—as in the helicopter-like high-angle shot of Stuart lying beaten next to his car. Worse, it works unceasingly to align our gaze as viewers with liveness's gaze, the gaze that situates us all, like the Simi Valley jury, as frightened suburbanites, all on one side of the thin blue line.

Black "Leadership"? Jonathan Rollins

Doogie Howser, M.D. and Televisual Instruction

The 1992 season premiere of *Doogie Howser* also sustains an extensive dialogue with liveness, foregrounding television sets broadcasting "live" news coverage throughout its mise-en-scène. But the first time we see a television in this program, no one is watching it at all. In the teaser, Doogie, his best friend, Vinnie DelPino, and Doogie's parents are gathered in the Howsers' kitchen. Vinnie is trying to convince the senior Dr. Howser to "invest" in the "classic" Nash Rambler he's trying to raise the money to buy, because such investments are particularly important, he claims, in "these troubled economic times." (Vinnie, the site of endless jokes about the adolescent male libido, is interested in the car because the back seat folds down into a bed.) Doogie's father replies that, on the contrary, he has "a very mature portfolio" and thus "no need to invest in a mobile bedroom." This exchange continues the generational banter about bourgeois masculinity and masculine sexuality that is one of the series' more persistent preoccupations, even as it reminds the audience of the class status of Doogie's family, which will later become implicated as an explanation for Doogie's particular view of the "riots." Indeed, the teaser connects the "problem" of white male heterosexuality, to which I will return, to the problems posed not only by the rebellion, but also by the project of representing the rebellion on television, for after the group disperses, the TV announces to the empty room that "we interrupt our programming to go live to Simi Valley, where the jury has reached a verdict in the Rodney King case."

With its pointedly unanchored diectic "we," this televisual proclamation comments uneasily and ironically on what Stephen Heath has called television's "universalization of the function of reception." "Television," he writes, "exists first and foremost as availability, as saying everything to everyone, all of us receivers, assembled and serialized in that unity." [17] But unlike *L.A. Law*, *Doogie Howser* knows, at least, that one lesson taught by the uprisings, perhaps *the* lesson, is the impossibility of such unity or universalization of reception: not all of us can embody the helicopter's-eye-view, the view of the police. Chiefly through the figure of Raymond, the black former gang member whom Doogie has befriended and rehabilitated as a hospital orderly, this episode registers, however problematically or self-servingly, that, as Doogie remarks, "the bell tolls a little louder for some of us than for others." Or, as Raymond puts it more prosaically, Doogie doesn't, during the rioting, "have to run to a pay phone to see if it's [his] home that's on fire." But *Doogie Howser*'s critique of liveness, signaled initially by this hostile fantasy of the unwatched live broadcast, is energized by more than its suspicion of liveness's claim to produce the unified gaze of the nation. This critique aims ultimately to replace universalized reception with scenes of instruction and to position fictional TV as the most crucial pedagogical technology for explaining race and history.

The episode works out most of these questions via the figure of Vinnie, who aspires to be a filmmaker and who, expanding on a long-standing trope of the show, arrives in the emergency room after the verdict (he and Doogie have planned to test-drive the Rambler that afternoon) with his video camera and proceeds to get in everyone's way as he pursues his art. Dr. Canfield, Doogie's boss, launches the first assault on Vinnie's vocation and his camera. "DelPino, what are you doing here?" he demands. Vinnie replies, "I'm recording history," to which Canfield responds, "Do it somewhere else," as he wrenches the camcorder from Vinnie. Undeterred, Vinnie hunts down Doogie, who is treating a firefighter who's been hit in the head with a brick. At this point, a group of small, mostly African American children arrives. Their day care teacher has been burned trying to put out a fire in her school, and they need looking after while she gets treatment. Doogie, eager to find something to take Vinnie out of the emergency room, tells him to take the kids to the pediatric lounge. In a reply crucially evocative of slavery, Vinnie tells Doogie, "I'm an auteur, not a wet nurse." Doogie loses his patience: "Vinnie, *look around*." Here the episode cuts to a point-of-view shot as Vinnie scans the emergency room. He reluctantly takes the children upstairs.

This entire exchange, with the exception of the final shot from Vinnie's point of view, takes place as he is taping. Thus, it seems the video camera itself prevents Vinnie from seeing what is so obviously going on around him. Indeed, Canfield's and Doogie's reactions gesture toward a powerful indictment of amateur video's capacity to see precisely what it purports to see. Furthermore, undermining the credibility of Vinnie's vision also discredits that of George Halliday, and of anyone else who would claim that his tape might be taken as self-evident. The episode thus refuses, albeit obliquely, to indict the Simi Valley jury for the drastic difference between its reading of the Halliday video and that produced by many of those who saw the tape in a different context, embedded in the flow of television news programming. In the process, it interrogates the presumptions that shore up the very live coverage it so voraciously cannibalizes: exhibiting a powerful distrust of video's allegedly privileged relation to immediacy, presence, and the real, *Doogie Howser* puts *its* stock in fictional television's representations, situating them as a better route to cultural understanding, both historically and in the contemporary everyday.

The show tips its hand, revealing its investments in fictional TV's mediation of the shocks of live catastrophe coverage, in a sequence in which Vinnie tries to manage his unruly charges. Here *Doogie Howser* sets up richly condensed relations between race and televisual pedagogy, imagined as a way for white men simultaneously to retain and share power. As a result, this scene is usefully emblematic of the larger project of this episode (and, arguably, the series as a whole) in providing a textual space in which white masculinity tries to re-negotiate its own hegemony, sometimes absorbing and containing, sometimes yielding to, real or imagined "threats" — material, representational, and sexual. The sequence opens with an unsteady, clearly handheld point-of-view shot from the viewfinder of Vinnie's camcorder, but since it is of Vinnie himself, reading *The Cat in the Hat,* the shot is immediately and unequivocally situated as the enunciation of one of the children. The viewfinder shots continue as Vinnie looks up from the book, sees the child, and heads over to retrieve the camera, saying, "Hey, put that down. That's not a toy, kid, that's my life." As Vinnie and the child wrestle for the camera — a struggle evidenced by a wildly unstable image, still from the point of view of the viewfinder — Vinnie intones, "I'm not a violent person, but I've got a copy of *Cat in the Hat* and I'm not afraid to use it," and an off-screen child's voice says, "Oh, I'm really scared." At this point, there's a cut from the viewfinder POV shot back to the more standard visual discourse of *Doogie Howser:* a medium shot of Vinnie, having retrieved the camcorder, walking across the lounge to try to dissuade another of the African American children from "playing" with the fire alarm. "Look, that's not a toy either," Vinnie says. "The toys are the brightly colored plastic things around here. Here, why don't you play with this fairy magic wand?" The children scream with laughter as the little boy hits Vinnie over the head with the wand.

If we understand the struggle over the camcorder in the opening of this sequence as related to the first struggle with Canfield and to Doogie's derisive "Vinnie, *look around*," the potentially disruptive appropriation of the enuciative powers of video technology by a child of color here is always already undermined. Vinnie's words "Put that down, that's not a toy" only serve to call attention to the fact that his camcorder has been "proven" by the episode to be just that: an annoying disruption to the real, immediate, embodied work of the hospital staff. The persistent dismissal of the possibility of camcorder activism is rendered all the more striking by the fact that the episode, most centrally concerned with the damage done to persons and property by fire, hints at the stakes of such representational appropriation, by aligning the video camera with the fire alarm that fascinates one of these children but that is "not a toy either." This show thus suggests that redistributing control over media representation might be an alternative way of putting out some urban fires. The show does no such thing, however, for the implications of this moment are thoroughly contained by conventions of TV comedy: "playing" with the video camera or the fire alarm is inappropriate in the same way it's inappropriate for a child to hit Vinnie with the "fairy magic wand."

What should we make of the interruption of this scene by the word *fairy*, which is, of course, completely unnecessary to describe this object? Ideologically, Vinnie's offer of the "fairy magic wand" embeds both a utopian promise and a rebuke. On one hand, it's an appropriate toy, unlike the camcorder and the fire alarm, and its magic might transcend the thoroughly material work the nontoys can perform. On the other, the "fairyness" of the wand is unstable, always threatening to transfer itself to its bearer and emasculate him. Thus, we might guess that when the boy hits Vinnie over the head with the wand, he is trying to transfer its effeminizing potential back onto Vinnie. The mock violence of the exchange of the wand between Vinnie and the boy thus mobilizes the threats — instabilities of racial, sexual, and hegemonic positions — that white heterosexual masculinity in general, and *Doogie Howser* in particular, must work to manage. Thus, in the context of *Doogie Howser*'s obsession with documenting the vicissitudes of suburban white adolescent male heterosexuality (the series' attention to sexuality is indeed this precise), the exchange of the fairy magic wand condenses several of the "others" of the sexual position the show likes to imagine for its main characters, others that are nonetheless always present in the show's production of Doogie and Vinnie's sexual subjectivity: African American male sexuality (elsewhere centered in the presence of Raymond), the sexuality of children (elsewhere located in the original boy-in-a-man's-world premise of the show), and gay sexuality (elsewhere and everywhere present within the abiding homosocial bond between Vinnie and Doogie).

That such condensation, particularly of black male sexuality and gay male sexuality as threats to white bourgeois masculinity, might find its way into an episode on Rodney King should not surprise us. As Butler has pointed out, the sexual iconography of the Halliday video — "the image of the police standing over Rodney King with their batons" — evokes "a punishment for [King's] conjectured or desired sexual aggression."[18] Part of the work the fairy magic wand does in this scene, then, is to invoke King and his beating, to stand in for the police batons whose "fairyness" is also shifting, unstable in relation to the "sexual aggression" that is widely and popularly assumed to reside in black men, and which is persistently conjectured or desired as containing within it the capacity to interpellate white men as its objects. As in the beating itself, the intensity of the sexualized aggression in the exchange of the wand threatens to undermine the stability of white masculinity: if Vinnie begins this encounter in the position of the police, purporting to respond to the child's unruliness with the violently gratuitous and contaminating deployment of the word *fairy,* the child is able to appropriate that position and hit back. In this way, the scene, as a fantasized reenactment of the beating, restages the "logic" of the Simi Valley jurors who imagined King to be "in complete control" and clarifies the intertwined roles racism and homophobia played in the production of the jury's reading of the video.

In the closing moments of the sequence, this collation of sexuality, race, and the televisual negotiations of white male hegemony meets up explicitly with *Doogie Howser*'s critique of liveness and its claims for the pedagogic potential of fictional television. Vinnie's solution to the magic wand problem is to turn on the television, forgetting that one of the markers of catastrophe is that one finds the same thing on every channel. Liveness — in this case, images of fire — generates questions that only fictional television can answer; faced with the children's queries about what they've seen, Vinnie seeks to instruct them on race relations by promising to tell them "the whole thing": "It all started with this guy called Rodney King . . . You know what? I'm going to have to go back further than this." Blank looks from the children. "Martin Luther King."

Another blank look. He pulls up a chair, looks at them earnestly, and says, "Once upon a time there was this guy called Kunta Kinte" — blank looks — "who came to America on Ed Asner's slave ship."

Vinnie's reference to *Roots* returns us to his remark to Doogie earlier in the episode that he is "an auteur, not a wet nurse," a remark in which Vinnie wards off the specter of finding himself interpellated as a black woman, but in which the gesture of warding off serves only to situate his own masculinity more firmly as beleaguered, and beleaguered specifically in relation to a complex and volatile reenactment of the scene of slavery organized by a series of mirroring binarisms. In other words, even though Vinnie is a white man, not a black woman, being asked to care for black children rather than white ones, the perfect symmetry of his position relative to that of the wet nurse threatens always to deconstruct his opposition to her. But the invocation of *Roots* undoes the abjection of Vinnie's earlier self-insertion into the narrative of slavery, and thus provisionally secures the ground of white masculinity and heterosexuality; here Vinnie deploys this narrative *not* from the position of the wet nurse; here, at least, he gets to tell the story of slavery from the outside, from a position something like that of the auteur.

And from that of the *lecteur:* Vinnie's lecture — situated in this scene as ridiculous, with the children's blankness played for laughs — is eventually shown to evolve into a productive discussion with at least one of the children about the beating, the verdict, and its aftermath. Fictional television — here, *Roots* specifically — thus turns out to be pedagogically useful by generating a scene of instruction in which the white teacher "explains" the racial history of the United States to six children of color. And through this consideration of pedagogy, these scenes inscribe the series's profound ambivalence about its own situation within the white-liberal culture industry, a situation in which *Doogie Howser* is both acutely aware of the specificity — and thus the limitations — of its privileged access to the airwaves, and is simultaneously completely unwilling to imagine sharing that access. The answer to this dilemma, as *Doogie Howser* imagines it, is for mainstream network television to function didactically in relation to its audiences of color.

But this gesture is itself complicated, in these scenes, by the children's persistent construction as a less than appreciative audience for Vinnie's lesson. Their disaffection echoes the unwatched verdict of the teaser, and returns us to the question of reception *Doogie Howser* is so worried about: if it rejects the falsely universal national gaze of liveness—which is, after all, a powerful fantasy of mass viewership in these days of cable's challenge to network hegemony—what might a plausible alternative be? How might *Doogie Howser* find an audience for its lectures? The answer to these questions may lie in the fact that network audiences, these days, are disproportionately of color, since predominately African American and Latino inner-city neighborhoods are the cable industry's final, and as yet unreached, frontier. The children in these scenes, and their parents, might plausibly be understood as stand-ins for the actual viewers *Doogie Howser,* and shows like it, must address.

Rodney King Dead

"For all its ideology of 'liveness,' it may be death which forms the point of televisual intrigue." In this line from "Information, Crisis, Catastrophe," Mary Ann Doane points out that liveness, as a crucial televisual rhetoric of catastrophe coverage, is always linked with catastrophe TV's primary object: death:[19] Live TV is always haunted by the possibility of death. If we take seriously this linkage between liveness and death, then what are the specters that trouble the texts of King TV? I'd like to conclude by proposing two answers to that question. First, as I've suggested in my reading of *Doogie Howser*'s extended meditation on liveness, one ghostly other of live TV is dead TV, or, more specifically, the long, drawn-out death of the major networks, gradually bled of their audiences by cable and VCR use. We can read the enthusiastic deployment of live catastrophe coverage and its fictional recyclings by network television as one of the ways in which the networks reinvent their own relevance to national life. And in this regard, King TV (like Thomas-Hill) was particularly efficacious from the network point of view, given their quest for African American audiences: at this moment in U.S. television's history, there is a particularly pressing market imperative to rehash endlessly the vicissitudes of race in America.

Second, the production and reception of Rodney King Live requires also the invocation and repression of Rodney King Dead. These requirements, I think, lie at the heart of the capacity of King's query—"Can't we all get along?"—to transfix the nation, and also at the heart of the necessity for that query to be so immediately and widely ironized; King's authority at that moment was so eerie because his was, in a sense, a voice from the dead. The power of the Halliday video, after all, lay in its spectacularly awful and thankfully unkept promise to finally catch Darryl Gates's LAPD in the act of beating a black man to death. In this respect, the video, and the wider televisual flow through which it circulated, placed King as a stand-in for the "invisible" or at least unvideotaped victims of police murder in L.A. and elsewhere: for Eulia Love, say, or Eleanor Bumpers, or Michael Stewart. It is their spirits who inhabit the margins of these texts.

Finally, though, both of these answers are in one way at least the same answer: network television, scrambling for African American viewers, self-promoting, and sensationalist, finds itself telling and retelling the story of U.S. race relations and, in the process, chronicling the violent eruptions of dreams deferred. Finds itself, in other words, fading to black.

Notes

Audiences at the University of Chicago, the University of Pennsylvania, Duke, and Harvard have helped me think through this work. I am indebted in particular to Elizabeth Alexander, Chris Amirault, Lauren Berlant, Amanda Berry, Jacqueline Bobo, Nahum Chandler, and Phillip Brian Harper for their suggestions and support.

1   Much has been written about the video, of course, but little has attended specifically to its intersections with mainstream broadcast practice; the latter will be my focus here. On the video, see, for example, Patricia J. Williams, "The Rules of the Game," in *Reading Rodney King/Reading Urban Uprising*, ed. Robert Gooding-Williams (New York: Routledge, 1993), 51–55; and Kimberlé Crenshaw and Gary Peller, "Reel Time/Real Justice," in the same volume, 56–70.

2   These events were also treated in episodes of *Melrose Place, The Fresh Prince of Bel Air*, and *A Different World*. My interest here on fictional television's cannibalizations of liveness leads me to focus on *L.A. Law* and *Doogie Howser*, both of which engage with liveness extensively. In the process, I sidestep the important questions that might be generated by a comparative analysis of these programs and *Fresh Prince* and *A Different World*, which target an African American demographic.

3   Herman Gray, "Television, Black Americans, and the American Dream," *Critical Studies in Mass Communication* 6 (December 1989): 376–386.

4   Jane Feuer, "The Concept of Live Television: Ontology as Ideology," in *Regarding Television: Critical Approaches—An Anthology*, ed. E. Ann Kaplan (Frederick, MD: University Publications of America, 1983), 12–21. Other important accounts of liveness include Stephen Heath and Gillian Skirrow, "Television: A World in Action," *Screen* 18, no. 2 (summer 1977): 7–59; Mary Ann Doane, "Information, Crisis, Catastrophe," in *Logics of Television: Essays in Cultural Criticism*, ed. Patri-

cia Mellencamp (Bloomington: Indiana University Press, 1990), 222–239; Stephen Heath, "Representing Television," in *Logics,* 267–302.

5   Feuer, 14.

6   Ibid.

7   Ibid., 19.

8   Judith Butler, "Endangered/Endangering: Schematic Racism and White Paranoia," in *Reading Rodney King/Reading Urban Uprising,* 17.

9   On direct address, see Margaret Morse's "Talk, Talk, Talk: The Space of Discourse in Television News, Sportscasts, Talk Shows, and Advertising," *Screen* 26 (1985): 2–15.

10   The helicopter's-eye-view of South Central Los Angeles had by now been thoroughly linked, by national media culture generally and by Hollywood film in particular, to the gaze of the LAPD. Consider, for example, the deployment of helicopters in *Colors* (1988), *Boyz N the Hood* (1991), and *Grand Canyon* (1991).

11   Butler, 21.

12   Rhonda Williams, "Accumulation as Evisceration: Urban Rebellion and the New Growth Dynamics," in *Reading Rodney King/Reading Urban Uprising,* 83. One of the many pleasures of Lynell George's chronicle of the rebellions, "Waiting for the Rainbow Sign," is the way in which it, as a street's-eye-view account, revises most of the assumptions and narrative conventions that have emerged in other representations of these events. See her *No Crystal Stair: African-Americans in the City of Angels* (New York: Verso, 1992), 9–16.

13   The most important consideration of these recombinatory practices is Todd Gitlin's, in his *Inside Prime Time* (New York: Pantheon, 1985).

14   What are we to make of the appearance of a character from *The Simpsons,* one of Fox's most successful, durable, and visible series, embedded in an NBC program? I would suggest that this intertextual reference does more than simply promote television per se, as Mimi White argues about such cross-network references in "Crossing Wavelengths: The Diegetic and Referential Imaginary of American Commercial Television," *Cinema Journal* 25, no. 2 (winter 1986): 51–64. *The Simpsons* after all, marked Fox as a new threat to the dominance of the big three networks when Fox programmed it against NBC's enormously successful *Cosby Show* in 1990, and it has of course outlasted both *The Cosby Show* and *L.A. Law* itself. Thus I argue that "Homer Simpson" functions here as the sign that allows this text both to register and to struggle against its own network's increasingly obsolete programming strategies and demographic self-understanding. I will return to these points in the section on *Doogie Howser.*

15   I am indebted for this point to Butler's suggestion that King's "body . . . received [the officers'] blows in return for the ones it was about to deliver, the blows which were that body in its essential gestures, even as the one gesture that body can be

seen to make is to raise its palm outward to stave off the blows against it. According to this racist episteme, he is hit in exchange for the blows he never delivered, but which he is always, by virtue of his blackness, always about to deliver" (19).

16   Here I am relying on the testimony of California Highway Patrol officer Melanie Singer, in the Simi Valley trial: "At that time, I withdrew my weapon, pointed it at the suspect and told him to get his hand away from his butt—I could not see where his hand was—and at that time he turned his . . . body around to where his rear end was facing me. He grabbed his right buttock with his right hand and shook it at me." See *The "Rodney King" Case: What the Jury Saw in California v. Powell,* Court TV compilation tape of the Simi Valley trial, 1992. Though Singer's testimony might lead us to assume that King's gesture was directed at Singer and thus heterosexually motivated, I think such a supposition would be a mistake, as Singer's irrelevance to the proceedings was adequately established by the Simi Valley trial. Rather, I propose to read King's gesture as addressed to and received by both Singer and the other officers, all of whom were men.

17   Heath, 270.

18   Butler, 21.

19   Doane, 233.

TELEVISUAL POLITICS

Negotiating Race in the L.A. Rebellion

John Caldwell

Ethnic diversity isn't just a fact of life, it's a fashion theme for spring.
—Mary Rourke, *Los Angeles Times*[1]

Here I am in my own backyard—and I'm covering a war.
—KABC television reporter Linda Moore, April 30, 1992

It has become an apparent truism that justice was defeated in Simi Valley be-cause the evidence of aggression was stylized and overworked. Why did the prosecution fail to establish that Rodney King was a victim? Because the tape of the beating was played in slow motion, freeze-framed, talked over, inter-preted, distributed, and—most damaging of all—closely analyzed.[2] To critics, the visual evidence had been tampered with through a highly publicized ritual of deconstruction and overanalysis.[3] Satiated with redundant images of King's beating, the audience-jury was thought to have been deadened as well to the reality of violence.

I hope to address several problematic issues surrounding this event and the supposed analysis-induced miscarriage of justice that accompanied it. First, the ever-expanding coverage of the King trial, the L.A. rebellion, and its after-math suggest that stylization and deconstruction are not aberrancies limited to televised legal proceedings, but are fundamental modes of mainstream televisual representation as well. In the way that difference is represented, and the other is packaged, these modes have clear political implications, but their effects depend ultimately on the context and functions given those modes. The Rodney King–L.A. rebellion phenomenon was less a crisis of style than a televisual form of crisis management.

Second, television coverage of the L.A. rebellion challenges some assumptions about the gendered nature of television and its depiction of the other. The ideas of television as feminine and mass culture as modernism's other have helped establish the field of contemporary television study in important ways.[4] Landmark work by Tania Modleski demonstrated how television narratives are organized around the daily rhythms and pleasures that culture sanctions for women.[5] Beverle Houston feminized the "endless consumption" of television by stripping the new critical theory of its phallocentric bias and arguing that the medium's defining properties were oral and maternal pleasures.[6] Extrapolations from these perspectives, however, have tended to underestimate fundamental masculinist aspects of the television apparatus, traits that have been operative in both the industry and its programming for many years. Even Lynne Joyrich's important demonstration of the rise of "hypermasculinity" as a reaction to increased feminization reinforces the notion that television's norm has somehow been feminine.[7] The linkage of television, distraction, and the feminine — typically set in binarist opposition to the spectatorial modes and desires of film — has come at a cost.[8] The L.A. rebellion and its aftermath suggest that the television apparatus is *also* clearly and problematically masculinist, especially in the ways that it performs style and fetishizes production technology.[9]

When Sgt. Stacey Koons cast Rodney King as "Mandingo," in a book manuscript that hit the press well before his trial, and anchor Paul Moyer and his Channel 7 Eyewitness News reporters targeted window-breakers as "hoodlums" and "thugs," television viewers witnessed classic ways by which the ethnic other is rendered marginal and alien.[10] But there was more at work the first evening that Los Angeles burned, April 29, 1992, than the invocation of these kinds of static stereotypes.[11] The anchors did occasionally apologize for their impulsive outbursts, as they did after calling on-camera window-breakers "creeps."[12] More than just attempts to reestablish news studio decorum, such outbursts and apologies betrayed the fact that the news readers were also simply taken-aback spectators. The same reporters then elaborated sociological justifications for their racial designations. Repeated reference was made to the fact that the senseless violence was being perpetuated by "people with nothing better to do" than to look for "an excuse to go out and trash buildings and start fires."[13] A persistent but not so subtle othering process was now in gear: there was no motive or reason for the violence; the hoodlums were simply inactive people with enough idle time on their hands to entertain themselves by creating a disturbance. With this kind of officially concerned verbal discourse on television, fifty years of Los Angeles social, political, and economic history—indeed, the very notion of causality or context in any form—simply vanished.

Although the mainstream has always created a center on the inside of culture with this kind of verbal discourse, television during the rebellion quickly brought to bear a large number of other, nonverbal tactics for containing the dangerous other. As much as any other recent phenomenon in television, the L.A. rebellion demonstrated the fundamental role that the ecstatic performance of style plays in constructing and managing the other. Once the conflict started, desperate news institutions appeared unable to keep up with the unfolding threat. Without their normal scripts and teleprompters, news-reading anchors and reporters merely free-associated. The sometimes incoherent verbiage that followed quickly indicted those who free-associated, as did their lack of actual knowledge about the communities in Los Angeles.[14]

The *televisual* apparatus, by contrast—construed by broadcast corporations as hard-wired, automatic, and omnipresent—quickly and immediately engaged with the chaos outside and presented it as knowable, understandable, and containable. In rebellion coverage—in both local and national manifestations—style was clearly more than icing on the cake. It was a fundamental way the other was managed and packaged, and it fulfilled an important role in television's crisis management. Coverage of the L.A. rebellion is important because the social uprising caused a simultaneous crisis in television's system of representation as well. Faced with a social rupture of this magnitude, television's privileged journalistic and narrative systems of representation were outrun by a furious performance of electronic televisual style. The coverage also stands as a challenge to a number of recurrent and privileged theoretical notions—especially those that link television inextricably with liveness, the glance, and the dehistorified present.

The analysis that follows uses two tripartite models—one historical, the other ideological—to understand television's crisis coverage of the L.A. rebellion. From an ideological perspective, crisis coverage convulsed with three

The borrowed and stolen icon, encrusted with graphics and legally reinscribed with time-code. The icon, anchored as political book and graphic postcard. (Fox, KCBS, KCAL)

recurrent control fantasies: hyperactive embellishments of masculinity, race, and autotechnologies were all thrown into the fray to establish and maintain television's command presence.[15] The ideological effects of this linkage among race, gender and technology during crisis provides one key to the politics of televisuality. From a historical perspective, on the other hand, television representations of Rodney King and the L.A. rebellion underwent three different phases and transformations as well, each with its own favored televisual tactics. Television's strategies of containment, furthermore, changed in each period, even as the threat of the dangerously racial other was redefined, managed, and naturalized. The term *televisual mill* describes aptly the first phase, a period that stretched from Rodney King's videotaped beating in March 1991 to the Simi Valley trial in April 1992.

The Televisual Mill: Rorschach, *Vanitas*, Stigmata

The great irony of the beating footage seen round the world was that people were reacting *perceptually* to very little. The handheld, low-resolution, monochromatic tape footage was essentially electronic noise. The form was amorphous and vague — a kind of Rorschach test that could be infinitely read into. But unlike the Abscam sting footage over a decade earlier, the King footage was not just legal evidence, it was also a visual schematic ripe for constant and immediate commercial and journalistic redefinition. Like a palimpsest, the grainy video slate would be scraped and erased, encrusted and reused in a seemingly infinite number of ways. Once on satellite, even its owner and originator, George Halliday, lost control, which led to suits and countersuits, threats and counterthreats about the video's use and exploitation.

An icon was being mass-produced, and its dispersion throughout culture seemed self-perpetuating. In fact, the mass production of the beating icon in the period between the actual beating and the Simi Valley trial clearly suggested that television is a kind of televisual mill — endlessly grinding out different stylistic permutations from privileged and charged visual fragments. The low resolution and amorphous source slate became, in many manifestations, highly stylized and visually complicated program openings, mural-size screens in newsrooms, and graphically constructed and flying visual artifacts. The beating icon had value as both an anchor for journalistic discourse and as a cutting-edge component in newsroom interior design and station marketing flash. The beating icon was continuously borrowed, stolen, and encrusted with graphics. NBC, CBS, CNN, Fox, and others fought to insert their own logos over Halliday's date graphics. Dispersed by satellite, the noisy image became a commodified "projective test" — a tabula rasa for mass market mental projections and readings.

The legal system continued and complicated the mass media's obsession with fixing the icon. In one of many courtroom variations, an alternate time-code system was keyed over Halliday's original time information to resecure its time. Electronically keyed style arrows pointed out details impossible to discern with the naked eye — and probably absent on the tape in any credible sense of the word. The obsession with fixation, however, did not just occur by time-place insertions and graphic anchors. In another case, the dispersed icon was objectified in book form for Amnesty International's legal case against the police system. Television stations regularly created graphic postcards out of the fragment for intros and previews. Other appropriators included fraternal and lobbying organizations who took partisan stances either for or against the police department. A legal hermeneutic was emerging that placed Rodney King's image at its center. The rhetoric of the trial itself centered around video-taped images and numerous mock-ups and derivations of images. Live television coverage of the trial positioned the audience both as jurors and as police officers. In over-the-shoulder close-ups, the audience was allowed to see from Stacey Koons's perspective, even as he struggled to make sense of the visual fragments and details. King's absence in court, by contrast, prevented any of this narrative camera language from fixing *his* point of view. On another day of the trial, a use of force expert dominated and anchored the video image in a kind of voice-over karaoke. Because the image the expert analyzed is so open and lacking in detail, the officer's performance evoked a Rorschach test, a projective exercise the openness of which allows subjects to invent and fix

Televised trial and visual analysis from Koons's spatial point of view. Use of force expert dominates and anchors the image in voice-over karaoke. (Ventura County Court)

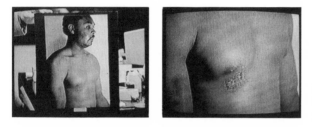

King's sacrificial body, his wounds transformed into stigmata. (Ventura County Court)

their own meanings. Continuous live coverage of the trial clearly made visual analysis and evidence the audience's business. Courtroom witnesses provided the audience with a surrogate model for participation, one that made visual anchoring and fixation the crucial viewing task.

A daily obsession with the credibility of the victim's flesh produced visible evidence that transformed King's wounds into postreligious, mass-cultural *stigmata*.[16] Cloned icons of this sacrificial subject were dispersed throughout the medium and wounds of the martyr were broadcast from the courtroom into the living room on a nightly basis. The original, open, and amorphous video evidence also initiated and replicated higher-resolution color images. Highly resolved 16-by-20-inch color photographic prints — a medium of superior ontological value when compared to video — were used to fix the authenticity of King's scars and flesh wounds. The legal and televised issue of credibility, then, hinged on a battle among three competing discourses: surveillance video, Catholic iconography, and medical diagnostics. The very authority of the image and the authenticity of King's body were at stake in the competition among these institutionalized but divergent image-discourses.

In the days before and during the trial, King was also transfixed in fake print form, embellished on videographic marble surfaces, and arranged tastefully in still-life fashion, complete with baton and badge. As evocations of the

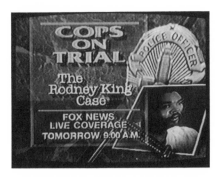

King's beating evidence transformed into moral *vanitas*. (Fox)

past and constructions meant to suggest nostalgia, digital arrangements like these evoked the *vanitas* of earlier European still-life paintings. In this tradition, painters self-consciously arranged and posed objects for viewers and patrons as symbolic moral messages: on temporality, on mortality, on the very meaning of life. The video *vanitas,* repeated nightly on national network feeds before and after each unfolding story, inscribed, prepackaged, and reduced the Rodney King story to the status of a singular tragic moral.

Crisis Management: Televisual Autopilot

Televisual autopilot describes the second and most intense period of local rebellion coverage—a phase of unstable crisis management—from the moment the verdicts were made public in late April through the weeks of armed conflict that followed in May. If the pretrial televisual mill ritualized electronic, mass-production moralizing as benign, then televisual autopilot betrayed another one of broadcasting's control fantasies: the idea and ideal that crisis coverage means hard-wired omnipresence and automated response. Even though reporters and anchors frequently seemed clueless about the chaos on the ground, the fact that television could see the unfolding spectacle, and could see it everywhere, justified and underscored the very authority of broadcasters to speak. Live coverage has always been the trump card of broadcasters, and crisis coverage on a massive technological scale legitimized two of television's most persistent mythologies: its cult of technical superiority (the result of years of heavy capital investment in concrete, satellite, and microwave technologies) and its cult of journalismo (the superiority of delegated professional reportage over democratic or populist media). Whereas the earlier milling of Rodney King

The visual chaos of unsanctioned camcorder footage. Bunkered news center and forward air-control stacked up over "flash points." Chopper pilots as mechanized eyes and surrogate interview subjects. (KCAL)

packaged him in rote moral guises—the stigmata and the *vanitas,* symbols that neatly fit the long tradition of tragic African American victimization—crisis televisuality attacked the now exploding threat of race through higher-tech ecstasies of masculinity and militarism.

Once the Simi Valley verdicts were handed down, community violence erupted in response to tentative police actions. A botched arrest attempt in the neighborhood near Florence and Normandy instigated a hasty and disorderly police retreat. The visual chaos of early unsanctioned camcorder footage taken by residents during this confrontation was clearly reminiscent of the King beating imagery. Like Halliday's earlier beating footage, these images were hand-held, sketchy, and unresolved glimpses of violence. Other unsanctioned footage evoked images of the apocalypse. In camcorder footage later snapped up by concerned tabloid *A Current Affair,* a cleric, Bible in hand, calls for divine protection above a recently slain victim. The street footage from the start of the crisis, like the King video before it, had the blurry and bewildering openness of a projective target.

This volatile openness was short-lived. Within minutes, the official news media called in the choppers—an immediate response that kicked the televisual apparatus into autopilot. Choppers were dispatched from bunkered, observation tower–like television studio control rooms. Refueled and in the air around the clock, swarms of chopper cameras eventually stacked up above flash points and acted as literal and symbolic extensions of the bunkered and centralized stations below. The pilots become mechanized eyes of the spectacle. As there were, apparently, no human subjects below to interview, much of the coverage in the next few days involved interviewing the pilots, who were essentially the station's own mechanized eyes, not rebellion subjects or victims. Television's relative lack of contact with actual human participants in

Olympian dialogue between station tower and skycam. The vertical hierarchy and an obsession with militarization during the crisis conflated Los Angeles with the Gulf war and the arsonists with crazed Iraqis. (KTTV, CBS, NBC)

the rebellion also led to a crisis of representation. Paired graphic boxes were set up to show dialogue between station tower and skycam. Anchors in front of control room vistas and mechanized camera eyes reflected on the meaning of the world cleanly above the misery spewing forth below them. KTLA Channel 5 proudly announced to the viewer, in their skycam dialogue boxes, that KTLA represented Hollywood in the violent spectacle that was unfolding below. *These* participants were not, then, just anonymous reporters. They were concerned industry players.

During crisis coverage, the obsession with stylistic fixation took many other less Olympian forms, including the metaphorization of the event in dramatic military terms. While the apparatus celebrated its automated technological abilities during the period of crisis coverage, television also actively worked to militarize itself. By drawing battle lines in explicit on-camera graphics, television conflated the multiplicity of participants and motives into a paradigm of the polar pitched battle, with an us and a them, with victims and assailants, good guys and bad guys. The decisiveness with which television militarized the situation is not so shocking if one considers the long history of strategic counterinsurgency plans espoused and formalized by the LAPD. Mike Davis has documented how militarization and Vietnamization were systematic and highly publicized parts of the LAPD during the 1980s. He describes the LAPD's "search-and-destroy missions" in South Central, the Vietnamization of large urban neighborhood assaults like "Operation Hammer," the construal of African American housing projects as "strategic hamlets," and LAPD's overall strategic goal of pacifying Los Angeles.[17]

The rebellion Rorschach, and the media's militarist response, then, were not subjectivist at all. Television reporters were not simply grabbing impulsive connections from a journalistic and individualist id—they were spewing forth

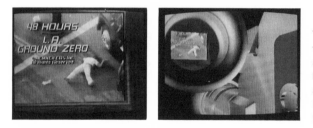

The specter of nuclear warfare. Florence and Normandy as ground zero. CBS's digital Betacam locks in on target for air superiority in Strangelove-like smart-bomb video opening. (CBS)

projections from a systematically manufactured social unconscious. So, too, the tactics of live coverage were not merely "determined" by the technologies of chopper-borne and uplinked video, nor were they as automatic and hard-wired as broadcasters imagined. They too were fabricated from a long tradition of logistic control and surveillance, honed from ritual aerial freeway chases on the nightly news and from years of spotlit aerial search-and-arrest missions in South Central. Although many on the streets celebrated the fact that the LAPD "was finally getting its ass kicked," few recognized that the conflagration and its coverage were actually self-fulfilling prophesies that followed years of civic and militarist strategic planning.

Repeated on-camera references likened the aerial spectacle to the endless oil fires in the Gulf war, as smoke billowed to the horizon from countless fires below. This reporting tactic did not just create a visual analogy, but forcefully inscribed the unfolding events within an existing, and easy to grasp, militarist framework. Through this televisual staging, the arsonists below assumed the unenviable symbolic role of crazed Iraqis. Significantly, the ploy suggested that the victims, like the oil reserves in the gulf, were positioned as the physical (rather than human) resources of Los Angeles: what was at stake was American property. The credibility problem created by calling these views "close-ups"—as NBC news did in their graphics—underscored the sense that the only thing the viewer was actually close to was the viewpoint of an individual pilot high up in the air. The aerial eyes were posed, then, as sensitive professionals, musing on the tragedy and lost physical resources of Los Angeles, as individuals filled with remorse and traumatized by declining property values.

CBS went further and hyped Florence and Normandy as "ground zero"—thereby invoking the specter of fifty years of paranoia over global nuclear destruction. This militarist and geographical fixation centered the conflict in a local skirmish rather than within the social system of Los Angeles or a broader

The "good" Mayor Bradley weeps over fallen people in 1930s-style montage, and the ever-sensitive Ted Kopple uses burned-out buildings as apocalyptic wallpaper. (ABC)

urban context. The Reginald Denny beating footage was recognized on the very day that it aired as a mirror image of the King beating. Reporters immediately and repeatedly characterized this incident in polar terms: as black retribution against the King beating and the white verdicts. The new Denny icon was further stylized and embellished by *48 Hours* as part of their high-impact opening. A computer-generated digital betacam locks in on the target, suggesting "air superiority"—a term with resonance dating back to Vietnam. The pilotless Betacam flies into the target at Florence and Normandy. By visually riding this Strangelove-like doomsday apparatus down to ground zero, CBS unwittingly identified its line of sight with a different kind of retribution, one made popular in smart Gulf war video-bombs. The network news heavyweights at CBS thereby positioned themselves both as a form of air superiority and as journalistic, but partisan, retribution against Denny's injustice. The network's militarist self-consciousness and high-tech air superiority did George Halliday's unwitting video-crusader–partisan mode one better, with one important exception: CBS clearly positioned itself on the other side—the official side—of the assault.

Having established sight in L.A. rebellion coverage as the preferred mode of observation, the complicated semiotic potential of the televisual apparatus shifted into high gear. Seemingly endless configurations and embellishments were spun out to manage, treat, and stylistically encrust rebellion imagery. ABC, for example, worked to fix the chaos with a personal center. Evocative of a 1930s-style montage, the good mayor Bradley is stylistically forced to weep over his fallen people and city. This form of fixation attempts to center the chaos by giving it a human and emotive core. Without a handle, the stations grasp for ways to personify an out-of-control social story. In another case, *Nightline*'s ever-caring Ted Kopple used burned-out buildings as apocalyptic wallpaper. This visual tactic made his special both relevant and centered

Televisuality's obsession with temporal fixation and context. An either/or moral binarism ruled, as when video was turned into electronic film negative. (KCBS)

around an accessible and knowing subjectivity, his own. In search of a tele-visual Kurtz, Kopple is quick to travel up river in South Central's heart of darkness. President Bush and Governor Wilson will soon do the same thing.

Although gnostic scholars like Neil Postman argue that television does otherwise, the rebellion footage immediately and continuously contextualized the event.[18] On KCBS, floating and transparent digital supergraphics were fused with fast-breaking images to fix the time and place of each incident leading up to the outbreak. In the days following the outbreak, television was in fact obsessed with temporal fixation. During the crisis, television worked hard to contextualize the rebellion in other ways as well. In one of many such instances, the itchy fingers of KABC's station director/switcher pulled in and combined two live images in a split-screen wipe. On the split screen that resulted, King's lawyer continued to translate and paraphrase to the press King's now-famous plea for Los Angelenos to "just get along." Even as the audience heard and viewed these pleas screen-right, the left side of the screen simultaneously showed armed Army National Guard troops storming off the back of a military truck in South Central. More than just an effort to show the audience what was going on at the same time that King made his plea for peace, the left screen also was the station's de facto warning about what would happen if the audience did not obey King's plea. Simultaneous and overlapping pictures, therefore, continuously editorialized the crisis. Visual diptychs like this one littered coverage with moral warnings.

The foreign view: L.A. as Dresden-like firebombing on Germany's ZDF. The domestic views: rebellion prefixed as a book, with neat chapters and a conclusion. (ITN, ZDF, KCBS)

A logic of binarism ruled rebellion coverage. Moral preachments were not just products of journalistic storytelling or free association by news anchors. Binarist judgments also occurred in the mundane ways that the conflict was visually pictured. In one case, the footage of the failed arrest at Florence and Normandy was freeze-framed, then electronically inverted as a photographic negative. The videographic negative, obviously, was an imported visual paradigm that dramatized and assigned a dark side to the struggle. At the same time, however, other visual paradigms and stylistic tactics implicitly encouraged the viewer not to worry. For example, television coverage during the rebellion attempted to describe the situation and the LAPD as a book, with sequential chapters and a conclusion. This graphic mode not only imagined an orderly transition from out-going chief Daryl Gates (widely perceived as one cause of the conflict) to incoming chief Willie Williams, the device also brought with it an artificial expectation of order. The digital transition used here brought with it confidence that one chapter would inevitably follow another, and that the Los Angeles conflict — like all bound books — would have a clean beginning and ending.

There was a pervasive sense during the first few days of the rebellion that television was struggling to gain control of the situation. One immediate response to this flood of fragmented and disorienting information was the shift by broadcasters to multiscreen video displays. Across the channels, viewers confronted double, triple, and quadruple screen configurations. The multi-

Loading up the screen: boxed spectacles as diversionary televisual defense against unruly in-studio guests. (Fox, KCBS, CNN)

screen device was useful for staging surrogate interviews between anchors and reporters as on Fox; staged video-conferenced fights between supposed ideologues on *Larry King Live* and cnn; and simple mischief in the newsroom, as in the case of one of Edward James Olmos's many in-studio interviews. Olmos was repeatedly set up as the voice of community calm and constructive action in many on-camera appearances during the crisis. In the live studio at kcbs, however, Olmos instead decried the systemic injustice of the economic and social system in Los Angeles. The uncomfortably surprised anchors — clearly hoping for a more docile mouthpiece, one who would simply encourage calm — became openly skeptical of Olmos's political critique. Increasingly impatient with the diatribe, the station pulled in a fourth box of imagery unbeknownst to Olmos, one that showed a fiery conflagration outside of the studio. While Olmos earnestly continued his critical discourse off-screen left to the now-absent anchors, his message was overwhelmed by the station's visual statement. Again, the political and social complications of the situation had been channeled into a polar dichotomy: calm or destruction. Olmos the political theorist had been silenced and contained, *framed as an expressionist picture in the newsroom's digital trophy case.*

Not only did television try to cover the crisis in as many different visual guises as it could, it was extremely conscious of how the world was reacting to its visual coverage and to the violence. American viewers were shown what was termed the "foreign" view of L.A.: gun-toting Korean vigilantes on Britain's itn, and the Dresden-like firebombing imagery displayed on Germany's zdf. American television was very conscious, then, of its own televisual performance and emphasized this awareness and facility. By reappropriating and showcasing even foreign, and potentially critical, readings of the rebellion,

Immediate visual historification of rebellion as race riot. Watts-era pleas for "passover" are replicated in 1992. Ahistorical? Television constructed a concrete then and now in desperate, crisis catch-up mode. Yet instant-history ignored the visual fact that some looters were Caucasian and Latino. (KCBS, KTTV)

U.S. television showed that it could play the game of textual one-upmanship as well.

Television also immediately historicized the rebellion as a race riot. Clearly challenging those academic theories that characterize television as ahistorical and obsessed only with presentness and simultaneity, crisis coverage, in fact, made historification a regular televisual strategy. Contemporary images from South Central were repeatedly paired with similar icons from the Watts riots. In one shot, the 1960s pleas for a "passover" of "negro-owned" properties are replicated in 1992. Televisuality may deal with the wrong history, but academics are misguided if they ignore the fact that historification is very much a central preoccupation of the televisual apparatus. This parade and facility with history was embraced by stations in the catch-up mode and helped them make sense of the apparent anarchy. Finding and constructing a concrete and connected then and now helped the stations visually reduce the conflict to race riot status—even as on-camera reporters verbally equivocated on whether or not the rebellion was induced by race.[19] This televisual and historical fixing and framing around race glossed over fundamental economic and class-based aspects of the rebellion. Television's inability to deal with both race and class exposed the leaky nature of the televisual apparatus. Stylized historification also conveniently ignored the newsroom's own evidence that many of the looters were Latino and Caucasian. What did not fit television's historicized and binary racial model, then, was simply ignored. The visual evidence showed that

Airlifted Chicago news anchor performs high-speed, journalistic drive-by shooting. Network reporter sets up live, on-camera tag-team wrestling match between Korean and African American in the ruins. Gates protests that Kopple hasn't even read the LAPD written document during their televisual summit. (WBBM, CBS, ABC)

the looters in many cases were not African Americans at all, especially as the rebellion spread to Hollywood and to the Pico-Union district. Partly as a result of technical changes in recording and storage technology, historification is now a very easy ritual that television routinely uses. The possibilities for historification now seem tantalizingly limitless, for most major stations have amassed large amounts of archival material from years of news production. Proprietary access to this raw material provides endless possibilities for historical reworking and hybridization. Constructing a history along binarist or reductive lines is dangerous, however, as this example shows, for images can belie the theses that news editors force upon them.

If digital graphics, file footage, and electronic stylization all worked to stylize and historically fix the onslaught outside—in a kind of televisual holding action—then dropping reporters onto the scene, after the fact, could help reestablish and legitimize the station's authority to say anything about what was going on. In one case, anchor Bill Curtis of WBBM Channel 2, the CBS affiliate in Chicago, was airlifted and inserted into the Los Angeles war zone. Curtis performed one of television's favored visual guises, the journalistic drive-by shooting. Rent-a-car wheel in one hand, microphone in the other, Curtis sped past rows of burning buildings to explain to viewers what is "really" going on in Los Angeles. A broken windshield later in the day served as proof of the extremes to which this reporter would go to bring back the inside story. "Inside" must, in this case, have referred to the inside of the reporter's car.

After the smoke cleared, another reporter covered his look back on the riot in a method more akin to tag-team wrestling. On-camera with a distraught and ruined Korean shop owner, the network reporter invited local African Americans to "come on down" and enter the dialogue about the riots even as the camera rolled. This done, the reporter crossed his arms in a defensive posture, even as the interracial argument that he arranged was set into ever more hostile motion. Before airing this reporter-staged racial grudge match, however, the segment producer/editor tastefully cut away to another scene before any overt violence actually ensued. This was, after all, CBS — good network journalism — not tabloid sensationalism.

In like manner, ABC's *Nightline* set up a heated on-camera exchange between Ted Kopple and Chief Daryl Gates. The event was pitched as a kind of televisual summitry between opponents of comparable power. After presenting an edited, point-by-point indictment of Gates and the LAPD, Kopple allowed Gates to appear on the set at show's end to even up the score. Far from an exercise in self-flagellation by Kopple, Gates was left with the impossible task of having to refute the dramatic visual evidence the audience had just seen. Behind Gates was a bank of monitors, a constant reminder to the audience that the rebellion violence stood as undeniable evidence against Gates. Gates convincingly accused Kopple of not having even read a lengthy written document that showed that the LAPD *did* have plans in place for dealing with urban riots (these plans were criticized by Kopple in his edited segment). Gates's angry jab at Kopple notwithstanding, ABC clearly mastered this televisual arena, for the chief was allowed only a token verbal rebuttal, even as he frantically waved a dense but unread written document. Kopple took his ceremonial lashes, but Gates clearly lost. Such is the image-driven world of televisual summitry.

Containment: The Big Response
Primetime's Transcendent Polis

Containment, the third and final stage, refers to the more ostensibly serious response of the industry and includes that period when rebellion-specific entertainment programs were showcased by the networks as season premieres in August and September of 1992. After the flames were out and local television had exhausted its angles on crisis coverage, orgies of technology and militarism lost both their anchoring power and command presence. Industry heavyweights now began to weigh in and formulated what might be termed the big response. Hollywood, cable, politicians, and network entertainment programmers all became active players in what appeared to be a more reasoned and planned strategy for reconciling the effects of the rebellion.

Reconciliation had, in fact, started within days of the violence, when the re-

Within days, rebellion footage is fair game for May political candidates. (Gil Garcetti Campaign, Barbara Boxer Campaign, Gray Davis Campaign)

bellion footage—like King's before it—became fair game for any and all takers. The political primaries in California in May made extensive use of the footage on both the Right and the Left. The district attorney attempted to novelize the riots with an epic textual opening. Future senator Barbara Boxer symbolically positioned herself as a lone and isolated photojournalist in front of the apocalypse. Senate aspirant Gray Davis, on the other hand, visually cast himself in contrast to all that was wrong with the state of California—that is, as antithetical to the decay symbolized by the hybrid incumbency of Gates, Wilson, and Bradley. Keys, mattes, and graphics stitched candidates into the fabric of the rebellion, even though most had little contact with the situation while the buildings actually burned. The historical causes of the riots, then, were now not nearly as valuable as the appropriation and exploitation of the rebellion as a historical cause. Like a loose historical cannon careening on deck, the rebellion was available to any who felt inclined to grab on. With the rebellion now overhauled and viewed after the fact as a *cause* rather than as an *effect,* any candidate could pitch himself or herself as the answer and not as a cause, which many of them were.

The favored metaphor for framing the event also shifted from the confrontational and binarist modes operative during the crisis period to an obsession with anatomy during the industry's big response. It is worth considering why viewing Los Angeles as a "body" served the needs of the media during a time of social crisis and its aftermath, that is, when society was trying hardest to contain and naturalize its threats. The body, implied by the L.A. rebellion special entitled *Anatomy of a Riot,* both unified and effaced difference, for the figure postures culture as a single organism. The metaphor also functioned as a more organic and ostensibly benign variant of the melting pot myth: a synthesizing paradigm erected on the myth of cultural effacement. Biology and

With time, favored metaphors shift from militarist to anatomical analogies. Biology and anatomy position threat in diseaselike terms. (A&E, ABC)

Commodification. "Traumatized by the horror?—Call ABC's 800 number." TV used an obsessively polar logic and grabbed callous and awkward images of Denny's jailed assailants. (ABC, KCBS, KCBS)

anatomy, in addition, are also useful in positioning social threats in disease-like terms. Although the rebellion can be looked at as a kind of social disease and symptom, the notion of sickness and disease also places the threat on the *outside* of the social body. Hence, the looters, rioters, and demonstrators — infections frequently conflated and identified as people of color — were pictured as threats to the equilibrium and health of the system. Anatomical figuration, then, repeatedly legitimized and reinforced television's favored inside/outside dichotomy as a response to contagion.

The big response also contained the threat by commoditizing it. At one point, the spectacle was sold by ABC directly to viewers on VHS for only $19.95. Anxiety and trauma about the horror and hate that you have just seen? Call ABC's 800 number and have your credit card available. During the big response, coverage unabashedly became commodity. Even in the more extensive phase of reconciliation after the rebellion, television thought in polar terms. One of television's visual pretenses was the promise that it could both think and

The big response: Doogie, Bill, and George in televisual Mt. Rushmore. (ABC, NBC, NBC)

interpret for the audience. Less than mindless, television actively paraded interpretation and analysis before the viewer's eyes. Infinite follow-ups to the rebellion fixated binary conceptual schemas. KCBS's options for response? There were really only two choices: "Recovery review—rebuild or rebel?" Binarism was now being institutionalized, especially in the service of rhyming headlines or couplets. No raw and decontextualized image leaked out of these televisual icons. Viewers were warned (how) to think.

Following the uprising, the courts were jammed with rebellion-related cases, giving television ample visual material to process throughout the months that followed. The images that resulted frequently discredited ethnic participants of *any* type. On one evening, Reginald Denny's African American assailants were caught by the cameras callously laughing behind the courtroom's barred holding area. KCBS left no doubt as to their guilt when it isolated the laughter. Korean shop owners were also forcefully discredited when KCBS broke its top story about how some merchants had set fire to their own stores. With this tortured visual attribution, even the groups most victimized by the rebellion were discredited by postrebellion association: the Koreans were also arsonists. NBC did a story months later about the hard-working blacks who were "also" victimized by the riots. In this segment, a self-made African American businessman sits alone on his property. Looking back on images of the conflagration, he provides a sad and tragic ending to NBC's follow-up. NBC's moral? The rebellion was shortsighted and self-defeating. The dangerous other here gave way to the domesticated and contained other—to a model of middle-class reflection and property-owning patience.

Episodic television, however, also enacted and relished the big response. By September, Doogie Howser had joined President Bush and network patriarch Bill Cosby as a member of the televisual Mt. Rushmore. Even as classical dramatic form seemed dwarfed by the social threat, this triumvirate regressed

L.A. Law and *Doogie Howser* do the camcorder ritual. Legal trajectory of Simi trial piggy-backed onto *L.A. Law*'s episodic arc. Large-screen TVs now pervasive on each set of *L.A. Law* for the first time. (ABC)

to one of the most basic forms of one-to-one communication. Each left his narrative world, took courage, faced the massive national audience in close-up and direct address, and appealed for calm and cooperation. Even prestige entertainment programming, then, gave in to direct address—to point-to-point unmediated communication with the audience—when the threat was great enough. Prime time used eye-to-eye contact when deck-clearing consciousness-raising was in order.

But the King beating and the L.A. rebellion also provided rich iconic templates that could be narratively used again and again in prime time. Visual configurations operated as master structuring allegories in ways once attributed only to narrative archetypes. *L.A. Law* and *Doogie Howser, m.d.* did the camcorder ritual as central parts of their programs. When the industry did not feel the need to address the audience directly with messages about containment, they acted out and performed pointed sociopolitical morals. Doogie's medical aid, for example, sensitively disarmed a young African American patient of his recently stolen consumer electronics contraband. *Doogie*'s master narrator, then, tastefully allowed another African American character to teach this lesson to the audience and to the shoplifting African American patient who had stolen "to get back at the system." This sort of heavy-handed social teaching is clearly no longer restricted to Mister Rogers's preschool province.

Episodic television danced around the threat in a number of other "sensitive" ways as well. An episode of *Fresh Prince of Bel-Air* used a sepia-toned

Doggie's African American medical aide is allowed to "teach" African American patient not to steal consumer electronics. The rebellion was an excuse to create South Central backstory in *Fresh Prince of Bel-Air.* Retrospective textuality provided the show with enough guilt to connect with its lower-class roots. [ABC, NBC]

L.A. Law's sensitive characters gaze at burning city like grieving family members. Sister Souljah is heavy-hitting import on *A Different World.* Prime time masqueraded with recognizable news photo templates during the big response. [ABC, NBC]

flashback scene to re-create an entirely new history for the show. This revised L.A. rebellion–based premise for the show revealed that the sitcom family now had its economic roots and origins in South Central. This form of crisis-induced textual regeneration provided the family the quantity of guilt necessary to enable them to reconnect with their lower-class roots. It also created comic opportunities whereby the Prince demonstrated just how easy it is for an African American to be mistaken for a looter. The bat-wielding Latino who attacked him in this episode actually turned out to be an old family friend. Retrospective textuality like this was in full force during the industry's big response.

The L.A. rebellion provided a rich visual menu from which episodic television could order up icons in September. Photographic icons of mass arrests

Prime time's repertoire of available L.A. rebellion icons? Gun-toting Korean shop owner fires 12-gauge shotgun into crazed African American mob leaping through plateglass store windows. The Denny icon was also rigidified into reusable cinematic motif in prime time, in a way that invariably placed the audience inside the glass, with surging African Americans outside. (ABC)

and urban wreckage taken directly from the pages of the *Los Angeles Times* were reenacted on both *Fresh Prince* and *L.A. Law*. Prime time also imported rebellion-related scenic imagery and wallpapered dramatic scenes with visual evidence of the conflagration. In *L.A. Law*, the cast's sensitive characters gaze at the burning metropolis and emote, less like Nero than like a saddened family member grieving a loss. Sister Souljah made a much-publicized appearance on *A Different World*. Her unabashed on-camera critique of the King beating trial—footage of which played behind her in the electronics showroom—was set up in the press as a special, insider's point of view. Having gone toe-to-toe with presidential candidate Bill Clinton over the racial implications of the rebellion weeks earlier, she was imported by the series producers to elevate the moral air and relevance of *A Different World*. Souljah doubled as a police brutality critic and as a high-profile advertising ploy.

L.A. Law, meanwhile, fused the legal trajectory of the televised Simi trial with its own episodic arc. This *textual piggybacking* heightened the constructed liveness of the show even though the trial footage seen in the episode clearly predated production of the prime-time drama. Absent during the previous seasons, large-screen TVs now popped up everywhere on the *L.A. Law* sets. Like the family and audience at home, the *L.A. Law* workplace family was now inside, looking out on the world through the television window.[20] Like middle-class home owners, they too would be forced to pull together in the face of the uncontrolled onslaught taking place around their property. The *L.A. Law* episode used the full repertoire of L.A. rebellion icons. A senior law partner on the way to his wedding, for example, confronted his worst nightmare: a crazed, gun-toting Asian, a Korean shop owner. The shopkeeper soon fired a double-barrel 12-gauge at African Americans who were wildly leaping through his

Empathizing with what it means to be Homer (that is, "black") "like me." (ABC)

plateglass windows. This racial stereotype of the Asian as strange and incomprehensible is as acute as *L.A. Law*'s depiction of the crazed looters. The show also rigidified the Denny beating spectacle into a reusable, high-angle scenic vantage point. In their variation on a theme, *L.A. Law* reinscribed one of *its* characters as the victim in the Denny aerial-beating guise. The *L.A. Law* characters and the audience both were placed on the inside of the shattered glass, with the surging African Americans on the outside. This repeated spatial rigidification of inside versus outside not only conflated the audience's point of view with that of the lawyers, but, more important and ironically, set up both the characters and the audience as the victims of the violence in Los Angeles. The L.A. rebellion provided drama's essential fuel: dangerous antagonists (the people of color coming at "us" from out there) and innocent victims (the white, disoriented characters and audience at home).

Each of the subplots in the episode also masqueraded with visual disguises taken from the earlier conflict. In one scene, a marshal acted as courtroom VCR operator. *L.A. Law* mimicked the Simi trial, then, but with some problematic differences. The victim in prime time was no longer a black man, was not Rodney King, but was a Homer Simpson impersonator employed by a theme park. The defense dramatized the wrongfulness of his firing by having the entire jury don Homer Simpson headgear. Arnie had to get the jury inside of Homer's skin, apparently, for them to truly understand victimization. The lesson is clear. The law firm wins. Now, apparently, the jury members can empathize with what it means to be Homer (that is, "black") "like me." One troubling implication of this plot line is that the Rodney King beating has been reduced to the level of peril that one finds at family-oriented theme parks. Furthermore, Rodney King is construed as the essential postmodernist mask — as a Matt Groening clone — his beating an empty foil available to one and all.

But perhaps the strangest of the many King–L.A. rebellion prime-time analogies was the bullet-in-the-breast motif—a highly privileged example of

The bullet-in-the-breast motif. Franchising victimization: "We are all erotic Rodney Kings." (ABC)

retrospective textuality. The previous season of *L.A. Law* ended with a cliff-hanger wherein a blonde lawyer was gunned down outside a courtroom. By September, however, the event had been redefined as a symbolic part of the L.A. rebellion. The female victim's anxiety about the violence, her scar, and the social implications of her career were only textually resolved in this episode by a man's kiss, through the man's oral acceptance of her scarred breasts. Once again, prime-time television was obsessed with creating opportunities and victim substitutes from the L.A. rebellion. Here, the affluent white woman bears the burdens for society's sins. Here, the sin can only be absolved by an erotic act. The jumping assailants depicted in *L.A. Law*'s earlier crisis-management scenes give way here to a much bigger picture: one that makes the substitute victim *erotic*.

The King–L.A. uprising conflict provided a rich visual score that was performed in many variations. In prime-time's *A Different World,* on the traffic-clogged streets of L.A., and in the courtroom, the police baton-beating of King became a widely recognized ritual that was repeated again and again by those with very different motives. The gestural performance of the baton blows was open to infinite appropriation. This subsequent popularity raises the question of why such televisual scores proved so attractive and pervasive to programmers. In one telling instance, an NBC segment proclaimed in hindsight that all crises can be summed up in single images. The segment directly compared the Rodney King and Reginald Denny beating images to the heroic man-against-tank icon from Tiananmen Square and to the infamous on-camera execution of a captured Vietcong prisoner during Tet in 1968. This singular thesis, then, was NBC News's retrospective analysis of the very same spring rebellion that had earlier overwhelmed both police and news media alike. Had amnesia set in at the news division? No, the network philosophized, the riots really could be reduced to one image. NBC, ironically, was ignoring the fact that during the period of crisis its own televisual apparatus spun out and proliferated as many different images as possible. By contrast, and after weeks of reflection and analysis, the high journalists of the big response tried to verbally summarize the rebellion's lessons by resorting to clichés of the most reductive sort: that a picture is worth a thousand words.

The progressive potential of this kind of verbal gloss is worth considering. The images that NBC points to as iconic markers could not ultimately be contained by either the South Vietnamese executioner during Tet or by the Chinese government during Tiananmen. In fact, the point-blank firing in Vietnam and the marshaling of Chinese tanks — like Stacey Koons's police assault against King — were staged by the powerful as explicit symbols of intimidation against the weak. Yet all eventually leaked from their constraints. The Vietcong execution, in fact, helped catalyze the American antiwar movement. The Chinese tank confrontation, once on satellite, garnered worldwide support from reformist sympathizers. And the Halliday beating footage was utilized by outsider independents and community groups, as well as by Spike Lee and others, to further various causes. Televisuality is indeed a leaky system. Those who describe it as an inherently illusory, hegemonic, and deceptive system fail to see that it is also an instrumental system, one that can be used by the marginal as well as abused by the powerful.

Conclusion: TV's Command Presence

The crisis of the L.A. rebellion, then, was not simply a matter of arson and anarchy outside the walls of the broadcasters. For television, the crisis was also very much an internal one. Faced with an out-of-control catastrophe in the streets, television marshaled a command presence by invoking three of its most enduring control fantasies. Exhibitionist displays of technology, masculinity, and race-based journalistic authority were all thrown into the fray on a commercial-free, twenty-four-hour basis. These frontline defenses, however, regularly faltered. Disheveled and unprepared local anchors like Paul Moyer — traditional bastions of calm and dispassion even in the face of earthquakes and serial killers — badly ad libbed their way through coverage. Network types like Kopple were caught making on-air statements that were factually wrong. Chief Gates, meanwhile, continued to insist that the LAPD had a systematic plan. Fantasies of information control — inevitably centered on-air around white, male figures — circulated both in law-and-order and journalistic circles.[21] The burning of Los Angeles—unfolding live before the viewer—made these assertions of authority far from credible.

As white masculinity staked its claim to control, television slotted people of color into a very different, but much more spectacular, role. Rodney King emerged as the latest in Hollywood's long line of tragic, suffering, and sacrificial victims of color, a lineage that includes the young Sidney Poitier, Paul Robeson, and even Rudolph Valentino. Olmos—despite his sometimes forceful efforts to the contrary—was continually stripped of informational and ideological authority during coverage. Television postured him first as an on-camera stand-in for victims, and then as a long-suffering street-sweeper picking up the city's tragic pieces with a push broom. Cosby turns in pain to the national viewer during his show, but is never quite able to jettison the entertainment aura NBC gives his sitcom patriarchy. Even Mayor Bradley is visually montaged as a tragic figure, as a wounded person verbally unable to account for his community's trauma. The racial bifurcation is clear: *white males struggle with little credibility to maintain information control, and men of color are spectacularized into recognizable roles defined by raw emotion and victimization.* Lynn Spigel has suggested that this racial split—between white male information control and black male visuality and victimization—mirrors television's favored binary split between entertainment and information. Perpetuating the myth of that division, a generic polarity under threat in contemporary programming seems to be continually at stake in this coverage as well, even as the very myth falls apart before our eyes.[22] Even the sometimes articulate and politically informed direct addresses thrown back at reporters by looters— fragments of which were captured on-camera as stores were being emptied —undermined the simplistic entertainment-versus-information model being forced upon persons of color as an explanation for the horrific spectacle. The social crisis of the L.A. rebellion, then, was also a crisis of masculinity and race, a threat to the clean ideological distinctions that prop up and feed fundamental program distinctions. High-tech embellishments of the spectacle notwithstanding, the televisual command presence faltered under the weight of its own insecurity and instability.

The Los Angeles rebellion and its coverage proved to be traumatic for a diverse coalition of forces: urban social programs and government policy were indicted; broadcasters (at least temporarily) questioned their image-hungry role in encouraging and fueling the conflagration; and scholars stopped to

NBC News muses in retrospect
that all crises can be summed up
in single images. (NBC)

consider their own methods and politics in light of the crisis. Coverage of the
King beating trial in particular created a crisis of conscience in media studies.
Much hand-wringing, for example, greeted the fact that police brutality was
exonerated in the legal system through close textual analysis. Since the same
kind of textual analysis, now bloodied by legal precedent, has been favored
in critical theory, one immediate temptation was to flee to more naïve conceptions of extratextual reality. This reaction, however, ignored two important
facts: (1) that televisual texts and representations *are* political acts, and (2) that
excessive televisuality can and is being used by independent groups to counter
the effects of mainstream television practice. Scholarly insecurities about concrete politics offer no credible basis per se for disavowing televisual practice.

For those interested in social change, the apparent power of televisuality to
manage crisis challenged the very idea of resistance. Certainly the months that
followed the uprising, however, demonstrated that resistance is possible. Young
African American protestors, for example, disrupted traffic in Los Angeles
and performed "the Rodney King." The legal system may have legitimized the
LAPD's blows, but it could not own the public ritual that soon took on a life
of its own. Street artists and taggers also made site-specific artworks in and
among the physical wreckage of the rebellion. In one case, a touristlike network news correspondent used a painted guerrilla counterwork as a kind of
pop supergraphic to frame his entrance to the rubble. The street artist gets network play; the network journalist gets some hip visual flash. Crisis televisuality

Uprising as widely available performance score: in traffic, on prime time, in the court-room. Site-specific artworks by street art-ists and taggers were used as pop super-graphics to frame the network correspondent. (NBC, Fox, CBS)

has also been used by community activists and organizers in public schools and in media workshops for urban children. Anna Everett, for example, has shown these stylistic modes to be operative in media programs of public elementary schools in Los Angeles County. Beretta Smith has shown that televisuality was performed by community video cooperatives to address and redress King's vic-timization.[23] Stylish, low-tech political videos proliferated in children's video workshops like those organized by KidVidco. The real victims of the conflict in L.A.—urban schoolchildren rather than the affluent characters on prime-time television—do speak the televisual language and can use it to engage the status quo.

Close analysis of the evidence from the period of crisis management, fur-thermore, shows a preoccupation with presentational modes that challenge a series of at least five privileged assumptions about television: (1) television's obsession with militarist guises and production performance underscores fun-damental masculinist aspects of an apparatus that is typically theorized as feminine; (2) television's penchant for immediate and visual historicization, along with its marshaling of contextualizing file footage, problematize the view that the medium is fundamentally defined by its ahistorical appetite for pres-entness and immediacy; (3) the favored theoretical paradigm that television is based essentially on the inattentive glance is undermined by the highly em-bellished and complicated images evident during the period of the rebellion and King's televisual milling; (4) television's pervasive and continuous efforts at fixation—to interpret and nail down the historical meaning of its televised images—undercuts the popular view that the televisual image is by nature both contextless and illogical because it is antithetical to reason; (5) finally, prime time's obsession with rituals of substitute victimization during the period of containment undercut the highly publicized liberal concern and social conscience of those shows. This retrospective textual performance, whereby dramatic shows inserted their characters as *the* victims of the violence, displaced the real rebellion victims and participants into symbolic positions outside of the showcase. Even in their calls for racial harmony and a sense of oneness, prime time stylistically positioned the other back on the margins and outside of the glass. The aesthetic potential and dramatic capital provided by this master visual ritual of victimization simply overwhelmed the industry's more immediate and explicit liberal interest in moralizing, educating, and pacifying. The industry's big picture response was at root a textual feeding frenzy—a wild performance of surrogate victimization.

What was dangerous in televisuality's crisis management during the rebellion was not its high-tech stylization of the event, but rather the use of those modes to bolster old-style class and racial politics. Even the big response of the industry, after months of concerned reflection, attempted to contain the real threat to the economic status quo with clichés of the most regressive kind. If crisis televisuality made the dangerous other exotic, alien, and stylized, the serious and liberal voice of the industry contained by covering over difference. The industry's explicit and heartfelt verbal appeals to calm, reason, and cooperation were belied by prime time's use of racial stereotypes and marginalizing representations of the most problematic and sometimes bizarre sort.

The fact that television was so quick to racialize the crisis should come as no surprise, given broad-based demographic changes in Los Angeles. For several years the media had tossed around the notion that whites now represented only 37 percent of the city's population, that whites were now a minority. The rosy picture of happy multiculturalism foisted during the Olympic era in 1984 had long since been dwarfed by the sense that Los Angeles was in decline. The decline mythology was invariably linked to the emergence of a new multiethnic monster and to race. Illegal immigration, white flight, gated communities for the affluent, and the collapse of public health and education all became evidence for decline in nightly news coverage. Seen in this context, crisis televisuality was also an act of desperation, a last-gasp exercise in control by upper-middle-class "victims" jostled into a corner defined by race and economic class. The smiling upper-middle-class Anglo faces that dominated newscasts leading up to the rebellion, then, were far from comforting: the air of decline and victimization was not a pretty picture. Desperate times called for desperate measures, and television was more than equipped with electronic and preemptive command and othering measures. A long-cultivated partnership between the televisual apparatus and its institutionalized fortress mentality had come of age.

There is a lesson in television's representation of the L.A. rebellion. The uprising so overwhelmed television's narrative and journalistic systems of containment and recuperation — systems that have claimed the lion's share of critical attention in the past — that the televisual apparatus was exposed for what it has been on many occasions: a stylistic architecture for managing difference, building consensus, and stylistically packaging the dangerous other.

Notes

This essay originally appeared in John Thornton Caldwell's *Televisuality: Style, Crisis and Authority in American Television,* and is reprinted here by permission of Rutgers University Press.

1   Mary Rourke, "Fashion," *Los Angeles Times Magazine,* 2 January 1993, 25.

2   Numerous articles and op ed pages in newspapers and news magazines made and perpetuated this mythology of the deadening effect of overanalysis. See, for example, Charles Hagen, "The Power of a Video Image Depends upon Its Caption," *New York Times,* 10 May 1992, 32; and "King: Video Blurs the Line in Beating Trial, Experts Say," *Los Angeles Times,* 14 February 1993, A34. This easy write-off of visual analysis probably results more from journalism's traditional distrust of the deceptions and lies of images, than from anything else.

3   Such a miscarriage was all too troubling to many academics, who saw in the trial's mode their cherished method of intellectual deconstruction, an analytical approach that had dominated critical theory in recent years. Simi Valley seemed to indicate that deconstruction — without reconstituting a human center, for proof or for justice — was in fact an empty and politically impotent exercise.

4   See, for example, Andreas Huyssen's discussion of mass culture as an antithesis to the masculinist impulses of high-modernist culture, "Mass Culture as Woman: Modernism's Other," in *Studies in Entertainment: Critical Approaches to Mass Culture,* ed. Tania Modleski (Bloomington: Indiana University Press, 1986), 188–208.

5   Modleski's work is important for it shows not only that the institutional and narrative logic of daytime television is organized around the desires of women, but

that such desires are not finally nor adequately satisfied by daytime soaps—a factor that leaves open the possibility of resistance. Tania Modleski, *Loving with a Vengeance: Mass-Produced Fantasies for Women* (New York: Methuen, 1982).

6   Beverle Houston, "Viewing Television: The Metapsychology of Endless Consumption," *Quarterly Review of Film Studies* 9, no. 3 (summer 1984): 183–195, was to become one of many articles that displaced the phallocentric assumptions of psychoanalytic-based criticism that was then being imported to the new medium of television by academics. Houston's account of television stood in stark contrast to Laura Mulvey's influential theory of the male gaze that had driven classical Hollywood cinema and dominated high film theory.

7   Lynne Joyrich's discussion of "hypermasculinity" as a cultural and programming reaction to the threat of feminism is found in "Critical and Textual Hypermasculinity," in *Logics of Television: Essays in Cultural Criticism,* ed. Patricia Mellencamp (Bloomington: Indiana University Press, 1990), 156–172.

8   Sandy Flitterman-Lewis is especially persuasive in defining television's spectatorial modes and viewing pleasures in stark, polar opposition to the masculinist modes of film, in her chapter "Psychoanalysis, Film, and Television," in *Channels of Discourse: Reassembled,* ed. Robert Allen (Chapel Hill: University of North Carolina Press, 1992), 203–246.

9   It is important to reiterate that these masculinist modes evident in television (word-based journalism, fetishized production technology, etc.) *coexist* simultaneously or alternately with guises, genres, and narrative forms that have been characterized as feminine. That is, the history of programming shows that these two tendencies are neither mutually exclusive nor singular.

10   Sgt. Stacey Koons's description of Rodney King as "Mandingo" was from the manuscript of his book on the beating incident and was widely reported by both the print and television media before and during the first trial. Koons described a confrontation between King and a white, female California Highway Patrol officer as a "Mandingo sexual encounter" (Jim Newton, "U.S. Loses Bid to Question Koons on Manuscript," *Los Angeles Times,* 26 March 1993, A1, 18).

11   Donald Bogle has demonstrated the power and importance of racist stereotyping in his book *Toms, Coons, Mulattoes, Mammies, and Bucks: An Interpretive History of Blacks in American Film* (New York: Viking, 1973). One of the lasting contributions of books like this one and J. Fred MacDonald's *Blacks in White TV: African Americans in Television Since 1948* (Chicago: Nelson-Hall, 1992) is that they describe media in concrete terms as political—and they do so without equivocating or transforming race into intellectual abstractions. Bogle stands against those who disguise or abstract the racist foundations of Hollywood, and MacDonald addresses head-on the important but frequently overlooked connections among television, politics, and civil rights. Yet studies of stereotyping can also become a more

static kind of content analysis, an approach that tends to overlook the more dynamic process of racial othering as a cultural ritual described in works like Hamid Naficy, "Mediawork's Representation of the Other: The Case of Iran," in *Questions of Third Cinema*, ed. Paul Willeman and Jim Pines (London: British Film Institute, 1990), 227–239. I hope in this study to examine some of the televisual rituals that "other" the person of color during crisis.

12   Paul Moyer's play-by-play commentary on KABC included the following: "There's some creep trying to break a window. . . . I'm sorry for using the word 'creep,'" (Thursday, 30 April 1992).

13   Live and on-camera, field reporter Linda Moore repeated the sociological explanation that described the hoodlums as otherwise bored and idle perpetrators: "People just need an excuse to do this" (KABC, Thursday, 30 April 1992).

14   On the second day of the uprising, reporter Linda Moore recounted—with an air of professional self-satisfaction—her earlier plight at being trapped in a gun battle between rioters and Korean store owners. "I never thought that I would cover battle—and here I am in *my own backyard*—and I'm covering a war." Yet her actual presence on camera suggested more the air of tourism. Her claim that this was her backyard was undercut by the economic, racial, and professional signals that her performance gave off. In what possible ways, for example, could glamorous Anglo Moore claim that these armed Korean merchants, Salvadorans, Chicanos, and African Americans had always been her neighbors? Like other journalists thrown into the fracas, she came across more like a picture-happy, career-building alien than a neighbor.

15   Command presence, the notion that some individuals are able to dominate social space by their physical appearance and authoritative demeanor and so encourage deference from others in the same social space, is a commonly appreciated ideal in the training of military officers, law enforcement officials, football coaches, and (shall we say it) academic lecturers—all roles that institutionalize authority in the social system. As we shall see, this linkage between media's command presence and law and order is far from gratuitous.

16   In art history and Catholic iconography, stigmata are bodily marks indicating or replicating the wounds or pains of the crucified Christ, marks that are frequently associated with religious ecstasy.

17   Mike Davis, *City of Quartz: Excavating the Future in Los Angeles* (New York: Vintage, 1990), 244, 258, 268.

18   Neil Postman argues that pictures—a synonym for disinformation—short-circuit introspection, analysis, and context, in *Amusing Ourselves to Death* (New York: Penguin, 1985), 101–108.

19   One of Michel Foucault's most enduring accomplishments was to demonstrate the fundamental importance and privilege given polar dichotomies by the insti-

tutions of power and oppression in Western culture. Television's race paradigm — white-black, us-them, inside-outside — is a perfect example of how an impossibly complicated social phenomenon is reduced to polar terms that seal power on the side of the discursive speaker, in this case, television.

20 Ella Taylor, *Primetime Families* (Berkeley: University of California Press, 1991), shows how the domestic, nuclear family was updated and situated in the workplace in the late 1960s and 1970s. The Caucasian *L.A. Law* family during the riots — even in its workplace home — appears as paranoid about the racial and violent threats rumbling outside its walls as any of the suburban families in the 1950s sitcoms were about what they defined as external threats.

21 There were, of course, many women reporters involved in rebellion coverage as well, yet their numbers and approach did not displace the authoritative masculinist command presence that held down the center of coverage, especially around the management functions associated with the in-studio anchor's desk.

22 I am especially thankful to Lynn Spigel for making this point, following a presentation of a draft of this chapter at the Console-ing Passions conference on feminism and television at the University of Southern California, Los Angeles, in April 1993. By connecting these binarist representations of race and masculinity to the generic distinctions between information and entertainment, she suggests that there is an institutional logic behind these awkward attempts to maintain racial distinctions.

23 Anna Everett, "The Emancipatory Use of Video in the Classroom," unpublished ms., UCLA, 11 December 1992. Beretta Smith, "Arming Youth: Video for the Revolution," unpublished ms., UCLA, 1 December 1992.

PEDRO ZAMORA'S REAL WORLD

OF COUNTERPUBLICITY

Performing an Ethics of the Self

José Esteban Muñoz

Pedro Zamora died on November 11, 1994. He was 22. The day after his death there appeared a cover story in the *Wall Street Journal.* The article explained that Pedro received thousands of fan letters a week.[1] It quoted one letter from a South Carolina woman who wrote: "I never thought anyone could change my opinion of homosexuals and AIDS. Because of you I saw the human side of something that once seemed so unreal to me." The letter speaks to Pedro's intervention in the public sphere. It bears witness to the difference this young Latino's life's work made. In this essay, I will suggest that although these interventions in the majoritarian public sphere were important, one would fail to understand the efficacy of the activist's tactics and the overall success of his life's work if one were to consider only such letters. Pedro's work enabled the possibility of queer and Latino counterpublics, spheres that stand in opposition to the racism and homophobia of the dominant public sphere. Through this labor one begins to glimpse new horizons of experience.

In what follows I will outline the cultural interventions of televisual activist Pedro Zamora. I will describe the way Zamora performed what I understand as a Foucauldian ethics of the self. This "working on the self" allowed Zamora to take a *next* step: a leap into the social through the public performance of an ethics of the self. I will also call attention to the ways this Cuban American cultural worker's performances accomplished tasks that enabled the enactment of queer and Latino identity practices in a phobic public sphere. These tasks include the denouncement of the dominant public sphere's publicity that fixes images and understandings of queerness and *latinidad;* the enactment of resistance to the reductive multicultural pluralism that is deployed against them; the production of an intervention within the majoritarian public sphere that confronts phobic ideology; and the production of counterpublicity that allows *the possibility* of subaltern counterpublics.

In *The Care of the Self,* the third volume of his *History of Sexuality,* Michel Foucault elaborated, through a tour of antiquity and its philosophical underpinnings, an ethics of the self—a working on the self for others.[2] The care of the self emphasizes an ethics around nourishing and sustaining a self within civil society. It is ultimately expedient to cite one of Foucault's more elucidating interviews at some length for the purpose of explicating the care of the self and its roots in Hellenistic and Greco-Roman culture:

> What interests me in the Hellenistic culture, in the Greco-Roman culture, starting from the third century B.C. and continuing until the second or third century after Christ, is a precept for which the Greeks had a specific word, *epimeleia heautou,* which means taking care of oneself. It does not mean simply being interested in oneself, nor does it mean having a certain tendency to self-attachment or self-fascination. *Epimeleia heautou* is a very powerful word in Greek which means "working on" or "being concerned with" something. For example, Xenophon used *epimeleia heautou* to describe agricultural management. The responsibility of a monarch for his fellow citizens was also *epimeleia heautou.* That which a doctor does in the course of caring for a patient is *epimeleia heautou.* It is therefore a very powerful word; it describes a sort of work, an activity; it implies attention, knowledge, technique.[3]

In this paper, I will consider the work of televisual activist Zamora as just such a sort of "work" that disseminated and "publicized" "attention, knowledge, and technique" that are consequential to the project of minoritarian subjectivity. I will suggest that Zamora worked within *The Real World,* which one should never forget is a product of the corporate entity MTV, and yet still managed to find ways to do this work *despite* the corporate ethos that ordered that program. Foucault had, at a later stage in his thinking, decided that our understanding of power could be augmented by richer discourse on the subject. Work on the ethics of the self ultimately allows us a new vantage point to consider the larger games of truth that organize the social and the relations of these games to states of domination. Within the structure of MTV, its corporate structure, Zamora performed his care of the self as a truth game that "was for others," letting them see and imagine a resistance to entrenched systems of domination.

It is important to note that Foucault's care of the self is based on the lives of citizens and not slaves in antiquity. George Yúdice has pointed out this limit in Foucault's project and has gone on to theorize how an "ethics of marginality" might be extracted from Foucault's project.

> The problem with Foucault's analysis, as I see it, is that the examples are drawn from the aesthetic practices of Greek freemen and, more important, modernist art. In both cases only elites engage in these particular types of self-analysis and self-formation. This does not mean, however, that Foucault's framework prohibits a priori other types of self-formation related to different social groups. On the contrary, insofar as knowledge, politics (power) and ethics mutually condition each other, despite their relative autonomy, the particularities of the group that engages in ethical practices (its knowledges, its politics) must be taken into consideration. If Foucault could trace the genealogy for dominant groups, it should be equally possible to trace that of dominated and oppressed peoples.[4]

Yúdice outlines the very specific origins of Foucault's paradigm. He suggests that even though elitist and first-worldist limitations exist within Foucault's paradigm, this does not mean that "Foucault's framework prohibits a priori other types of self-formation related to different social groups." Yúdice uses Rigoberta Menchú's *testimonio, I . . . Rigoberta Menchú: An Indian Woman in Guatemala,* as an example when unfolding his theory of an ethics of marginality. He uses the case of Menchú to amend Foucault's notion of "an aesthetics of existence" and transforms it into an ethics in which practical politics plays a central role. Yúdice explains, "We might say that a 'practical poetics' is the ethical 'self-forming activity' in which the 'self' is practiced in solidarity with others struggling for survival. Menchú, in fact, has turned her identity into a 'poetics of defense.'"[5]

The example of Menchú and her *testimonio* potentially elucidates our understanding of the politics that undergird Zamora's uses of the self, his care of the self for others. *The Real World* employs what it calls *video confessionals.* These confessionals have been small rooms within the cast's living space where individual members are encouraged to "confess" to the camera outside the space of social negotiation. These spaces have been used by the cast as sites where they could perform their selves solo and in private. Real Worlders have used these solo performances to argue for themselves and their identities. These spaces of self-formation are, of course, highly mediated by MTV, even more mediated than Menchú's *testimonio* that has been transcribed and heavily edited by Elisabeth Burgos-Debray. Yet I want to argue that this corporate mediation does not foreclose the counterpublic-building possibilities within these video *testimonios*. Although his housemates and cast members from other seasons used the video confessionals to weigh in on domestic squabbles, Zamora used them as vehicles to perform the self for others. Zamora's work, these quotidian video performances, function like video *testimonios* that convert identity into a "poetics of defense."

In this essay, following Yúdice's lead, I am disidentifying with Foucault's paradigm insofar as I am redeploying it and, to a certain extent, restructuring it in the service of minoritarian identity. In this essay I am interested in imagining an ethics of the minoritarian self. Within a Foucauldian framework recalibrated to consider the minoritarian subject's care of the self, to work on oneself is to veer away from models of the self that correlate with socially prescribed identity narratives. The rejection of these notions of the self is not simply an individualistic rebellion: resisting dominant modes of subjection entails not only contesting dominant modalities of governmental and state power but also opening up a space for new social formations. The performance of Latina/o, queer, and other minoritarian ontologies—which is to say the theatricalization of such ethics of the self—conjures the possibility of social agency within a world bent on the negation of minoritarian subjectivities. My project here is to map and document a minoritarian ethics of the self and, more important, the ways representations of and (simultaneously) by that self signal new spaces within the social. I will also suggest that the televisual dissemination of such performances allows for the *possibility of counterpublics:* communities and relational chains of resistance that contest the dominant public sphere. Within radical movements that already exist, Zamora's work may not register as progressive enough or may be seen as redundant. The fact that he agreed to work within the tepid multicultural frame of the corporate entity MTV might immediately diminish his significance to already established activist communities. It is my contention that Zamora's work was not for other activists, queer or Latino, but was instead for a world of *potentially* politicized queers and Latinos; for a mass public that is structured by the cultural forces of homophobia and racism; for those who have no access to more subculturally based cultural production and grassroots activism. Thus, Zamora's activism preaches to the not-yet-converted and in doing so may not seem as radical as the work of other activists but nevertheless should be acknowledged as frontline struggle and agitation.

My focus on a nexus of identity markers that circulate around queer and Latino is of importance for various reasons. The AIDS emergency has become a painful habit of being for many of us. Those of us who live inside and around Latino communities and queer communities know the ways in which so much has been lost, indeed, that the present and far too many futures have been robbed. The necessity of publicizing such ethics of the self, of moving these ethics beyond the privatized zones of individual identities, is great during our current health crisis.

But AIDS is only one of the reasons why publicizing and performing an ethics of the self seems so essential for Latina/o and/or queer politics. The disjunctures between queer and Latino communities are many. The mainstream gay community ignores or exoticizes Latino bodies, and many Latino communities promote homophobia. Yet, as of November 1994, the month in which Zamora died, the linkages between queerness and *latinidad* have never seemed so poignant. The congressional elections, nicknamed "the Republican revolution" by some news media pundits, made the headlines by establishing the New Right's majority status in the U.S. Senate and House of Representatives. This reactionary tidal wave also included legislation that was calibrated to legislate against certain identities. Although two antigay amendments were barely defeated in Idaho and Oregon, California's Proposition 187, a measure that further erodes the nation's civil rights by denying health care and education to immigrants who have been classified as "illegal" by the state apparatus, was passed. The targeted immigrant communities are non-Europeans, especially Latinos. An anti-lesbian/gay amendment passed in Colorado in 1992—which read very much like the barely defeated ordinances in Idaho and Oregon—proposed that lesbians and gays be stripped of any basic civil rights that would acknowledge and protect their minority status. The 1992 Colorado proposition was eventually overruled by the Supreme Court. Nonetheless, the popularity of such initiatives tells us something about the national body: homophobia, racism, and xenophobia are being codified as legislation. It can certainly be argued that these hate discourses have always been the law of the land, yet there is something particularly disturbing about the fact that the majoritarian public sphere announces these prohibitions and discriminatory practices as sites to rally around. Indeed, homohatred and Latino-bashing are two of the New Right's most popular agenda issues. The 1992 Republican conventions made all of this quite clear as countless speakers at the podium and delegates interviewed on the floor voiced their anti-immigrant and "pro-family" (which is always antiqueer) rhetoric. The 1996 GOP convention chose to remove ultra-right zealots like Pat Buchanan and Pat Robertson from roles of visibility, thus allowing much of these politics of exclusion to be relocated just below the surface of the televisual proceedings. Despite this prime-time camouflage and a hollow rhetoric of "inclusion," the New Right's agenda, spelled out in the GOP platform, still promised a repeal of civil rights legislation, further attacks on immigrants, xenophobic welfare reform, and more family values.

In this essay, I am interested in unveiling moments in which the majoritarian public sphere's publicity—its public discourse and reproduction of that discourse—is challenged by performances of counterpublicity that defy its discriminatory ideology. Counterpublicity is disseminated through acts that are representational *and* political interventions in the service of subaltern counterpublics.[6] The philosopher Nancy Fraser, following the work of other writers, has criticized Jürgen Habermas's account of the public sphere for focusing primarily on the constitution of one monolithic bourgeois public sphere at the expense of considering other possibilities for publicity. Even though Habermas's work is essentially a critique of the bourgeois public sphere, his lack of recourse to counterpublics essentially reinscribes the exclusionary logic and universalism of the bourgeois public sphere. Counterpublics, for Fraser, "contest[ed] the exclusionary norms of the 'official' bourgeois public sphere, elaborating alternative styles of political behavior and alternative norms of public speech."[7] Fraser goes on to point out the significance of subaltern counterpublics for women, people of color, gays and lesbians, and other subordinated groups. Alexander Kluge and Oskar Negt describe the public sphere as being comprised of various forms of publicity that are connected to different communities and modalities of publicity. Negt and Kluge's work maintains that counterpublics often emerge out of already existing industrial and commercial channels of publicity, especially the electronic media.

The act of performing counterpublicity in and through electronic/televisual sites dominated by the dominant public sphere is risky. Many representations of counterpublicity are robbed of any force by what Miriam Hansen has called the "marketplace of multicultural pluralism."[8] The practices of queer and Latino counterpublicity—acts that publicize and theatricalize an ethics of the self—that I will be mapping present strategies that resist, often through performances that insist on local specificities and historicity, the pull of reductive multicultural pluralism.

The best way we can understand the categories *queer* and *Latina/o* or *latinidad* is as counterpublics that are in opposition to other social factions. What is primarily at stake is space. The mode of counterpublicity I am discussing makes an intervention in public life that defies the white normativity *and* heteronormativity of the majoritarian public sphere. Thus, I am proposing that these terms be conceptualized as social movements that are contested by and contest the public sphere for the purposes of political efficacy—movements that not only "remap" but also *produce* minoritarian space.

The theoretical schools I am blending here, social theory influenced by Habermas and Foucault's discourse analysis, are more often than not pitted *against* each other. Habermas's thinking appeals to and attempts to reconstruct rationality. Foucault's, in its very premise, is a critique of rationality. The mappings that public sphere social theory provides are extremely generative ones. Yet, as I leave the work of social theorists like Negt and Kluge, Hansen, and Fraser and return to the major source of these paradigms, Habermas, I find myself having various misgivings with his project's philosophical tenets, namely, his use of and investment in communicative reason.[9] Habermasian communicative reason presupposes that within the framing of all communicative gestures there exists an appeal to an undeniable "good" that would alleviate all disagreements within the social. Foucauldians and others find the category of a universally defined good to be an exceedingly easy target.

My post-Habermasian use of the public sphere is primarily indebted to Negt and Kluge's critique of Habermas, especially their move to critique the underlying concepts of universal reason that they identify in his project. Their critique utilizes Kant's critical philosophy to problematize the category of an abstract principle of generality. Their work then opens up space to conceptualize multiple publics, complete with their own particularities.

Jon Simmons has explained that it is indeed difficult to locate Foucault on any map of politics that we inherit from nineteenth-century philosophy. But he goes on to add:

> Foucault does belong to a "we," though this "we" is not easily classifiable according to traditional categories. How does one define the gay movement, feminism, youth protests, the movements of ethnic and national minorities, and the diffuse discontents of clients of educational, health and welfare systems who are identified as single mothers, unemployed, or delinquent? His transgressive practices of self with writing, drugs, gay friendship and s/m operate in the space opened by these movements. Those whose designated desires, genders, ethnic identities, or welfare categorizations do not seem to fit in this space. It is in this space where some women refuse to be feminine and become feminists; in which black-skinned people refuse to be Negroes and become African-Americans; and in which men who desire other men might refuse to be homosexuals and become gay. Like Foucault, they practice the politics of those who refuse to be who they are and strive to become other.[10]

The space that Simmons describes is what I consider the transformative political space of disidentification.[11] Here is where Negt and Kluge function for me as valuable supplements to Foucault's mappings of the social. This space, what Simmons calls Foucault's "we," can be given a new materiality and substance when transcoded as counterpublics. Fredric Jameson, in a fascinating essay on Negt and Kluge, sees this connection between the German writers and Foucault, despite the fact that he is ultimately opposed to Foucault and valorizes Negt and Kluge: "The originality of Negt and Kluge, therefore, lies in the way in which the hitherto critical and analytical force of what is widely known as 'discourse analysis' (as in Foucault's descriptions of the restrictions and exclusions at work in a range of so-called discursive formations) is now augmented, not to say completed, by the utopian effort to create space of a new type."[12]

The definition of counterpublics that I am invoking here is intended to describe different subaltern groupings that are defined as falling outside the majoritarian public sphere; it is influenced by a mode of discourse theory that critiques universalities and favors particularities, yet it insists on a Marxian materialist impulse that *regrids* transgressive subjects and their actions as identifiable social movements. Thus, my notion of a counterpublic resonates alongside Simmons's description of "those whose designated desires, genders, ethnic identities, or welfare categorizations do not seem to fit." The object of my study, Pedro Zamora, was, from the purview of the dominant public sphere, one of those who did not seem to fit. In this way, his work can be understood as a counterpublic response to dominant publicity.

The young Cuban American activist disidentified with that dominant publicity, working with *and* on one of its "channels," MTV. Habermas, following the example of Frankfurt School predecessor Theodor Adorno, would probably see MTV as the providence of monopoly capitalism, locked into a pattern of sameness that was only calibrated to reproduce the consumer. A strict Habermasian reading could never see MTV as a stage on which radical work could be executed. Negt and Kluge understand that in this postmodern moment, the electronic media is essential to the reproduction of state capitalism and counterpublicity. Zamora also understood this. Using his keen sense of counterpublicity, he spotted *The Real World*'s potential as an exemplary stage. One only needs to consider the cover letter he sent MTV when he was applying for the show to understand how the young activist immediately saw the political potential of the medium. I will first cite a section of the letter where his pitch challenges the producers to consider the possibility of having a person living with AIDS on the show:

> So why should I be on *The Real World?* Because in the real world there are people living productive lives who just happen to be HIV+. I think it is important for people my age to see a young person who looks and feels healthy, can party and have fun but at the same time needs to take five pills daily to stay healthy.
>
> On one of your episodes this season [season 2] you had an HIV+ guy come in and talk about AIDS/HIV with the group. He was there a few hours and he left. I wonder what kind of issues would have come up if that HIV+ guy would be living with the group, sharing the bathroom, the refrigerator, the bedroom, eating together? Everyday for six months. Things that make you go hmmmm. . . .[13]

Here Zamora describes the dramatic and televisual energy his inclusion in the show would generate. He does not pitch his project in all its political urgencies. He understands that one needs to disidentify with the application process to be given access to the stage that the cable program provided him. He plays up the fact that his inclusion would make for good TV as well as an important political intervention. He next speaks to his willingness to sacrifice his own privacy for the sake of his activism:

> I know that being on *The Real World* would mean exposing the most intimate details of my life on national television. How comfortable am I with that? Well, I do that through my job every day. If I can answer the questions of an auditorium full of fifth graders with inquiring minds, I am sure I could do it on national television.

He is willing to sacrifice his right to privacy because he understands that subjects like himself never have full access to privacy. Although the dominant public sphere would like to cast him in the zone of private illness, it is clear that any fantasy of real privacy, as *Bower v. Hardwick* signals, is always illusory. In this statement, the young activist conveys his understanding that his desires, gender identifications, health, and national and ethnic minority status keep him from having any recourse to the national fantasy of privacy to which other subjects in the public sphere cling.

Magic Johnson, who achieved celebrity before he tested positive for the virus, uses his celebrity and the mass media in ways that are similar to those used by Zamora, who came into celebrity through *The Real World.* Hansen offers a reading of Johnson's case that is relevant here:

> When basketball player Magic Johnson used his resignation upon having tested positive to advocate safe sex he did more than put his star status in the service of a political cause; he made a connection, albeit a highly personalized one, between the industrial-commercial public sphere of sports, its local reappropriation within the African-American community, and the counterpublic struggle surrounding AIDS. While the latter is by now organized on an international scale, it continues to be marginalized domestically as a "special interest," to be denied public status with reference to its roots in gay subculture. Johnson's gesture not only made public a concern that the neoconservative lobby has been trying to delegitimize as private; it also, if only temporarily, opened up a discursive arena, in both mainstream publicity and within the African-American community, in which sexual practices could be discussed and negotiated, rather than merely sensationalized or rendered taboo. Not least, it provided a way to return sex education to schools from which it had disappeared under Reagan.[14]

Although there is much to say about the vastly divergent strategies of negotiation that Johnson and Zamora employed, I want to suggest that it is useful
to consider how the two men's examples are similar. Both used the power of
celebrity to make counterpublic interventions by way of using the mainstream
media, a mode of publicity that is usually hostile to counterpublic politics.
Both used their national stages to appeal to various publics, including a mass
public and the minoritized counterpublics from which they locate their own
identities. They also decided to combat the neoconservative strategy of relegat-
ing public health emergency to privatized and individual illness. Practicing a
public ethics of the self, both men thematized and theatricalized their illness
as public spectacles. The New Right is bent on removing AIDS from the public
agenda, nourishing ignorance through the suppression of safe-sex pedagogy
and, finally, cutting off federal support to persons with AIDS (PWAS) and medical AIDS research. To better understand Zamora's example, it is useful to review
the show's five-season run, noting shifts in each incarnation of the show.

Since its inception in 1991, MTV's *The Real World* has included queers in
its "real-life" ensemble cinema verité–style melodrama. The show's premise is
simple: to watch seven videogenic young people, all strangers, not actors, live
in a house together. The twenty-something individuals are selected through an
application process, and the producers strive to collect a group that is somewhat racially diverse. Its gender breakdown is usually four men and three
women. Cameras follow them throughout the day, and heavy editing results in
single episodes.

As of this writing, the show has had five different "casts" and five different
incarnations in five different cities: New York, Los Angeles, San Francisco, London, and Miami. Each season has included a gay or lesbian character. The New
York cast included Norman, a white man who sometimes identified as bisexual
and sometimes as gay. Although rather charismatic, Norman was something of
a minor character on the show; most of that season focused on the contrived
sexual tension between innocent country girl Julie and Eric, a New Jerseyian
Herb Ritts model who was nominally straight and went on to host the illus-
trious MTV dance-party show, *The Grind*. Much momentum was lost in the
show's second season, in which the queer came as a midseason replacement.
Beth was a white lesbian who worked in B-horror movie production. She received probably less screen time than any other character in the show's five
seasons. Norman and Beth both dated, but their sexual lives were relegated to
"special episodes." The way these two characters were contained and rendered

narratively subordinate to the show's straight characters is a succinct example of the inane multicultural pluralism that Hansen has described. It also clearly displays some of the ways queers and the counterpublicity they might be able to disseminate are rendered harmless within the channels of the electronic media and the majoritarian public sphere. Zamora was the third season's house queer. However, he did not fall into obscurity in the way his queer predecessors had. Rather, Pedro managed to offer valuable counterpublicity for various subaltern counterpublics that included U.S. Latinos, queers, and people living with AIDS.

For five months Pedro was one of the only out gay men appearing regularly on television.[15] He was also one of the only Latinos seen regularly on national television. Furthermore, he was one of the only out people living with AIDS on television. Let's make no mistake as to MTV's motives in selecting Zamora. He was as handsome as a model and rarely looked "ill" in any way. He was a Cuban American, a group that comes as close as any Latino community in the U.S. to qualifying as a "model minority." Although articulate and skilled as a public speaker, he possessed a thick Cuban accent that must have sounded very "tropical" to North American ears. In fact, one could argue that he walked a road that was paved by a previous Latino star, Desi Arnaz.[16] He was selected because of these features and his agency in this selection process was none. He fit a larger corporate schema as to what MTV wanted for the show, and these reasons led to his being represented. Yet Zamora was more than simply represented: he used MTV as an opportunity to continue his life's work of HIV/AIDS pedagogy, queer education, and human rights activism. Unlike his queer predecessors, he exploited MTV in politically efficacious ways; he used MTV more than they used him.

The fourth season of the show was set in London. At this point, the show broke from its pattern of having an out house queer. The *Real World* London was less contentious than the San Francisco show. It included only one ethnic minority, a black British jazz singer, and not one out lesbian, gay, bisexual, or transgendered person. It would seem that the ethnic, racial, and sexual diversity that characterized the show's first three seasons was put on hiatus after the explosive San Francisco season that I will be discussing here. I will argue that the soft multicultural pluralism that characterized the series was exploited and undermined by Zamora and some of his peers. I am suggesting that the fourth season of *The Real World* can be read as a backlash of sorts, which is to say it was an escape from North American politics and social tensions to a storybook

England, a fantasy Europe that had none of its own ethnic or sexual strife. (The roommates actually lived in a flat that was made up to look like a castle.)

The fifth season, set in Miami, represents a back-to-basics approach, where the tried and true formula of nominal racial and sexual diversity was reestablished. The Miami cast included two women of color: Cynthia, an African American waitress from Oakland, California, and Melissa, "the local girl," a Cuban American woman from the Miami area. The house queer spot went once again to a white man, as it did on its classic first season. Dan, a college student from Rutgers University, was raised in the Midwest, where he grew up watching the show like many queer kids in the U.S. In a feature article in *Out* magazine, Dan spoke about the way he, as a pre-out youth, marveled at seeing an out Norman on the show's first season. In that article, he expresses his understanding that he was now, thanks to the show, going to be the most famous gay man in America. The young Real Worlder's statement testifies to the counterpublic-making properties of the program. Dan aspires to be a model and a writer for flashy fashion magazines. His interviews on the program and in the print media indicate that he was cognizant of a need to be a public "role model" for queers, but his performances fell short of the radical interventions that Zamora produced.

Dan understood the need to perform a positive image; Zamora, on the other hand, was conscious of the need to take the show's title seriously and be radically *real*. A coffee-table fan book that MTV published in 1995 while the fourth season was airing prints "sound bites" by many of the show's stars, producers, and crew; the book's revenues go, in part, to the Pedro Zamora Foundation. In that book, story editor Gordon Cassidy comments, "The one thing I feel best about in this show is what Pedro enabled us to present to the rest of the country, and not just about AIDS, but about who he was as a person, things that networks can't get away with. You think of the problems networks have portraying gay relationships, interracial relationships, and he was all of those."[17] The fact that Zamora was indeed all of these things is especially important. The "realness" of Pedro and the efficacy and power of his interventions have much to do with the manner in which he insisted on being a complicated and intersectional subject: not only gay but a sexual person; a person of color actively living with another person of color in an interracial relationship; a person living with AIDS. While Cassidy's comments could be read as an example of MTV's patting itself on the back, much of what he is saying is accurate. As of this moment, with few exceptions, broadcast network television is unable and unwilling to represent queers who are sexual yet not pathological, interracial relationships, and stories about AIDS that portray fullness and vibrancy of such a life narrative.

To understand Zamora's intervention one needs to survey the status of homosexuality on television at the time of his death in November 1994. A *Los Angeles Times* feature article cites Richard Jennings, executive director of Hollywood Supports, a group promoting positive gay portrayals in film and television, who sees the resurgence of gay characters in the media. Jennings explains that, "As gays have increasingly 'come out,' many viewers have become aware of gay brothers, sisters and friends. Together with gay viewers, they are increasingly asking for sympathetic gay portrayals." This lobbying is opposed by right-wing activists like the Rev. Louis Sheldon, head of the Orange County–based Traditional Values Coalition. Sheldon is quoted in the same article as saying that "Homosexuals should not be portrayed at all on TV." Sheldon, the deranged bigot who is perhaps most famous for "picketing" outside of AIDS memorials and funerals, feels that sympathetic gay role models confuse viewers; he contends that "If young males need to identify with someone, they should identify with Clint Eastwood."[18] While we might want to dismiss Sheldon's speech as the demented ravings of an Eastwood groupie, we cannot underestimate the influence that such zealots continue to exercise over mainstream broadcasting.

Although some advertisers seem to have become more accepting of queer representation—Ellen DeGeneres's very public coming out in the spring of 1997 and the appearance of a black gay supporting character on ABC's *Spin City* evidence this—very few queer characters on television have, as of this writing, performed their sexualities on the screen. For example, when producer Darren Star wanted to show his gay character, Matt, kissing another man on the season finale of *Melrose Place* in the spring of 1994, the Fox network balked and asked them not to, afraid that advertisers would withdraw their advertising as they did for a 1989 episode of ABC's *thirtysomething* that showed two gay men in bed together.

Within this context, Zamora's performance of self, his publicized care of the self, especially as represented in an episode that featured an exchanging of rings ceremony with boyfriend Sean, can be seen as radical interventions. In that episode, originally broadcast on November 3, 1994, the two men kiss no fewer than seven times in the half-hour program. Zamora's romance was, according to producer John Murray, significant within the history of the show, as it was "probably the deepest we've ever gotten into a relationship in our three seasons." [19] (Since then, Dan dated two men on the show's fifth season, one a closeted white man, the other an out Cuban American. Although both these relationships seem significant insofar as they were *real* queer couplings on television, neither bond seemed as serious or ultimately memorable as Pedro and Sean's.) When I suggest that such performances function as counterpublicity, I am imagining the effect that such performances might have on a queer child or adult, whose access to queer cultures or energies may be limited or nonexistent. These highly mediated images, brought into the fold through the highly mediated channels of corporate broadcasting, still served as sites where children and others could glimpse a queer *and* ethnic life world. What started out as tokenized representation became something larger, more spacious: a mirror that served as a prop for subjects to imagine and rehearse identity. This, in part, enables the production of counterpublics.

It would be a mistake to elide the representational significance of Zamora's work on the mainstream. Pedro, as Bill Clinton put it, gave AIDS a very "human face." Beyond that, he gave it a vibrant, attractive, politicized, and brown face. He showed an ignorant and phobic national body that within the bourgeois public's fantasy of privacy, the binarism of public health and private illness could no longer hold, that the epidemic was no longer an abstract and privatized concern. He willfully embodied and called attention to all those things that are devastating and ennobling about possessing a minority subjectivity within an epidemic. And although MTV gave Zamora a stage on which to do this work of education and embodiment, it should not be too valorized for this contribution, for they often attempted to undercut it. In what follows, I will offer a quick synopsis of Pedro's role and work on *The Real World*. I will focus on those episodes that are pertinent to Pedro's story or the story I am telling in this essay. I will then consider the show's nineteenth episode in more elaborate detail.

The show begins with Cory, a college student from California who rendezvoused with Pedro on a train. The young Anglo woman is very taken with Pedro, and Pedro, for his part, as he explains in a voice-over, was expecting to meet a woman who would be very much like Cory, very "all-American." The roommates include Judd, a Jewish cartoonist from Long Island; Pam, an Asian American medical student; Mohammed, an African American Bay Area musician and writer; Puck, a white male bicycle messenger; and Rachel, a Republican Mexican American[20] from Arizona who is applying to graduate school. (I am aware that these descriptions are somewhat stock, but they were the primary identity accounts that the program offered.) That first episode concluded with Pedro's sharing his scrapbook with his roommates. The scrapbook consisted of newspaper clippings from around the nation of his activist work. This outed him to the rest of the cast as not only queer but also as a person living with AIDS. Rachel was put off by this display and proceeded, during an interview in the confessional,[21] to voice her AIDSphobic and homophobic concerns about cohabiting with Pedro. Thus, that first episode began with the "all-American girl" meeting the handsome young stranger on a train and concluded with a conservative Latina expressing a phobic position against the young AIDS educator. This episode framed Pedro as one of the show's "star" presences, unlike the queers from previous seasons.

Episode 2 presents an early confrontation between Pedro and the show's other star presence, Puck. Pedro objects to Puck's postpunk hygiene in the kitchen and throughout the living space. Although the show hoped to frame this confrontation as a sort of Odd Couple dilemma, it ignored the very material fact that Puck's lack of hygiene was nothing short of a medical risk for a person living with a compromised immune system. While Rachel goes to an "Empower America" fund-raiser and meets the New Right's beloved Jack Kemp, one of her personal heroes, Pedro goes on a first date with Sean, an African American HIV-positive pastry chef with a disarming smile. Sean and Pedro's relationship advances, and the couple falls in love by episode 6. Puck makes homophobic jokes about Pedro during this episode. According to interviews with the cast after the series was completed, these comments from Puck were a regular household occurrence that were, through editing strategies, downplayed by the producers.

In episode 8, Pedro goes for a medical examination. He discovers that his T-cell count has dropped significantly. This moment represents an important one in TV history: a painful aspect of a PWA's quotidian reality is represented as never before. This sequence is followed by one in which Pedro gives a safe sex and risk prevention seminar at Stanford University. Puck, always vying for the house's attention, schedules a beachcombing expedition at the same time. Pam and Judd choose to watch and support Pedro, and Cory and Rachel join Puck. The show crosscuts both sequences, emphasizing the divisions in the house. Tensions mount during episode 9. Pedro and Sean become engaged, and Puck reacts with what is by now predictable homophobia. The house confronts Puck on his behavioral problems in episode 11. Puck won't listen and Pedro delivers an ultimatum to the house: it is either he or Puck. The members vote, and Puck is unanimously ejected from the house.

In episode 11, Pedro travels with Rachel to Arizona to meet her Catholic, Republican family. Pedro is exceedingly diplomatic with the family and connects with them as Latinos. Rachel's parents, both educators at a local school, invite Pedro to talk about AIDS at their workplace. One student asks if he still has sex and whether or not he has a girlfriend. There is a tight shot of Rachel's mother looking worried and seemingly holding her breath. Pedro pauses, then answers that he is in "a relationship" and continues to practice safe sex. There is a cut to a shot of Rachel's mother looking relieved. This maneuver shows what is for many antihomophobic spectators a difficult and problematic moment. Deciding *not* to be out and *not* to perform and inhabit his queerness at that moment was a worthwhile compromise in the face of his professional work as an AIDS educator dealing with adolescents in a public school. It can also be understood, at least in part, as a moment of Latino allegiance, where queerness is displaced by the mark of ethnicity. I want to suggest that understanding this disidentification with his queerness as a disservice to queers or his own queer identity would be erroneous insofar as these shuttlings and displacements are survival strategies that intersectional subjects, subjects who are caught and live between different minoritarian communities, must practice frequently if they are to keep their residences in different subcultural spheres.

Episode 13 is focused on Pedro's returning home to Miami and his best friend, Alex. The homecoming is cut short when Pedro becomes sick. Zamora, in a post–*Real World* interview, explained that he wanted to show it all, the good days and the bad days.[22] Representing as much as he could of the totality of living with AIDS was very important for his ethics of the self, his performance of being a self *for* others. That episode gives a family history and background. Pedro emigrated to the U.S. through the Mariel boat lift at the end of the Carter administration. He lost his mother to cancer at the age of fifteen, a tragedy that rocked his family. His family is represented as a very typical blue-collar, Cuban American family. Cuban Americans, especially Miami Cubans, are associated with right-wing politics and values; it is thus important to see this family embrace their son and brother without hesitation. The image of Cuban Americans loving, accepting, and being proud of a gay son complicates the map of *latinidad* that is most available within U.S. media. The better-known map positions Cubans on the far right and Chicanos on the far left, which, although demographically founded, is a nonetheless reductive depiction of *latinidad.*

Episode 16 depicts Pedro's bout with pneumonia, which eventually leaves him hospitalized. The housemates experience a feeling of helplessness that is common in support communities for people with AIDS. By the next episode, Pedro is out of the hospital and accompanies the rest of the cast on a trip to Hawaii. By the twentieth and final episode, Pedro has become very close to Cory, Pam, and Judd. The cast is shown moving out of their Lombard Street flat.

In reading the penultimate episode, episode 19, I want to point out the restraints that the show's producers put on Zamora's performances and the way the young Cuban American responded to them. Pedro's romance became the major romance of the show; Sean never fell out of the picture like Norman's and Beth's partners and flirtations. Sean became part of Pedro's quotidian reality. Both made their presence continuously known in the San Francisco flat. A few weeks into their relationship, Sean proposed marriage to Pedro and Pedro accepted. In response, the show's other "star" presence, Puck, decided to one-up the queer couple by proposing marriage to his new girlfriend, Toni. Puck stands as proof that not all counterpublics challenge the way the social is organized by dominant culture. Puck's counterpublic is a juvenile version of rugged individualism; it represents a sort of soft anarchism that relativizes all political struggles as equivalents to his own exhaustive self-absorption. The competing modes of counterpublicity between Pedro and Puck eventually contributed to the breakdown in the domestic space that concluded with Puck's being asked to leave.

The episode I want to consider tracks Pedro's and Puck's respective romances. Pedro's queerness is played against Puck's heterosexuality; the episode crosscuts between the two pairings. One questions the producers' rationale for juxtaposing Puck and Toni's romantic relationship with Pedro and Sean's commitment ceremony. After Puck was ejected from the house, producers continued to film his encounters with his former housemates Cory, Rachel, and Judd. But except for this penultimate episode, there was no presentation of Puck independent of his housemates until that episode.

Early in the episode, Sean and Pedro are shown in bed together, lying on top of each other and planning their commitment ceremony. To MTV's credit, there has never been any scene of queer sociality like it on television. The scene of two gay men of color, both HIV-positive, in bed together as they plan what is the equivalent of a marriage is like none that was then or now imaginable on television. The transmission of this image throughout the nation and the world is a valuable instance of counterpublicity.

Edited within this scene are individual video bites by both participants. Sean explains: "Being with Pedro, someone who is so willing to trust and love and sort of be honest with, is refreshing. I think that knowing that Pedro does have an AIDS diagnosis and has been getting sick makes me recognize the need to be here right now. I know that one of us may get sick at sometime but [it is this] underlying understanding or this underlying feeling that makes it a lot easier." Sean's statement and his performance in front of the video camera explain their reason for having a formal bonding ceremony as being a response to a radically refigured temporality in the face of AIDS. This, too, is an important instance of nationally broadcast counterpublic theater that provides an important opportunity for the mass public to glimpse different lifeworlds than the one endorsed by dominant ideology.

Yet the power of this image and Sean's statement is dulled when the program cuts to its next scene. The previous scene of coupling is followed by Puck and Toni's coupling ritual. Puck, in a voice-over, announces that he and Toni are made for each other, that they are, in fact, "a matched pair." When they go window-shopping for a wedding ring and Toni eyes a ring that she likes, Puck scolds her and tells her that the item is a cocktail ring, not a traditional wedding ring. He then offers to buy her a tie clip instead. This scene is in contrast with a scene of the other couple actually selecting bands. Sean's voice-over is narratively matched with the playful Toni, who explains, "When I first met Puck he was stinking and looking for a mate. I think we're in love. I know we're in love."

While Sean and Pedro are preparing for an actual ceremony, Toni and Puck are shown hanging out. Toni and Puck are not planning any sort of ceremony. The producers' strategy of matching the story lines and making them seem equivalent is resolved by a strategy of crosscutting the commitment ceremony with one of Puck's soapbox derby races. Toni is shown cheering on Puck as he races his green car. Since the inception of *The Real World*, its producers have always hoped for a romance to erupt on the set between cast members. That has yet to happen.[23] In lieu of such a relationship, the producers hope for an interesting relationship between a cast member and an outsider. Sean and Pedro's romance emerged early on as the show's most significant relationship. I am arguing that the series' producers were unable to let a queer coupling, especially one as radical as Sean and Pedro's, stand as the show's actual romance. Pedro's and Sean's individual performances and the performance of their relationship were narratively undermined by a strategy of weak multicultural crosscutting that was calibrated to dampen the radical charge that Pedro and Sean gave *The Real World.*

Despite these efforts by the show's producers to diminish the importance of Pedro and Sean's relationship, the ceremony itself stands as an amazingly powerful example of publicly performing an ethics of the self while simultaneously theatricalizing a queer counterpublic sphere. The ceremony begins with a shot of a densely populated flat. Sean and Pedro are toasted by Eric, a friend of the couple who has not appeared on previous episodes, who delivers an extremely touching toast: "It gives me a lot of pleasure and I see it as a real pleasure to speak on behalf of Sean and Pedro and to them. In your love you remind us that life is about now and love is about being there for one another. It is with real bravery that you open your hearts *to each other,* and I think it's with real hope that you promise your lives to each other. *We stand with you* defiantly and bravely and with real hope. To the adorable couple [emphasis mine]." This toast is followed by equally eloquent statements by both Pedro and Sean. Eric's statement is significant because it marks the way in which Pedro and Sean's being for themselves ("to each other") is, simultaneously, a being for others ("we stand with you"). This ceremony is like none that has ever been viewed on commercial television. It is a moment of counterpublic theater. The commitment ceremony not only inspires the gathering of spectators at the ceremony to stand together "bravely," "defiantly," and with "hope," but also, beyond the walls of the Lombard Street flat and beyond the relatively progressive parameters of San Francisco, it inspires a world of televisual spectators.

The Real World is overrun by queers. Queer bonds are made manifest in ways that have never been available on cable or broadcast television. Pedro's insistence on mastering the show's format through his monologues, domestic interventions, and continuous pedagogy are relaxed in the sequence I have just described. Here the public sphere is reimagined by bringing a subaltern counterpublic into representation. The real world is overrun by queers, queers who speak about those things that are terrifying and ennobling about a queer and racialized life world. The commitment ceremony sequence in many ways sets up the show's closure. Puck's antics, crosscut and stacked next to the commitment ceremony, are narratively positioned to lessen the queer spin put on

The Real World by Pedro. Such a strategy is concurrent with the show's pluralist ethos. Queer commitments, energies, and politics are never quite left to stand alone.

The way Puck's relationship is used to relativize and diminish the emotional and political impact of Pedro and Sean's relationship is reminiscent of Pedro's selection to be included in the cast *with and in contrast to* Rachel, a young Republican Latina. Again, the ideologically bold move of representing an activist like Pedro as a representative of *latinidad* is counterbalanced by a reactionary Latina. The fact that Rachel and Pedro later bond as Latinos, despite their ideological differences, is narratively satisfying, producing a sense of hope for the spectator invested in pan-Latino politics.

The performance of a commitment ceremony itself might be read as an aping of heterosexual relationships. Such a reading would miss some important points. In a voice-over before the ceremony, Pedro discusses the need to "risk" being with Sean. He points to the ways in which this relationship, within the confines of his tragically abbreviated temporality, forms a new space of self, identity, and relationality. It is, in Foucault's terms, a new form. The couple form, crystallized as the bourgeois heterosexual dyad, is shattered and reconfigured. Indeed, this is a disidentification with the couple form. When one is queer and knows that his or her loved one is dying, the act of "giving oneself" to another represents an ethics of the self that does not cohere with the prescribed and normative coupling practices that make heterosexuals and some lesbians and gay men want to marry. I want to suggest that Pedro and Sean's ceremonial bonding is *not* about aping bourgeois heterosexuality. Rather, it is the enacting of a new mode of sociality. Foucault, in an often-cited interview on friendship, suggested that we understand homosexuality not so much as a desire but, rather, as something that is *desirable*. He explains that we must "work at becoming homosexual and not be obstinate in recognizing that we are." [24] Homosexuality is desirable because a homosexual mode of life allows us to reimagine sociality. The homosexual needs to "invent from A to Z a relationship that is formless" and eventually to arrive at a "multiplicity of relations." [25] Becoming homosexual, for Foucault, would then be a political project, a social movement of sorts, that would ultimately help us challenge repressive gender hierarchies and the structural underpinnings of institutions. Thus, I want to mark Sean and Pedro's union as something new, a new form that is at the same time formless from the vantage point of established state hierarchies. [26] The new formation that Sean and Pedro's performances of self bring into view is one that suggests worlds of possibility for the minoritarian subject who experiences multiple forms of domination within a larger system of governmentality.

When considering Zamora's life's work, one is struck by his list of accomplishments, interventions within the dominant public sphere that had real effects on individuals, like the woman from South Carolina whose letter opened this essay, and other interventions on the level of state activism. Zamora tested positive for HIV while still in high school, a few years after he arrived in the United States with his parents and two siblings in 1980 with 100,000 other Cuban refugees who sailed to the U.S. in the Mariel boat lift. His activism began not long after he tested positive for the virus. Zamora testified before the Presidential Commission on AIDS and twice before congressional committees, he took part in a public service ad campaign for the Centers for Disease Control and Prevention, and was appointed to a Florida government panel on AIDS. Furthermore, he gave multiple interviews in the print and electronic media. I first encountered Zamora before his tenure on MTV. I saw him and his father on a local Spanish-language television news program in South Florida while I was visiting my parents during college. As I sat in the living room with my parents, I marveled at the televisual spectacle of this young man and his father, both speaking a distinctly Cuban Spanish, on television, talking openly about AIDS, safe sex, and homosexuality. I was struck because this was something new. It was a new formation, a being for others. I imagined countless other living rooms within the range of this broadcast and I thought about the queer children who might be watching this program in their homes, with their parents. This is the point where I locate something other than the concrete interventions in the public sphere. Here is where I see the televisual spectacle leading to the possibility of new counterpublics, new spheres of possibility, and the potential for the reinvention of the world from A to Z.

Notes

1   The show itself used only first names. Thus, when I discuss the narratives of actual episodes, I will employ *Pedro;* I will refer to the man and cultural worker outside of the show's narrative as *Zamora.*

2   Michel Foucault, *The Care of the Self, vol. 3 of The History of Sexuality,* trans. Robert Hurley (New York: Vintage, 1986). Also see "The Ethic of the Care of the Self

as a Practice of Freedom," in *The Final Foucault,* ed. James Bernauer and David Rasmussen, trans. J. D. Gauthier (Cambridge, MA: MIT Press, 1987).

3   Michel Foucault, "On the Genealogy of Ethics: An Overview of Work in Progress," in *Ethics: Subjectivity and Truth,* ed. Paul Rabinow, trans. Robert Hurley and others (New York: The New Press, 1997), 269.

4   George Yúdice, "Marginality and the Ethics of Survival," in *Universal Abandon: The Politics of Postmodernism,* ed. Andrew Ross (Minneapolis: University of Minnesota Press, 1988), 220.

5   Ibid., 229.

6   It is important to clarify that my use of public sphere theory and the notion of a counterpublic sphere is indebted to Oskar Negt and Alexander Kluge, *Public Sphere and Experience: Toward an Analysis of the Bourgeois and Proletarian Public Sphere* (Minneapolis: University of Minnesota Press, 1993), and to Anglo-American commentators of Habermas. One can thus characterize my deployment of this critical vernacular as being post-Habermasian.

7   Nancy Fraser, "Rethinking the Public Sphere," in *The Phantom of the Public Sphere,* ed. Bruce Robbins (Minneapolis: University of Minnesota Press, 1993), 4.

8   Miriam Hansen, foreword to Negt and Kluge, xxxvii.

9   For an excellent reading of the political and philosophical disjunctures between Foucault and Habermas, see Jon Simmons, *Foucault and the Political* (New York: Routledge, 1995).

10   Ibid., 103.

11   By disidentification I am referring to practices and spaces where identities are negotiated through a series of tactical and partial identifications within the majoritarian public sphere. I elaborate this project in my study, *Disidentifications,* forthcoming from University of Minnesota Press.

12   Fredric Jameson, "On Negt and Kluge," in *The Phantom Public,* ed. Bruce Robbins (Minneapolis: University of Minnesota Press, 1993), 49.

13   Hillary Johnson and Nancy Rommelmann, *The Real Real World* (New York: MTV Books / Pocket Books / Melcher Media, 1995), 158.

14   Hansen, xxxviii–xxxix.

15   He has continued to be, even after his death, a beacon of queer possibility thanks to MTV's policy of airing *Real World* reruns.

16   Both Arnaz and Zamora are figures of ambivalence insofar as, though they both held pioneering roles in the history of Latino representation in the media, they also seemed to have no qualms about performing for white people. Of course, this comparison falls apart when one considers the motivations that organized these performances for whites. Zamora's motivations were not about promoting an individual career but, instead, about being an activist and a pedagogue in a larger

health emergency. But these men are icons, and their iconicity is a troubling thing; although we might wish that they were less willing to assimilate, we cannot discount the influence of their work on a larger cultural imaginary. This footnote is a response to a conversation with Jorge Ignacio Cortiñas, a Cuban American activist and cultural worker whose astute skepticism and critical ambivalence have helped me nuance this discussion of Zamora's work. Cortiñas also urged me to consider a comparison between Arnaz and Zamora.

17   Johnson and Rommelmann, 90.

18   Joseph Hanania, "Resurgence of Gay Roles on Television," *Los Angeles Times,* 3 November 1994, 12.

19   Ibid.

20   I use the term Mexican American to describe Rachel because I imagine her political ideology would not be aligned with the politics of the Chicana/o movement.

21   The confessional is a room where house occupants perform a personal monologue for a stationary camera. The confessional footage is later intercut with the show's narrative.

22   Hal Rubenstein, "Pedro Leaves Us Breathless" *POZ* 1, no. 3 (August–September 1994): 38–41, 79–81.

23   Judd and Pam did eventually begin dating, but only after the show stopped filming. Failed on-the-set couplings include Eric and Julie during the first season, Puck and Rachel in the third, and Kat and Neil in the fourth.

24   Michel Foucault, quoted in Sylvere Lotringer, ed., *Foucault Live,* trans. John Johnston (New York: Semiotext[e], 1989), 204.

25   Ibid.

26   The Pedro Zamora Memorial Fund was established after his death. The fund was set up to educate women, young people, minorities, and the poor about HIV/AIDS and to fund AIDS service organizations. The fund, part of AIDS Action, can be reached at 202-986-1300, ext. 3013.

GAME THEORY

Racial Embodiment and Media Crisis

Stephen Michael Best

We, over a period of time, have apparently decided that within American life we have one great repository where we're going to focus and imagine sensuality and exaggerated sensuality, all very removed and earthly things — and this great image is the American negro.
— Lorraine Hansberry[1]

The Celebrated Body

The televised spectacle of pedestrians in Los Angeles (a rarity in that city) cheering a fugitive O. J. Simpson from along the embankments of Interstate 405 turned more than a few stomachs, no doubt, in this country and elsewhere. Los Angelenos appeared to have bought wholesale their city's most famous and valuable products; image and celebrity. The spectators who rooted for Simpson with signs reading "We love the Juice!" and "Save the Juice!" accompanied by chants of "Go, O. J., go!" chose celebrity over their own moral judgment, not because they were in some way immoral but because they were caught up in the state of social weightlessness that *is* celebrity, a state of suspended animation that makes moral choice an impossible option. And this state of pure rapturous fantasy — the "unreality" of O. J. celebrity — must have felt more real than the saga of sex, violence, and murder unfolding within arm's reach of O. J.'s fans.

What O. J.'s fans most likely failed to register was not their own morality (I'm sure most of them faced that issue at some point), but rather the libidinal exchanges between themselves and O. J. — the desires and identifications that are always already surrogates for sex, violence, and a vicarious encounter with death. The fans mistook the degree to which O. J. had already come to "live" for them. For celebrity is, in many ways, the permission we grant our heroes to usurp our place in the world, to live off (and die from) the fat of our adulation. But the O. J. saga also tells us that, in places devoid of royalty and a respected and revered political class, celebrity is, as the sportswriter Frank Rich put it, "next to Godliness." [2] We believe in celebrities and in God for the same reason: "their omnipotence and invincibility, however illusory, hold out the promise that we, too, have a crack at immortality." [3] If O. J. Simpson could defy murder charges, pursuit by the LAPD, and suicidal impulses — if he could defy *death* — then "there was a vicarious victory over mortality for his audience as well." [4] O. J.'s fans found in him a safe surrogate for life in this world and, potentially, death beyond it. [5] Celebrity, by freeing fans of morality, allowed them more nakedly to face mortality.

This televised exercise in going to the precipice and back, of tarrying near death, owes more than a mere nod to the representational exonomies of television itself. Television creates and re-creates this rhapsody in black and blue that *is* celebrity. In this instance, it grows from a discrete arena of accomplishment and prowess: the football field. O. J.'s celebrity transforms the public sphere into an arena of sport. The spectators who cheer his white Bronco along the freeways of Los Angeles are not applauding the act of murder. Caught in the ecstasy of celebrity, they urge O. J. on in his final mad run for the end zone, his last desperate rush for a place in the record books: the Crime (and Trial) of the Century. Those spectators, momentarily, individually, unconsciously even, transform the endless sprawl of Los Angeles into the comparatively modest arena of a football field. As one spectator confessed, she wanted "to be part of history," [6] a participant in the drama. And, if they worked fast enough, she and many others could participate in the spectacle and hurry home to "see themselves in replay" like sports stars themselves. [7]

O. J.'s fans are blindly, delusionally fixed on the legitimate drama of athletic pursuit, not complicit in what from all other angles looks an awful lot like an act of lawlessness. This moment of catharsis and inversion cannot be divorced from either the mechanisms of television or the cultural construction of black masculinity. In fact, television constructs black masculinity as the moment of crisis that we all collectively witnessed. Television, like a thief in the night, was waiting for O. J.

Local and national television networks provided endless and uninterrupted live broadcasts of the LAPD's pursuit of O. J. through the aid of helicopter-mounted camera teams, video simulcast, and satellite hookups. Liveness amplified and buttressed the vicarious nature of the spectacle, manifesting a global presence both of and at the scene of pursuit. As was true in the videotaped and endlessly televised beating of Rodney King, television helped to secure the nation's investment in and responsibility for the unfolding narrative of criminality. Furthermore, the pursuit of O. J. involved a black man who ab initio embodied core national ideals to which much of the nation had already assented. O. J. lived the Horatio Alger myth, America's most enduring rags-to-riches saga. He also embodied the promises of the civil rights and Black Power movements, praised for both his winning good looks *and* his dazzling displays of "speed, power, and finesse,"[8] for both the sense that he suits nearly perfectly many of television's formats (e.g., sports, commercials, miniseries, and movies) *and* his physical prowess. Finally, he provides one link in a chain of black male athletes who embody many of the same characteristics — from Jackie Robinson, Muhammed Ali, and Arthur Ashe before him, to Kareem Abdul-Jabbar, Magic Johnson, Mike Tyson, Carl Lewis, Michael Jordan, and Shaquille O'Neal after. But his troubles also represent the most recent in a series of breaks in this chain, and it is television's affinity for these breaks that will concern me in this essay.

On 8 November 1991, Magic Johnson acknowledged publicly that he had tested seropositive for antibodies to the HIV virus, which suggested that even the most treasured of American heroes engage in behavior believed by some to be less than "heroic." Arthur Ashe's later admission in April 1992 that he, too, had tested positive forced the nation once again to come to terms with the virus's disrespect for our culture's putative shields of "innocence." Both Mike Tyson's conviction on charges of date rape in February 1992 and allegations that Michael Jordan suffered from an "addiction" to gambling brought those issues into national consciousness. Finally, the charges that O. J. Simpson abused his wife for years and ultimately killed her and her friend have given the issue of spousal abuse national significance.[9] In the 1990s, scandals involving black male athletes have brought intense media scrutiny to the discussion of such issues as HIV infection, date rape, addiction, and spousal abuse. The energies of a phalanx of reporters, social workers, lawyers, and expert witnesses seem, in fact, to have produced a string of celebrity scandals in the twentieth century consistently linked by the subjects of blackness, celebrity, and crisis.

Clearly, there is some symbiosis between media discourse and moments of black male crisis. Concurrent with the above scandals were several involving such notables as Leona Helmsley, Woody Allen, Tonya Harding, and others. Though these scandals received substantial media attention, none triggered a national debate on employer tyranny and exploitation, father-daughter incest, or unsportsmanlike behavior, respectively. Furthermore, none spawned the type of national self-assessments that accompanied the scandals involving black male athletes. The nation responded to Leona Helmsley's economic violence with amused shock, yet took allegations of Michael Jordan's financial indiscretions deeply seriously. Media coverage of Woody Allen's incestuous transgressions included discussion of his idiosyncrasies, yet coverage of Mike Tyson's predations found them to be the penultimate expression of his "animality." These comparisons suggest the presence of invisible, *mediated* links between these black bodies and the media's racial unconscious. Something occurred in these spectacles of blackness that has to do not only with personal failure and the pressures of celebrity, but also with the social and cultural apparatus through which black bodies are brought into visibility and kept there. The scandal of black male celebrity marks a breakdown in the calibrated visibility that the sports stardom of Magic, O. J., and their peers was meant efficiently to maintain — a visuality in which the physical prowess of black sports icons abides by "the rules of the game" but against which flesh itself often collides. Why have the recent scandals involving black sports celebrities captured the nation's attention in ways that the scandals involving other nonblack celebrities have not? Why does the scandal of black celebrity figure so prominently in the media? What in blackness interests television so? The answers lie in the visual economies of television.

By way of a more general history of the trope of black physical prowess as an alive, enfleshed, palpitating human being (what Hansberry calls an "exaggerated sensuality" or "all very removed and earthly things"), I will use these accomplished athletes and their recent scandals to register how the sign "black male" produces certain meanings specific to television and the media. I will adumbrate the ways in which "black male" functions as a shibboleth for television's primary principle of structuration, liveness. A number of televisual discourses, particularly the notions of liveness and celebrity, construct black male bodies as "alive," making them the hyperefficient sites for the transformations of flesh into cultural capital (i.e., physical prowess, athletic achievement) within a capitalist economy of money, ideology, and images. The mechanism driving this logic of flesh-into-capital at the site of black male bodies is revealed in all its nakedness at moments of crisis or "scandal," when an excessive, unrestrained blackness arrests television's seemingly untrammeled temporal "flows."

My argument evolves in two stages. First, I distinguish between two competing levels of representation with regard to black masculinity, the scene of "the body" — an array of visual clichés we know most familiarly in the forms of black man as militant, sex object, homeboy, gladiator, or playground jock — and the time and space of the body's rupture, called (with due homage to literary critic Hortense Spillers) "the flesh." The collisions between body and flesh, flow and arrest, are rehearsed ad infinitum in the arena of sport. Sport depends upon moments of temporal arrest, moments that are given form in the instant replay, slow motion, and statistical assessments of player's performances. I aim next to show how nearly indistinguishable the representation of black male bodies is from the economies of sport. Finally, I reveal the ways in which television works according to the same logic, of time-in-motion against time arrested, and to argue that the phenomenal affinity of television for moments of black male crisis reflects a conceptual harmony between sport's temporality of arrest and television's temporality of crisis.

Black Male

An oblique yet appropriate starting point is the career of the ever-suffering Michael Jackson. Since he left the Jackson Five, Jackson's body has undergone a series of naturally occurring and man-made mutations whose outcome would best be described as a receding physicality. This admittedly multifarious process can be broken down and assessed in three stages. From the time of Jackson's first surgical operation, his nose has grown progressively slimmer, approaching sheer implosion. Like his nose, other parts of his body have tended to recede. His hair was consumed in a shower of flame during the filming of a commercial for the Pepsi Cola Corporation. And, as we discovered recently, he claims to suffer from the skin impairment vitiligo, a condition that progressively destroys the skin's deposits of melanin, resulting in large patches of depigmentation. Jackson has now withered to a ghostly apparition of his former self. He suffers increasingly from a heightened etherealness, a withering corporeality. And, most important for the concerns in this essay, his body recedes in inverse proportion to his media celebrity. It signifies his encroaching physical obsolescence and threatens with the specter of his reduction to pure (intense, imploded) media presence. Jackson is painfully, ironically, a "black hole." But Jackson's dialectical crisis of embodiment and celebrity has added dimension. His blackness and maleness are truly apparitional quantities, something *more* than he is presently, in a strictly material sense. "Black male" signifies, in Jackson's case, as a fleshly excess or, again, following Hansberry's phrasing, "all very removed and earthly things."

Clarence Thomas, particularly during his confirmation hearings in 1991, constitutes the pole opposite Jackson's withering corporeality. Thomas's body figured centrally in the staging of his nomination to and confirmation for the Supreme Court. Toni Morrison observes that the *New York Times*'s initial article on President Bush's controversial nominee refers puzzlingly to his accomplishments in weight lifting.[10] She notes further Senator Pete Domenici's confession that he "wanted to find out as best [he] could what [Thomas's] life *from outhouse to the White House* . . . has been like," a substitution of detritus for "home," "birthplace," and "Pinpoint, GA," through which there can be little doubt Domenici aimed to signify both surgically *and* obliquely the matter of race.[11] Of course, few can forget the signal moment of Thomas's embodiment: the pubic hair on a Coke can. Thomas's body figures so excessively in discussions of him that it seems to be everywhere, bursting through his business suit to cover all discussion of his intellectual capacity and judicial ability. Morrison notes the durability of this haunting and ubiquitous black physical presence: "a reference to a black person's body is *de rigueur* in white discourse. . . . The black man's body is voluptuously dwelled upon in biographies about them, journalism on them, remarks about them."[12]

Jackson's dialectical persona and Thomas's oscillation between his mental and his physical ability speak to a collision between a conception of black men as icons, clichés, or shibboleths (i.e., "celebrity"), and one of them as flesh, substance, superabundant embodiment or, crudely, overendowment. Together, Jackson's and Thomas's receding and encroaching corporeality mark the extremes in a field of media representations, extremes for which sports celebrity, arguably, serves as a mediating ballast. The meanings that congeal around Jackson and Thomas express a tension between celebrity and embodiment I mark with the terms *body* and *flesh*. The way television dwells "voluptuously" on Jackson and Thomas, and on black men in general, speaks both to the affinity of television for this particular figuration of blackness and to the internal representational economies of television itself.

Hortense Spillers, in her essay "Mama's Baby, Papa's Maybe: An American Grammar Book," insists on this distinction between *body* and *flesh,* an axiomatic that distinguishes "liberated" from captive subject-positions, respectively.[13] *Body* refers to a second-order domain of metaphor and iconography for which *flesh* provides a first order of distinction. *Flesh,* the "zero degree of social conceptualization that does not escape concealment under the brush of discourse, or the reflexes of iconography," precedes and buttresses *body. Flesh* is the template for the "high crimes" of bondage. It "register[s] the wounding" of New World enslavement in its "seared, divided, ripped-apartness, riveted to the ship's hole, fallen, or 'escaped' overboard." Needless to say, in the experience of Africans and their descendants on Western terrain, the journey from flesh to body, captivity to "freedom," is never clean, surgical, and complete. Flesh haunts body in the guise of "altered human tissue," in the form of "undecipherable markings" that register its own "kind of hieroglyphics." Spillers continues: "Even though the captive flesh/body has been 'liberated,' and no one need pretend that even the quotation marks do not *matter,* dominant symbolic activity, *the ruling episteme* that releases the dynamics of naming and valuation, remains grounded in the originating metaphors of captivity and mutilation so that it is as if *neither time nor history,* nor historiography and its topics, *shows movement,* as the human subject is 'murdered' over and over again by the passions of a bloodless and anonymous archaism, showing itself in endless disguise."[14] Thus, while the body instantiates the mythic meanings congealed around black people in American public discourse (the "American grammar book"), the flesh ruptures such coherencies in the form of a critical memory of captivity, a brush with violence, a tarrying near death. Flesh obstructs the epic and mythic progress of time-in-motion (or its Janus-faced twin, "history or historiography"). Considered in light of Spiller's axiomatic, flesh expresses a writhing corporeality: the condition of incarnate, palpitating, dark, abiding embodiedness. It is peculiarly alive *and* a mere beat short of death. The scene of the flesh registers a temporal arrest or crisis. A riotous embodiedness, it is revealed in all its gory splendor in the time and place where "neither time nor history . . . shows movement." Flesh throbs with the horror of that moment when "time stands still."

The signs of blackness articulate a temporality of crisis or, perhaps more accurately, the representation of crisis as arrested time. Black flesh is soaked to excess with the effluent of time. In turn, moments of crisis, represented as ruptures in the body, appear as eruptions by the flesh; flesh punctures and, in the process, punctuates. Whereas body signifies a tense we might designate "future perfect," flesh signifies an insistent "present-ness."[15] Yet this distinction does not seem adequate to address television's and media's specific interest in black flesh and black bodies. That interest lies in television's unique structuration of time in the twin forms of liveness and crisis. To understand what tethers black male bodies to the apparatus of television we have to assess both the construction of black sports celebrities as unique forms of embodiment and the temporal structures of television.

A Record of Accomplishment

If Michael Jackson and Clarence Thomas represent the extremes of black male bodies, black male sports stars mediate those extremes. Black physical achievement marks a certainty of the flesh *and* a set of physical ideals, a zero degree of physical accomplishment rooted in the body *and* an abstract measure of the human body's potentials. Take, for example, Arthur Ashe's 1975 win at Wimbledon, the first win of a Grand Slam title in tennis by a black man. O. J. Simpson won the Heisman by the largest margin in the trophy's fifty-nine-year history, receiving 82 percent of the first-place votes after setting single-season collegiate records by rushing for 1,654 yards on 394 carries in 1968. He also holds the distinction of running for 2,003 yards in 1973 while playing for the NFL's Buffalo Bills, the first time any player ran in excess of 2,000 yards in a single season. And, as a final example, Michael Jordan's average of 36 shots per game—the highest average in the NBA—secures for him a statistically certain place in basketball's record books.

Ashe's, Simpson's, and Jordan's achievements, as statistical "measurements" of their abilities, can never be taken from them. Neither can they be taken from their fans as a source of their pleasure. But the physical accomplishments of these black athletes appear paradoxical when viewed from the broader vantage point of sports discourse. Statistics function as a physics of the body, as a system that establishes economies of exchange in which "the laws which drive the mechanism [of sport] appear as universally objective as any of Newtonian physics."[16] Statistical knowledge, to cite John Fiske, "individuates, examines, ranks and orders with seductive precision both *extensively*—the scope of the data it can know stretches, literally, to infinity (which it has turned from a mystical concept into a statistical one) —and *intensively* so that there is no detail of our everyday lives too small to be quantified and assessed against a norm." [17] Statistics establish an incontrovertible relationship between individual physical accomplishments and the universal limit of human capacity. Football grids, digital clocks on scoreboards, instruments to measure the speed of pitches and serves, all work to divide the world of sport into spatial and temporal grids "that enable each play and player to be precisely plotted" [18] and registered within a knowledge system, a system of cultural capital that circulates among experts, commentators, and fans alike. Through the vehicles of product sponsorship, fandom, and general media hype, this institution of knowledge production becomes a system of capital production. Knowledge of the unambiguous and quantifiable accomplishments of Ashe, Simpson, Jordan, and others is thus the medium through which they become the "hard currency" in this ever expanding system of value. They are the best kind of currency to have in the market of late-advanced media capital. For, with each triumph and accomplishment, a new horizon of human potential is drawn. We purchase access to this economy in the form of knowledge and on the assumption that these athletes embody *our* potential, that they do our living in the world. As Fiske notes in conclusion, "Knowing is continuous with doing. The investment in knowledge pays its dividends in social life, otherwise knowledge would have no power." [19] In fact, as Pierre Bourdieu has gone on to argue, the very nature of athleticism confirms the profitable exchanges between cultural capital and economic capital.

In his study *Distinction: A Social Critique of the Judgment of Taste*, Bourdieu uses the notion of "the body schema" to designate how economic classes produce ideal, distinct relationships to the body. A body schema is, in his words, "the depository of a whole world view and a whole philosophy of the person and the body." [20] Starting from the assumption that the body is "the most indisputable materialization of class taste," Bourdieu argues that sport functions as a "class's relation to the body at its deepest and most unconscious level." [21] Thus, working-class fans of sport are more "attentive," he claims, to "the strength of the (male) body" and more likely to follow a "practical philosophy of the male body as a sort of power, big and strong, with enormous, imperative, brutal needs." [22] Sports of a "popular" nature that manifest an instrumental relation to the body that emphasizes *youth,* "a high investment in *energy, effort* or even *pain . . .* and which sometimes *endanger*"[23] are less likely than others to offend this body schema. Popular sports are, generally, "credited with a sort of temporary license, expressed, inter alia, in the expending of excess physical (and sexual) energy."[24] Rugby, football, basketball, boxing, motorcycling, automobile racing, and, to some extent, all "contact" sports fall within this category. Working-class sports, Bourdieu adds, manifest an affinity for more popular dispositions and disciplines such as "the cult of manliness and the taste for a fight, toughness in 'contact' and resistance to tiredness and pain," and are sometimes mingled with "an aestheticism of violence and man-to-man combat."[25]

By the same token, sports predisposed to a bourgeois bodily schema express a sense of "the high dignity of the person."[26] Typically bourgeois activities such as tennis, golf, yachting, riding, and swimming reinforce "the indisputable image of [the bourgeois subject as the master of] his own authority, his dignity or his distinction."[27] The motions of the body, Bourdieu observes finally, are accompanied by "a certain breadth of gesture, posture and gait, which manifests by the amount of physical space that is occupied the place occupied in social space."[28]

These class distinctions are not "natural," but are thoroughly palpable. Sports affinities are, like matters of taste more broadly, "a class culture *turned into* nature,"[29] a system that helps to shape the class body. The body is not a material vessel for the ego, but is, more accurately, a system of "sign-bearing [and] sign-wearing";[30] the incorporation (or "embodiment") of a principle of classification, that is, race, gender, or class. What distinguishes class bodies, then, is the perceived measure of benefits that accrue from certain forms of incorporation, and this "profit" distinguishes one body schema from the next. As Bourdieu explains, "the different classes do not agree on the profits expected from sport, be they specific physical profits, such as effects on the external body, like slimness, elegance or visible muscles, and on the internal body, like health or relaxation; or extrinsic profits, such as the social relationships a sport may facilitate, or possible economic and social advantages."[31] Despite crucial differences, then, sport clearly expresses a class-specific understanding of abstract human potential.

Yet, arguably, black male athletes manufacture consent within this system of physical, internal, and extrinsic profits, a system that looks almost too neatly oppositional. O. J. is a football star, one of the best in the sport, and he plays out a working-class relation to sport that emphasizes strength, power, youth, and an almost brutal force. Yet he is also, like a gymnast or an ice skater, adored for his "dazzling displays of speed, power and finesse."[32] Michael Jordan, a basketball star whose singular achievements on the court represent a working-class sport imperative toward "excess physical . . . energy" and a "resistance to tiredness and pain," is also celebrated for managing to have effected a unique "stylization of the body over time and space."[33] Ashe, finally, is remembered fondly for providing his fans, as the title of his memoir suggests, "days of grace." Thus, although in general terms the links between economic capital and cultural capital in sport are not simply metaphoric but part of the material structures that inform the institutions of capitalism, black athletes such as Simpson, Jordan, and Ashe are clear exceptions. As *bodies,* "sign-bearing [and] sign-wearing" entities, Simpson, Jordan, Ashe, and many of their black male peers manifest both an "excess physical (and sexual) energy," a high degree of effort, pain, and danger associated with working-class sport, *and* a dignity, distinction, and breadth of gesture expressive of a command of social space associated with bourgeois sport. Their athletic prowess overcomes rigid class-specific institutions of desire under capitalism. Thus, by the same measure used by Bourdieu but contrary to his established conclusions, black athletes provide race- and class-*neutral* articulations of the limits to human being expressed in the world at large. They are both iconic (bourgeois) and incarnate (working class), metaphoric and sensual.

Richard Dyer makes two astute observations on these matters. First, he notes that black people are "the primary sites where the problem of the body is worked through" in American culture.[34] Black men in sports form a single node in a media web that privileges blackness as embodiedness. Second, Dyer notes that capitalism, and not biology, forms the root of the problem of the body in American culture. "The rhetoric of capitalism," he states, "insists that it is capital that makes things happen."[35] Capitalism's narcissistic emphasis on itself mutes the extent to which human labor and the labor of the body, in particular, really makes things happen. Of this silencing, Dyer notes further: "It is no accident that blacks should figure so crucially in this [capitalist] scheme of things. Through slavery and imperialism, black people have been the social group most clearly identified by and exploited for their bodily labour. Blacks thus became the most vivid reminders of the human body as labour in a society busily denying it. Representations of blacks then function as the site of *remembering and denying* the inescapability of the body in the economy."[36] Thus, any cultural capital that accrues to black athletes for reasons of their blackness, such as superior athletic ability, is immediately leveraged off as the rightful property of the institutions of capital. Black power is siphoned into the domains of capitalist economy. The corporation comes into being in and through the corporeality of black male athletes. Incorporation is the primary corporate use for the black athletic body.

Contrarily, television works to maintain a grip on the flesh. Corporations and their ancillary webs of sponsors, athletic gear chains, and broadcast stations leverage off of blackness in a process both wildly profitable and riddled with danger. Black athletes' physical qualities and the meanings tethered to them must be, in Dyer's words, "deactivated" to function effectively in the racial visual field. "They must not be shown to be effective qualities in the world. Even when portrayed at their most vivid and vibrant, they must not be shown to do anything."[37] Today, television "deactivates" black athletes through the individuating, arresting, ordering work of statistics. Early in this century, however, the media negotiated this relationship to blackness in different ways. The career of the boxer John Arthur "Jack" Johnson displays the contradictions between power and powerlessness, physical prowess and languid celebrity, that operate under the sign "black male" as managed by the visual media.

Jack Johnson was one of the first black prizefighters to do battle with white opponents. In December 1908, Johnson became the first black to rise to the status of world heavyweight champion. From that day forth, numerous white constituencies determined to knock Johnson from that revered pedestal. They resurrected the retired boxer Jim Jeffries as their "Great White Hope." In contrast, Johnson figured in the African American imaginary as something of a "Great Black Hope," a figuration so powerful that on 5 February 1910, the *Chicago Defender,* a black newspaper, would observe unambiguously: "The Future Welfare of His People Forms a Part of the Stake."[38] Later that year, on Independence Day in Reno, Nevada, Johnson destroyed Jeffries while the former was garbed in navy blue trunks with an American flag inserted through the belt loops. Any "hopes" tethered to Jeffries's rise fell in a punishing fifteen-round assault. The next day, the *New York Times* reported numerous lynchings throughout the country. In all, thirteen blacks were killed and hundreds wounded in retaliation for Jeffries's loss. Town councils in Washington, D.C., Atlanta, Baltimore, and elsewhere soon thereafter moved to ban all films of the fight. The U.S. Congress was spurred by the defeat of a white fighter at the hands of a black one to censor boxing movies as a whole genre, voting to ban the films from interstate commerce.[39]

Following the fight, Johnson faced major legal difficulties outside the ring. On 7 November 1912, a grand jury indicted him on charges of violating the Mann Act, an early form of federal interstate commerce law known popularly as the "white slavery law," which made it a crime to transport anyone across state lines for immoral purposes.[40] Johnson's betrothal to Lucille Cameron, the fifth and last in a series of white women with whom he became involved, was the proverbial last straw. Under the provisions of the Mann Act, Johnson was found guilty on 13 May 1913 of three counts of prostitution, two counts of debauchery, three counts of unlawful sexual intercourse, two counts of crimes against nature, and one count of inducement to prostitution.

The pivotal moment in the construction of a calibrated visibility around Jack Johnson's image came at the moment when the U.S. Congress attempted to halt all traffic in his image. Many had longed to censor boxing movies for some time, yet it took the defeat of a white man by a black man to mobilize these desires for censorship. This suggests a great deal about the racial dynamics of the time, but it suggests as well the degree to which Johnson's physical accomplishments exceeded the capacity of the technology of cinema to "handle," manage, calibrate, and domesticate the representation of blackness. Johnson's physical accomplishments had reached a point where they continued to seem wildly profitable, vivid and vibrant, yet began increasingly to signify in potentially dangerous ways, ways that did a great deal of ideological work for himself and for his black fans, if not for others. Johnson's body began to signify in excessive and chaotic ways, spinning uncontrollably beyond his corporeal self, to the point that, following his triumph over Jeffries, the law emerged to halt interstate traffic both in his image and in the white women he was alleged of "stealing." *Traffic* signifies doubly in this case, for the attempts to bring Johnson's sexuality to a halt, criminalizing his desire for white women by marking it as "prostitution" and "debauchery," arrest prosthetically his violent physical threat, the dangerous iconography he makes available from the space of the ring. Johnson presents a knotted mass of sexuality and violence, a twinned embodiment of celebrity and crisis. In the management of his image, the signification of black male physical achievement as a Janus-faced embodiment of pleasure and threat begins to come into focus.

Johnson appears both to provide an abstract measure of human accomplishment and to pose a live, dangerous, and violent threat. When he appears in the latter guise, the film media functions as the tool of his domestication. His career at the limits of film media is admittedly more pertinent to a discussion of cinema in the early twentieth century, but it also urges us to investigate the medium of television and the contemporary phenomenon of black sports celebrity. Though O. J., Tyson, Ashe, Magic, and their peers occupy a different historical time and space, they too are celebrated for reaching physical peaks that extend the limits of human possibility, and their accomplishments become the measure (at moments of crisis) of the limits to their "human being." This slippage between their celebrity and their human being led one reporter to ask of O. J.: "[W]ho ever thought of O. J. as a mere human being? He was much too big for that, too big by now for the television screen that had created the O. J. who came to bestride the medium itself." [41] For black male athletes, the limits to their celebrity harmonize with the limits to television, and both limits signify the border between life and death. Without the life-giving gaze of television, celebrities "die."

The Moment of Crisis

Media theorists Beverle Houston, Jane Feuer, Robert Stam, and Mary Ann Doane have argued that television, in the pursuit of epistemological guarantees unique among those of competing technologies such as cinema and radio, emphasizes liveness, "flow," and immediacy. [42] Television's primary mode, Feuer observes, is one of absolute presence, a mode in which representations appear to be lived (to be alive) precisely for not being ostensibly *re*-presentations. Televisual presence results from the medium's ability to transmit and record simultaneously. "Live television is *not* recorded," Feuer observes ironically, "live television is *alive,* television is living, real, not dead." To watch television is thus to be sutured into its " 'imaginary' of presence and immediacy." [43] Houston proposes, in addition, that television's liveness is tethered to its domesticity; its powers of expressive simultaneity are the product of a "coextensiveness" or physical proximity: "Not only does [TV] lean on the world's body—that is to say, in its liveness—but it is available domestically at all moments—that is to say, in its *livedness.*" [44] The televisual apparatus, Robert Stam adds, not only limns its unique relationship to liveness to its equally unique claims on the domestic sphere, but it also "prosthetically extends human perception, granting an exhilarating sense of visual power to its virtually 'all-perceiving' spectator, stretched to the limit in the pure act of watching."[45] Television spectators thus find their ideal surrogate in the television camera itself, which is, in many ways, "the instrument of [their] presence, the viewer's presence."[46]

Mary Ann Doane captures the essence of much of this work when she observes simply that "[t]he major category of television is time. Time is television's basis, its principle of structuration, as well as its persistent reference."[47] Doane extends the interventions of Feuer, Houston, and Stam with regard to liveness to claim not only that television manages "an insistent 'present-ness' — a *This-is-going-on* . . . a celebration of the instantaneous" but that, largely inevitably, television maintains "an intimate relation with the ideas of death and referentiality [through] the potential trauma and explosiveness of the present."[48] Thus, television's investment in liveness means ultimately that the specter of death haunts the medium at every moment.

Death appears in numerous guises, the most obvious of which is television's oft-noted fascination with violence and crisis. Crises such as hijackings, drive-by shootings, and suicide bombings signify in Doane's formulation as "condensation[s] of temporality," situations that demand resolution "and hence always see[m] to suggest the necessity of human agency."[49] The monotonous reportage that accompanies such human-rendered scenes of mass destruction as the World Trade Center bombing, the Waco assault, and the Oklahoma City bombing reveal how centrally human crisis figures in the construction of tele-visual and spectatorial pleasure. A second guise is the catastrophe. Into this category fall more technologically oriented disasters such as airline crashes, nuclear accidents, and oil and chemical spills. A third, less obvious guise for the specter of death is the threat of "dead television" itself or the fear that the tech-nology will break down — a suspicion that television's flows will be interrupted, causing viewers to be cut off from the steady stream of daily "newsworthy" events that Doane calls "information." There is an even deeper connection be-tween death and the "break" in technological advance. Doane observes: "The time of technological progress is always felt as linear and fundamentally ir-reversible. . . . [T]echnological evolution is perceived as unflinching progress toward a state of control over nature. If some notion of pure Progress is the utopian element in this theory of technological development, catastrophe is its dystopia."[50] "For all its ideology of 'liveness,'" Doane concludes, "it may be death which forms the point of televisual intrigue."[51] Catastrophe, in both its technological and human form, embodies concern with the body and the encounter with death. Catastrophe represents the disruptive nature (the "flesh"?) technology has long been instituted to repress and control.

These issues of life and death, "liveness" and "dead TV," frequently congeal around the signifier of race. By the most abstract conceptual schemas, to experience television's liveness or, better yet, its "livedness," one needs, to paraphrase Lauren Berlant, to experience another's body, to wear another body "like a prosthesis."[52] This surreptitious, vicarious occupation of a body not one's own is in large measure, and certainly within Western epistemes, the reigning experience of otherness we call race. The phenomena of crossover and of passing are useful paradigms for such moments when cultural marginality translates into a vicarious embodiment. This embodiment is also characterized by the experience of otherness we call celebrity. Through celebrity, fans escape their own lives and troubles by participating in their celebrities' lives and troubles, and they find in the latter's omnipotence and invincibility "the promise that [they], too, have a crack at immortality."[53] Moreover, in terms of black athletic prowess, the more black flesh is marked as "alive" and a figure in television's presentation of its own "liveness," televisual blackness distinguishes the living from the dead, the animate from the inanimate, and live TV from dead TV. Blackness marks the limit beyond which lies nothing but dead TV, a collapsed and failed technology, pure and unimaginable absence. Blackness orients television's phenomenology of limits.

Our celebration of Simpson's, Jordan's, Ashe's, and Tyson's accomplishments fits neatly (and with good reason) into this conceptualization of race and time in the space of television. The gridding, ordering, and individuation that occur beneath the lens of instant replays, slow and attenuated motion, and the abstract measure of statistics provide assessments of their bodily motions that calibrate them to the ordered, rhythmic, measured flows of television itself. Statistics correlate the motions of the "body" with the temporal and spatial frameworks of television. Our knowledge of the extreme limit to the number of yards O. J. can run, the number of shots Jordan can make, and the number of serves Ashe can return, domesticates (or, in the words of Richard Dyer, "deactivates") their potential threat. On the field, on the court, or in the ring, black "bodies" are shown at their most "vivid and vibrant,"[54] but they are also shown to lack any power beyond the arena of sport and out in the world. Their accomplishments form part of television's banal, steady stream of "information" and buttress its structuration of time as steady, continuous, and ordered.

Yet, Jordan's "addiction," Tyson's predations, O. J.'s alleged murderous ram-page, Ashe's diagnosis, and Magic's sexual exploits—the traumas of the *flesh* that are AIDS, date rape, addiction, spousal abuse, and homicide—remind us again, yet in a different manner, of the correspondence between black sports celebrity and the mechanisms of television. As their physicality made them more "alive" to us than perhaps we were to ourselves, their crises also brought them much closer to death. Ashe has already, sadly, passed away. Tyson, O. J., and Magic all seem to be tarrying nearer to death, both real and metaphoric, than the rest of us. Jordan's father, in many ways, died *in his son's place* and in-sulated Jordan himself from a close brush with flesh and death. Jordan's come-back from retirement (a sort of "little death") is evidence of this evasion.[55] And it is not without due cause that these athletes' crises have been haunted by the specter of death. As I argued above, the moment of the flesh's revelation, the node where "time stands still" against its "swift and imperceptible" flowing or when (in Spillers's words) "neither time nor history . . . shows movement," warns of the proximity of (in Doane's phrasing) "death . . . [in the guise of] the potential trauma and explosiveness of the present." Our "livid" and "volup-tuous" interest in these black athletes' falls from grace and celebrity maintains a precise, if unspoken, relation between our understanding of their achieve-ments and their place within our collective media unconscious.

Notes

1 Lorraine Hansberry, *Variety*, 27 May 1959, 16; quoted in Richard Dyer, *Heavenly Bodies: Film Stars and Society* (New York: St. Martin's Press, 1986), 137.

2 Frank Rich, "Addicted to O. J.," *New York Times*, 23 June 1994, sec.A.

3 Ibid.

4 Ibid.

5 Fred Exley, a lifelong fan of the New York Giants, testifies to football's ability to help him overcome a deadening sense of separation from others in his world. "Why did football bring me to life?" he queries. "I can't say precisely. Part of it was my feeling that football was an island of directness in a world of circumspection." Watching the Giants play on TV, he was able to join in the game and "took high swimming passes over [his] right shoulder and troddled [*sic*], dipsy-doodle-like, into the endzone." John Fiske contends, based on Exley's remarks, that popular culture provides peaks of intense experience when spectators identify with their bodies' external conditions, shaking the body "free from the repressive difference between *their* [the players'] control and *our* sense of our identity." "When our indi-

viduality, our bodies and our immediate environment are experienced as a unity, we feel free. We feel free because this unity is a sign that we have shaken our locale free from their control and made it, however temporarily, our own at last" (Exley quoted in John Fiske, *Power Plays, Power Works* [London: Verso, 1993], 89).

6   Cited in Walter Goodman, "Television, Meet Life. Life, Meet TV," *New York Times*, 19 June 1994, sec. 4.

7   Ibid., sec. 6.

8   Robert McG. Thomas Jr., "Fleeing Poverty, He Ran to Limelight," *New York Times*, 18 June 1994, sec. A.

9   Add to O. J.'s difficulties the charges of spousal abuse against the baseball star Darryl Strawberry, the basketball star Moses Malone, and the boxer Sugar Ray Leonard and one begins to see that he is not alone in his troubles. Strawberry admitted beating his wife and pointing a gun in her face. Malone was accused by his wife of physical and verbal brutality. And Leonard's wife, Juanita Leonard, testified in divorce court that he punched her, threw her around, and harassed her "physically and mentally in front of the children." See Mariah Burton Nelson, "Bad Sports," *New York Times*, 22 June 1994, sec. A.

   This paper was written before Simpson's acquittal on charges of murder on 3 October 1995. Since that time, many have come to doubt the significance and effect of the discussions of spousal abuse that flourished in the months following his indictment.

10 Toni Morrison, introduction to *Race-ing Justice, En-gendering Power: Essays on Anita Hill, Clarence Thomas, and the Construction of Social Reality* (New York: Pantheon, 1992), xiii.

11 Ibid., xiv; emphasis added. As Kendall Thomas observes in the same publication, the Thomas-Hill hearings were soaked to excess with "the metaphorics of dirt" and "associated figures of pollution, contamination, and defilement" (377). And few groups, he notes, have been as thoroughly assigned the status of filthiness as blacks. The blackness of black skin, Thomas adds, "has been fused with the idea of dirt, and more generally, with the image of anything that can pass out of the body, such as feces" (385). See Kendall Thomas, "Strange Fruit," in Toni Morrison, ed., *Race-ing Justice*, 364–389. See also Joel Kovel, *White Racism: A Psychohistory* (New York: Columbia University Press, 1984), and Mary Douglas, *Purity and Danger: An Analysis of Concepts of Pollution and Taboo* (New York: Routledge, 1991).

12 Morrison, xiv.

13 Hortense Spillers, "Mama's Baby, Papa's Maybe: An American Grammar Book," *Diacritics* 17, no. 2 (summer 1987): 65–81; quotes that follow are from p. 67.

14 Ibid., 68; emphasis added.

15 On the tenses of mechanical and electronic reproduction, see Mary Ann Doane,

"Information, Crisis, Catastrophe," in *Logics of Television: Essays in Cultural Criticism,* ed. Patricia Mellencamp (Bloomington: Indiana University Press, 1990), 222.

16 Fiske, 83.

17 Ibid.

18 Ibid.

19 Ibid., 85.

20 Pierre Bourdieu, *Distinction: A Social Critique of the Judgment of Taste,* trans. Richard Nice (Cambridge, MA: Harvard University Press, 1984), 218.

21 Ibid., 190, 218.

22 Ibid., 190, 192.

23 Ibid., 212–213; emphasis added.

24 Ibid., 212.

25 Ibid., 213.

26 Ibid., 218.

27 Ibid.

28 Ibid. Though he riddles his analyses with masculinist and biologistic biases, Bourdieu provides a number of incontrovertible statistics to buttress his argument. As one example, he produces some rather persuasive numbers on the matter of class variations in sports activities and opinions on sport. When asked if they would like their children to become sports champions, manual workers in his sample responded positively 61 percent of the time, whereas professionals did so only 33 percent of the time. Or, when asked if they have ever regularly practiced any sport, manual workers responded positively 48 percent of the time, whereas professionals did so 22 percent of the time. Yet, when asked if they regularly practiced tennis, manual workers responded positively 1.5 percent of the time and professionals 15.5 percent of the time. For the same constituencies, the numbers were 2.5 percent versus 10 percent for swimming, and 6 percent versus 4 percent for football, working versus professional classes, respectively.

29 Ibid., 190; emphasis added.

30 Ibid., 192.

31 Ibid., 211.

32 Thomas, 11.

33 James Ledbetter, "Cornell U.," *Vibe* (September 1993): 66.

34 Dyer, 138.

35 Ibid.

36 Ibid., 138–139.

37 Ibid., 115.

38 Details of the Johnson-Jeffries fight are taken from Arthur Ashe's *A Hard Road to Glory* (New York: Warner Books, 1988), 30–42.

39   Daniel Leab, *From Sambo to Superspade: The Black Experience in Motion Pictures* (Boston: Houghton Mifflin, 1975), 18; Thomas Cripps, *Slow Fade to Black: The Negro in American Film, 1900–1942* (New York: Oxford University Press, 1977), 18.

40   Ashe, 40.

41   Goodman, sec. 4.

42   Much of the media studies work on television has focused on the technology's immediacy, which is figured, alternately, through the concepts of "liveness" (e.g., Feuer, Stam, Heath, and Skirrow), "presence" (e.g., Houston) or "*flow*" (e.g., Williams). For pivotal articulations of these concepts, see Raymond Williams, *Television: Technology and Cultural Form* (New York: Schocken Books, 1974); Jane Feuer, "The Concept of Live Television: Ontology as Ideology," in *Regarding Television,* ed. E. Ann Kaplan (Frederick, MD: University Publications of America, 1983), 12–21; Beverle Houston, "Viewing Television: The Metapsychology of Endless Consumption," *Quarterly Review of Film Studies* 9, no. 3 (summer 1984): 183–195; Robert Stam, "Television News and Its Spectator," in *Regarding Television,* 23–40; Stephen Heath and Gillian Skirrow, "Television: A World in Action," *Screen* 18, no. 2 (summer 1977): 7–59; and Doane, 222–239.

43 . Feuer, 14.

44   Houston, 184.

45   Stam, 24.

46   Paolo Carpignano, Robin Anderson, Stanley Aronowitz, and William DiFazio, "Chatter in the Age of Electronic Reproduction: Talk Television and the 'Public Mind,'" in *The Phantom Public Sphere,* ed. Bruce Robbins (Minneapolis: University of Minnesota Press, 1993), 109.

47   Doane, 222.

48   Ibid.

49   Ibid., 223.

50   Ibid., 230–231.

51   Ibid., 233.

52   Lauren Berlant, "National Brands/National Body: 'Imitation of Life,'" in *Comparative American Identities: Race, Sex, and Nationality in the Modern Text,* ed. Hortense Spillers (New York: Routledge, 1991), 111.

53   Rich, 1.

54   Dyer, 115.

55   I thank Sasha Torres for suggesting this idea.

HERE COMES THE JUDGE

The Dancing Itos and the Televisual Construction

of the Enemy Asian Male

Brian Locke

If for nothing else, Lance Ito will be remembered as the presiding judge in the 1995 O. J. Simpson murder trial. This third-generation Japanese American son of wwii internees directed the proceedings of the most extensively covered criminal trial in U.S. history. Consequently, Ito seemed to be everywhere on television during the trial. Court TV and CNN devoted several hours of programming a day to its ongoing coverage. In addition, his figure, a stern face behind his glasses, mustache, and beard, surfaced in the program lineups of both news and entertainment television.

Like any celebrity in the news, Ito became the butt of countless topical jokes, especially on late-night talk shows. This humor suggested vaguely that Ito may have been hiding something beneath his robes; the jokes of guests and hosts expressed a desire to investigate and expose what hid underneath the black judicial wrapper. On one episode of NBC's *The Tonight Show with Jay Leno,* the host asked the African American comedian, George Wallace, to voice his opinion about Ito, and he responded with the punchline, "You know, he's really naked under there." *The Tonight Show*'s late-night CBS rival, *The Late Show with David Letterman,* also participated. A "Top Ten List" from early February 1995, "Ways to Annoy Judge Ito," included the following two entries: "Pull robe over head. Spin. Push into street," and "Ask permission to have a television camera in his pants."

The Village Itos.
The Can-Can Itos

During the spring of 1995, *The Tonight Show* repeatedly televised its own fantasy of Ito, providing ample opportunity to peek underneath the judge's robes. In these skits, the show presented the Dancing Itos, a troupe of a half-dozen smiling men performing standard chorus-line routines. The dancers were marked as Judge Ito by their long black judicial robes, straight black hair parted on the side, glasses with thick lenses, and exaggerated black mustache and beard. In addition to these costumes, the Dancing Itos also impersonated well-known dancing groups such as the 1970s gay disco band, the Village People, and Parisienne can-can dancers.

Both of these impersonations relied on exposure for their comedic power. In their routine, "The Village Itos" lip-synch and dance to the tune of the band's signature pop song, "YMCA," here rewritten as "OJ LA." They begin the dance in a single-file line, then move into wedge formation with the lead dancer at the apex, nearest to the camera and the audience. At the climactic moment, the lead dancer reaches down to the hem of his robe and pulls it up over his head to reveal his crotch, gyrating his hips wildly. On a subsequent episode, "The Can-Can Itos" cartwheel onto the stage, then move into a single-file line, shoulder to shoulder. Their costumes resemble those of French chorus-line dancers except that their skirts are judicial-robe black. After doing the splits and rolling backwards *ensemble,* they bend over, flip up their skirts, and expose their rear ends to the audience.[1]

The Dancing Ito skits proved to be very popular. During the introductions to most performances, Leno mentioned the unusually high home audience response, once stating, "We've gotten thousands of letters asking when they'd be back!" And in the studio, the audience response was clearly ecstatic. As the band played lively music, the cameras panned an audience clapping in rhythm. The finales of each routine pushed the audience to scream with satisfaction. Usually Leno appeared unable to contain his own laughter, hopping and twisting his body as he announced the night's guest and cut to commercials. During one appearance, the camera focused upon a young Asian man amidst the gaiety who, laughing and clapping with the rest of the audience, smiled and waved to the home viewer.

This essay will analyze these and other representations of Lance Ito from several episodes of *The Tonight Show*. In doing so, it seeks to disrupt the black-and-white binary of contemporary racial discourse in the United States by showing how visual markers of "Asianness" play a central role in these representations. While it serves as a tacit critical comment upon more traditional paradigms of visual and televisual theory that do not take race into account, let alone racial constructions that fall outside of the duality that predominates racial discourse, at the same time it engages the issues of race and representation without trying to explicate exactly what constitutes Asians and Asianness. Instead, this essay uses the figure of Lance Ito to illustrate how certain depictions of Asian and Asian American men have been constructed by, and deployed in, U.S. mass culture.

An interview with Jay Leno's original bandleader, Branford Marsalis, helps to explain how television deploys race to fit its programming needs and in turn establishes a critical context for reading the show's representations of Ito. Marsalis came to *The Tonight Show* with considerable recognition and appeal. Prior to his arrival, Marsalis had established himself as one of the most critically acclaimed saxophonists in jazz circles. Furthermore, by touring with popular rock singers like Sting and acting in Spike Lee's movie, *Mo' Better Blues,* he became one of the most recognizable musicians in jazz.

Jazz connotes spontaneity, agility, and cool — all traits sought by *The Tonight Show.* As a predominately African American cultural production, jazz is deeply inflected by race. This connection between race and jazz became a significant factor in *The Tonight Show*'s quest to win the late-night talk show contest for ratings. Race played a central role in the decision to move from Doc Severinson, the white male jazz bandleader under Johnny Carson, to Marsalis, an African American, a decision that transpired in the midst of a ratings war with two other late-night talk shows. *The Late Show with David Letterman* made its successful debut on CBS on August 30, 1993, consistently garnering the highest weekly ratings of the three. At the same time, Fox's *Arsenio Hall Show,* hosted by the brash and confident African American comedian, appealed to the principal late-night target demographic of eighteen- to thirty-four-year-olds. When Hall's show went off the air in May 1994, NBC sought Hall's ex-viewers, using Marsalis as a lure. According to one NBC insider, the network was "desperate to hang on to him" because, "with Arsenio gone, and Letterman kicking butt in the ratings war, Branford is the hippest thing they have going for them. They may not understand him, but they sure don't want to let him go."[2] Both as a black man and a jazz musician, Marsalis was a hip television commodity.

For Marsalis, however, the show's use of his "jazzy blackness" had other, unintended effects. For example, Marsalis felt that the show failed to incorporate jazz successfully. Whereas jazz requires spontaneity, television counts on predictable dialogue, rehearsed audience participation, and tight on-air scheduling. Discussing the contradictions that arise when jazz is folded into the production of a television talk show, Marsalis explains, "People who work in television seem to believe that you can successfully *can* spontaneity, and open it up any time you feel like it. Real spontaneity drives a lot of TV people crazy, because it kind of usurps *their* authority."[3] The show sought to capture the spontaneity of jazz to provide a hip aura that would attract viewers, yet the show could not be truly spontaneous, for real spontaneity is antithetical to a predictable televisual product. Instead, *The Tonight Show* relied on the appearance of spontaneity, signified by the presence of Marsalis.

In addition, although the genre of the talk show seeks to evoke the impression that dialogue is spontaneous, real spontaneity would threaten to usurp the authority of the host, as Marsalis's comments suggest. *The Tonight Show* host's authority rests upon his ability to appear confident, agile, and witty. The host's affectation of this style, in turn, is contingent upon prior knowledge of what will happen on the show. Therefore, a rough plan for the dialogue is constructed prior to shooting, with the explicit purpose of making the host look as if he is conversing spontaneously. Yet, the real spontaneity upon which jazz thrives can be highly disruptive in a talk show setting.

This is especially true when real spontaneity is coupled with the bristly topic of race. A visit by a *Tonight Show* guest in early April 1995 illustrates such disruptions and reveals the presumptions about race upon which the show relies. After a Dancing Itos routine, stand-up comedian Jack Cohen appears and tells a series of jokes dealing with sensitive topics: gun control, treatment of the elderly, the misogyny of divorced husbands, the Jeffrey Dahmer murder trial. The white comedian's material also explores issues of race in general and the Simpson trial in particular: black solidarity with Simpson, black people and criminality, racism in the Los Angeles Police Department and in the criminal justice system.

Despite the topicality of the material, neither Leno's monologue nor Cohen's routine included the biggest news at that time regarding race and the trial. Only a day before, the media had been abuzz with a story concerning Ito and Alphonse D'Amato, a Republican senator from New York and the chair of the Whitewater hearings. Two days prior to Cohen's appearance, D'Amato was interviewed by nationally syndicated radio talk show host Don Imus. During the live broadcast, D'Amato had complained about the duration of the Simpson trial and its potentially disruptive impact on the hearings; he called Ito an egomaniac, dubbed his performance "a disgrace," and blamed him for dragging out the trial unnecessarily.[4] Whereas these comments were not particularly remarkable, the stereotypical "Oriental" accent he used to imitate the judge was. The radio listener could easily imagine the senator's face during the interview, squinting his eyes and speaking through top front teeth stretched over his lower lip, simulating the slanty eyes and buck teeth of the stereotypical Asian man of popular American cultural production.[5] The story of the senator's racial slur surfaced on the front pages of major newspapers the next morning.

Although it is not unusual that Cohen's practiced routine would fail to mention D'Amato's slur, it seems very unusual that Leno would fail to mention the day's hot political story. Prior to coming to *The Tonight Show,* Leno had made a name for himself as a political comedian. Furthermore, the show relies consistently on topical news like the Simpson trial for much of its comedic content, especially for the introductory monologue. This particular episode was no exception; nearly half of the jokes in a nine-minute monologue revolved around the trial, including several about Ito. Clearly, D'Amato's slur was somehow too fraught for the show.

In Leno's postperformance chat with Cohen, the reason behind this structuring absence becomes clear. When Leno asks his first question, "Do you ever worry about hurting anybody's feelings?" Cohen responds, "I don't worry about it much because we're comics. . . . It's not like we're . . . senators." Immediately, Cohen's brief reference to D'Amato's racial slur disrupts the show. As Leno leans back in his chair and replies monosyllabically, Cohen retorts, "How stupid! Did you see that?" pushing Leno to explain the reference to the audience. Leno improvises awkwardly, "Oh . . . D'Amato . . . He did his . . . Alphonse D'Amato, he did his . . . impression of Judge Ito . . . the most racist thing."

Cohen's unexpected reference to D'Amato and Leno's shaky response illuminate an insoluble contradiction. The show wants to include the popular Dancing Itos, yet the naked racial aggression of D'Amato's recent slur makes such an inclusion a very tricky matter. Had Leno mentioned the slur, the juxtaposition of the slur and the Dancing Itos skit would have threatened to expose *The Tonight Show*'s own televisual "impression of Judge Ito" as equivalent to D'Amato's "most racist thing" — a point not lost on Cohen. Laughing at Leno's efforts to contain the damage, Cohen responds, "Yeah. Too bad he didn't have a robe and was dancing. He would have been all right." Once again, Leno flounders; the band plays its punchline tag; the audience starts to clap and hoot.

In this brief moment, the spontaneity of Cohen's astonishing joke usurps Leno's televisual authority as host. Just as quickly, Cohen realizes that he has made Leno look bad and strives to repair the damage himself, although it seems that he is too late:

> c: You know I'm going to get in trouble because they told me . . .
> l: You got me on that one. Man, you nailed me on that one.
> c: They told me not to do it, too . . .
> l: No. That's a great joke.
> c: They're all panicky. "Don't. Don't. Don't say that."
> l: So you don't come back. Who cares?
> c: I'm sorry.
> l: But very funny stuff.
> c: Thanks Jay.
> l: Very funny stuff. Jack Cohen, ladies and gentlemen.

Asserting his role as the host who determines which guests return and which are banished, Leno regains his momentarily lost authority. Yet, in the exchange, Cohen's flustered responses reveal that the show is deeply threatened by the spontaneous eruption of race.

Cohen's surprise jokes about D'Amato question the innocence of the Dancing Itos and translate the show's discourse into terms that are explicitly racial. This translation, in turn, provides insights into the structure of contemporary racial discourse of which the D'Amato event and *The Tonight Show* are symptomatic. In the political atmosphere of the mid-1990s, D'Amato would surely not have characterized an African American on national radio in such terms. Such a slur would have hailed our commonsense notion of what counts as race, and therefore as racism, in a much more familiar way. In turn, the polarized black-and-white structure of racial discourse renders the status of any position that is neither "black" nor "white" more uncertain, or at times even invisible, as a racial position. The structure of racial discourse thus creates a space in which *The Tonight Show* can deploy a racist parody without invoking the vexing issue of race or provoking charges of racism.

Cohen's jokes expose the show's rules regarding the inscription of race. The show needs race in the form of the Dancing Itos or Marsalis's jazzy persona, but it must also dictate the ways in which race is deployed. As it turns out, Marsalis failed to meet one requirement for the job. Apparently, he did not smile often enough at work. As Marsalis put it, "[A] lot of times when Jay says something to me I'll retort, but I won't smile when I do it—much to Jay's chagrin."[6] Frequently, when Leno made a joke, the camera cut to Marsalis and found him unsmiling, an abrupt arrest of the show's televisual attempt to appear spontaneous. In this way, Marsalis threatened, rather than solidified, the show's crucial element of spontaneity.

Much has been made about this reported lack of on-camera accord between the white host and the black bandleader. In *The Late Shift: Letterman, Leno, and the Network Battle for the Night,* one of the show's executives comments, "Marsalis always looked as though he regretted in some way being in the studio."[7] Similarly, James Wolcott, the television critic for *The New Yorker,* claims that Marsalis "begrudged every smile for fear it might betray the rich legacy of jazz."[8] Contrary to Wolcott, I would argue that Marsalis's reluctance to smile has more to do with a concern regarding the history of African Americans than the betrayal of jazz. The smile connotes agreement. It smoothes the contours and ensures the easy flow of the televisual talk show interaction by letting the interlocutor know that things are as they should be. Marsalis implies that he would smile if he thought something was funny. A smile that is compulsory on the set of *The Tonight Show,* however, is too reminiscent of a long American tradition of compulsory smiling to fool those who dominate you. That is to say, systems of domination such as slavery often gave African Americans no option except to visually signify agreement with a smile, even if in truth there is no agreement at all. Marsalis's terms of participation reserved the right to refuse such agreement.

A smile on the lips of the bandleader also connotes a willingness to play the role of the sidekick. We can understand the show's terms of racial inclusion by considering the function of the colored sidekick. From Tonto and the Lone Ranger to Kato and the Green Hornet, the racialized sidekick performs in a way that supports the notion of the superiority of whiteness. Race

Eubanks's "real smile"

is thereby included, but the figure must behave as a willing subordinate to the white hero. After taking his leave, Marsalis commented on *The Tonight Show*'s terms of racial inclusion and subordination, focusing on the African American man who replaced him as band director, Kevin Eubanks, another critically acclaimed though less recognizable jazz musician: "The show's going to take a different direction, probably for the better, with Kevin Eubanks as the bandleader. For one thing, you can see his teeth. My top lip is too long. Look. See what I mean? My top lip is at least an inch-and-a-half over my teeth. But Kevin, he's got a real smile. So he'll do fine."[9]

By comparing Eubanks's smile and his own lack of one, Marsalis indicates that *The Tonight Show* codes blackness in explicitly stereotypical visual terms. Marsalis remarks that his own smile is inadequate, ridiculing the show by revealing how it appropriates a common stereotype about the physiognomy of Africans and African Americans. He states that his lips are too big and prevent him from giving a proper smile on the set, whereas Eubanks will "do fine" because of his "real smile." As it turned out, Marsalis's prophesy regarding Eubanks came true: since Marsalis left the show, virtually every exchange with Leno has Eubanks smiling and laughing. Even without cutaways, the viewer can hear quite well his laughter from the offscreen bandstand.

The visual marker of Eubanks's "real smile" helps to explain how the show desires race, and provides an approach for understanding the Dancing Itos and other representations of Asianness. When forced to describe the racial aspects of the Dancing Itos, however, one runs into a paradox. If the figures somehow convey Ito's status as a person of Japanese ancestry, then one would expect to find scrutable markers of Asianness. But at first glance, one is hard-pressed to find any; it is not immediately clear how the representations deploy race. Nearly every part of the body is covered, most notably the face. Indeed, the costuming hides a key facial detail, for the viewer cannot see the shape of the dancers' eyes. Because the glasses reflect the glare of the stage lights, two bouncing circles of brightness usually fill the spaces where the eyes should be. The eyewear overshadows the one physiognomic aspect that most typically serves as a foundation for the stereotypical visual establishment of Asianness: eyes with epicanthic folds.

The costuming gives the overall impression that the Itos hide themselves deliberately, make themselves inscrutable: the eyeglasses, the thick black mustache and beard look like a mask. This easily recognizable mask corresponds to the show's interest in exposing. The Dancing Itos become flashers, lifting their robes to wild applause. But what is the link between Ito's representation, inscrutability, and the fascination with exposure? Initially, it is difficult to make the case that race plays a significant role in *The Tonight Show*'s representation of Ito because the Dancing Itos' costumes tend to obscure visual markers of race. But, as John Fiske explains, in a culture that purports to be color-blind, racial signifieds are often expressed through signifiers that, at first glance, seem to have no connection to issues of race.[10] This strategy of recoding allows the producer of the sign to refute easily any charges of malicious racial intent. Thus armed, the show can convey Marsalis's blackness, for example, through the signifier of music, a category not necessarily read as explicitly racial. Similarly, *The Tonight Show* recodes race in the case of the Dancing Itos. Rather than accepting Ito's inscrutability as a marker of the impossibility of reading race into the representations, we must instead *read* that inscrutability as a racial signifier.

In fact, the signifier has a long history. Asians have been coded in U.S. popular culture as a threat, a people who keep their motives and means well hidden. Bret Harte's 1870 poem, "That Heathen Chinee," represents an earlier version of this view.[11] Characterizing "Chinese cheap labor" as possessing "dark ways" that hide "vain tricks," the poem is a thinly veiled warning to Americans about a Yellow Peril overwhelming the nation via our western shores. Similarly, the figure of Dr. Fu Manchu, the evil genius and namesake of Sax Rohmer's popular series of dime-store novels of the 1930s, evokes the inscrutable Asian; the difficulty of fighting the doctor stems from the inability of any Westerner to fathom his brilliant, but twisted, Chinese mind.

When China became an ally of the United States with the advent of wwii, anti-Japanese sentiment blossomed and required a reconsideration of the signifiers of Asianness. Shortly after Pearl Harbor, federal authorities began drawing up plans to intern every person of Japanese ancestry living on the West

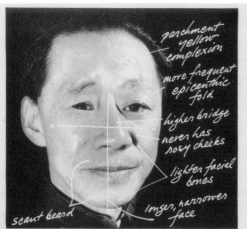
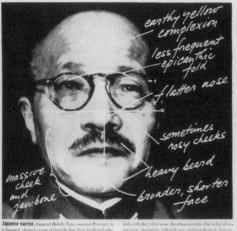

"How to Tell Japs from Chinese"

Coast, regardless of the specifics of citizenship, nativity, or status as resident aliens prohibited by law from U.S. naturalization. Despite the fact that the Axis alliance included other countries, persons with ancestral ties to Germany and Italy were never seriously considered for federal relocation, forced or not. America feared sabotage by the loyal subjects of the Emperor of Japan. Even if U.S. citizens of Japanese ancestry behaved as if they were loyal to the United

States, many assumed that such loyalty was merely a cover for sinister motives.[12]

The new political culture dictated a rehabilitation of the Chinese character. Two weeks after Pearl Harbor in December 1941, stories appeared in two national newsmagazines, *Time* and *Life,* about the need to distinguish between Chinese and Japanese people, between friend and enemy Asians. These articles reveal that the signs of Japaneseness, the connection between certain visual signifiers and the signifieds of inscrutability and threat, have remained remarkably stable over the years, despite vastly different historical contexts. Both articles conflate nationality and race, and they rely on physical anthropology's central premise that different national/racial groups can be distinguished by examining the body for unique physical signifiers. The articles state that precise knowledge of these signifiers equips one to distinguish between individual foes and allies.

Both articles deploy physiognomy as a key strategy for finding the truth of national/racial identity.[13] *Time*'s "How to Tell Your Friends from the Japs" asserts that "[t]hose who know them best often rely on facial expression to tell them apart" and tells us exactly what to look for: "the Chinese expression is likely to be more . . . open" than the Japanese, implying that the latter hide their intentions by hiding their faces. Facial hair figures prominently as well. The *Time* article holds that the "Chinese, not as hairy as the Japanese, seldom grow an impressive mustache."[14] The *Life* article asserts that Chinese exhibit a "scant beard," whereas a "heavy beard" marks one as Japanese.[15]

Finally, the articles emphasize the eyes. If one can examine only the face, *Time* states, then the only scrutable marker for Japanese identity is the "almond-eye[s]."[16] The article notes their importance: "[s]ome aristocratic Japanese have thin, aquiline noses, narrow faces and, except for their eyes, look like Caucasians." Furthermore, *Time* claims that "[m]ost Chinese avoid horn-rimmed glasses."[17] To reinforce this point, the *Life* article includes a photograph of the Japanese premier and general Hideki Tojo wearing horn-rimmed glasses, whereas the Chinese man in the photo directly above does not.[18]

Taken together, the articles warn that the enemy Japanese will try to hide their racial otherness and identity by hiding their eyes. Indeed, were it not for the eyes, these "aristocratic Japanese," posing as U.S. citizens, would be racially indistinguishable from whites. They would be able to infiltrate the United States without detection—an invisible, inscrutable enemy within.

Growing out of this history, the masks in the Dancing Itos skits signify the

"Peace Talk"

inscrutability of Japanese men. The Dancing Itos seem to have no scrutable racial signifiers due to their costumes. They prevent the possibility of examining the person behind them and thus of making a "racial" determination, the eyes hidden by the glare of the television lights. Furthermore, there are no buck teeth, Orientalized accents, Charlie Chan fortune cookie syntax. Yet the history of representations of Japanese men makes it clear that such inscrutability, coupled with a lack of direct racial markers, constitutes a hidden racial threat. In a manner that recalls the wwii-era articles, the show codes the Dancing Itos as Japanese figures who hide their own unique racial signifiers and thus render themselves inscrutable.

The visual markers of heavy facial hair and glasses surface again in another Pearl Harbor–era periodical, a political cartoon that ran in the *New York World Telegram* right after the attack and was reprinted in *Life*.[19] This representation, like the D'Amato slur of Ito, does not hide its racial aggression. The cartoon shows a coiled, deadly rattler whose head looks suspiciously like the head and face of a Dancing Ito. The face sports a wide, toothy smile similar to the smiles of the Dancing Itos. In the context of the cartoon, however, the smile that signifies harmony is merely the specific manifestation of Japanese deception that helps lay the groundwork for the Pearl Harbor attack. The Japanese snake has used the mask of the smile to cover his murderous plot against the United States.

The smile in this cartoon also connotes a specific type of pleasure. The snake seems pleased by recent events. There is liquid dripping from the white buck teeth of the grinning mouth, suggesting that he has recently struck prey.

"Bring Your Daughter to Work"

Given the context, the liquid must be "American" blood. The juxtaposition of the pleasure conveyed by the smile and the tragic loss of human life at Pearl Harbor paints a scenario of the Japanese enemy's depravity. The cartoon exposes the Japanese as the deadly, subhuman, and uncivilized enemy. It constructs a narrative of deceit through inscrutability: the Japanese behave well when under scrutiny by "Americans," but they use the cover of peace talks to cloak the sinister Pearl Harbor plan.

Although the blatant racial aggression of the cartoon would seem radically different from the Dancing Itos, another *Tonight Show* skit makes it clear that the presumption of inscrutability can lead to other jokes concerning another kind of enemy invasion: miscegenation. During a monologue in early April 1995, Leno begins a joke about the judge and the annual Bring-Your-Daughter-to-Work Day. He introduces the skit by telling the audience that Ito recently brought his daughter to his workplace, the courtroom. The piece opens with a tight close-up shot of Ito's face. His stern, unsmiling face fills the screen. Again, the figure wears the predictable visual markers: large heavy glasses, fake black beard and mustache. The shot widens out and we see that he is sitting down behind the bench, with a young, unsmiling, long-haired Asian girl on his lap. The girl wears the same glasses, beard, and mustache, giving her the appearance of a bearded lady in a circus freak show. The hairy little girl raises a gavel and raps it on the desk, father and daughter Ito look at each other briefly in recognition, then smile at the viewer.

Although the skit uses the same Ito visual markers as do the Dancing Itos, it is different in at least one crucial way. The close shot of Ito and his daughter makes it clear that the actors playing the father and daughter are "really" "Asian." Through the proximity of the camera and an absence of strong frontal lighting, the show has exposed their physiognomic racial characteristics by allowing us to see through the lenses of the eyeglasses. As we have seen with the wwii-era articles, "almond-eyes" are the most durable visual signifiers for the signified of Asianness, and the show works very hard to make these signifiers plain in this skit. In this reading, the joke about Ito's progeny exposes the threat of a racially compromised future: the daughter as the freakish, miscegenated offspring of Ito and his white American wife. Like the cartoon of the smiling wwii Japanese human/snake, *The Tonight Show*'s startling vision of Ito and his child relies on the specter of racial taint. The supposedly nonracial image of Ito, in this contextualized final analysis, is connected to the racialized trope of blood.

This essay has shown how one television show deploys race under specific terms of representation that are typically delimited by the culturally predominant, binary discourse of black and white. That *The Tonight Show* could stage a series of skits that are generally considered safely nonracial—at one point, Leno even claimed that Ito himself "loves the Dancing Itos"—demands that we reconsider how this binary discourse determines our sense of what counts as racial in the first place. This exploration of some of the consequences of a binary discourse suggests that those interested in race and representation must examine how cultural productions code a variety of racial groups and how these different codes work together within a larger economy of racial discourse.

Notes

1   I leave much unsaid here. The staging of the Dancing Itos as the Village People and French can-can dancers requires analysis about how drag and camp figure into these representations. I hope this essay will serve as an aid to such a critique, especially one that addresses how issues of gender and sexuality articulate with racial construction.

2   Vic Garbarini, "Branford Marsalis Knows Why the Caged Bird Sings," *Musician*, July 1994, 42.

3   Ibid.

4   Lawrence Van Gelder, "D'Amato Mocks Ito and Sets Off Furor," *New York Times*, 6 April 1995, B1.

5   The accent was not unlike the one employed by Mickey Rooney as the hotel proprietor in the film *Breakfast at Tiffany's*.

6   Garbarini, 44.

7   Bill Carter, *The Late Shift: Letterman, Leno, and the Network Battle for the Night* (New York: Hyperion, 1994), 200.

8   James Wolcott, "Sleepless Nights: Letterman v. Leno Is Becoming a Frantic War of Attrition," *The New Yorker,* 5 June 1995, 107.

9   Don Heckman, "Leno for Lefonque? Not the Standard Career Trade," *Los Angeles Times,* 30 January 1995, F1.

10 John Fiske, *Media Matters: Everyday Culture and Political Change* (Minneapolis: University of Minnesota Press, 1994), 37–38.

11 Bret Harte, *Selected Western Stories and Poems* (New York: Walter J. Black, 1932), 255–257.

12 For a concise historical account of the Japanese American community in Seattle, Washington, and the Pacific Northwest throughout the WWII years, see David Takami, *Executive Order 9066: Fifty Years Before and Fifty Years After* (Seattle: Wing Luke Asian Museum, 1992). Along more literary lines, see John Okada, *No No Boy* (Seattle: University of Washington Press, 1979). For a video account, see Lise Yasui, *A Family Gathering* (Alexandria, VA: PBS Video, 1990).

13 Elaine H. Kim, *Asian American Literature: An Introduction to the Writings and Their Social Context* (Philadelphia: Temple University Press, 1982), 281, n. 1.

14 "How to Tell Your Friends from the Japs," *Time,* 22 December 1941, 33.

15 "How to Tell Japs from the Chinese," *Life,* 22 December 1941, 81.

16 "How to Tell Your Friends," 33.

17 Ibid.

18 "How to Tell Japs," 81.

19 Will Johnstone, "Even a Rattlesnake Gives Warning," *Life,* 22 December 1941, 7.

SELECTED BIBLIOGRAPHY

Auletta, Ken. *The Underclass.* New York: Random House, 1982.

———. "Working Seminar on the Family and American Welfare Policy." In *The New Consensus on Family and Welfare: A Community of Self-Reliance.* Washington, DC: American Enterprise Institute, 1987.

Barnouw, Erik. *Tube of Plenty: The Evolution of American Television.* 2d rev. ed. New York: Oxford University Press, 1990.

Baudrillard, Jean. *Simulations.* Trans. Paul Foss, Paul Patton, and Philip Beitchman. New York: Semiotext(e), 1983.

Berlant, Lauren. "National Brands/National Body: 'Imitation of Life.'" In *Comparative American Identities: Race, Sex, and Nationality in the Modern Text,* ed. Hortense Spillers. New York: Routledge, 1991.

Bhabha, Homi K. "The Other Question . . ." *Screen* 24, no. 6 (1983): 18–36.

Bobo, Jacqueline, and Ellen Seiter. "Black Feminism and Media Criticism: The Women of Brewster Place." *Screen* 32, no. 3 (1991): 286–302.

Bodroghkozy, Aniko. "'Is This What You Mean by Color TV?' Race, Gender, and Contested Meanings in NBC's *Julia.*" In *Private Screenings: Television and the Female Consumer,* ed. Lynn Spigel and Denise Mann, 143–167. Minneapolis: University of Minnesota Press, 1992.

Bogle, Donald. *Toms, Coons, Mulattoes, Mammies, and Bucks: An Interpretive History of Blacks in American Films.* New York: Continuum, 1989.

Bourdieu, Pierre. *Distinction: A Social Critique of the Judgment of Taste.* Trans. Richard Nice. Cambridge, MA: Harvard University Press, 1984.

Campbell, Richard, and Jimmie L. Reeves. "Covering the Homeless: The Joyce Brown Story." *Critical Studies in Mass Communication* 6, no. 1 (1989): 21–42.

Carter, Bill. *The Late Shift: Letterman, Leno, and the Network Battle for the Night.* New York: Hyperion, 1994.

Certeau, Michel de. *Heterologies.* Trans. Brian Massumi. Minneapolis: University of Minnesota Press, 1986.

Churchill, Ward. *Fantasies of the Master Race.* Monroe, ME: Common Courage Press, 1992.

Clifford, James. "Introduction: Partial Truths." In *Writing Culture,* ed. James Clifford and George E. Marcus, 12. Berkeley: University of California Press, 1986.

Collins, Patricia Hill. "A Comparison of Two Works on Black Family Life." *Signs* 14, no. 4 (1989): 875–884.

———. *Black Feminist Thought: Knowledge, Consciousness, and Politics of Empowerment.* New York: Routledge, 1990.

Coontz, Stephanie. *The Way We Were: American Families and the Nostalgia Trap.* New York: Basic Books, 1992.

Cripps, Thomas. *Slow Fade to Black: The Negro in American Film, 1900–1942.* New York: Oxford University Press, 1977.

———. "Amos 'n' Andy and the Debate over American Racial Integration." In *American History/American Television: Interpreting the Video Past,* ed. John E. O'Connor, 33–54. New York: Ungar, 1983.

Dates, Jannette L., and William Barlow, eds. *Split Image: African Americans in the Mass Media.* Washington, DC: Howard University Press, 1990.

Davis, Mike. *City of Quartz: Excavating the Future in Los Angeles.* New York: Vintage, 1990.

Deloria, Vine, Jr., and Clifford M. Lytle. *American Indians, American Justice.* Austin: University of Texas Press, 1983.

Dent, Gina, ed. *Black Popular Culture.* Seattle: Bay Press, 1992.

Dippie, Brian. *The Vanishing American.* Lawrence: University of Kansas Press, 1982.

Doane, Mary Ann. "Information, Crisis, Catastrophe." In *Logics of Television: Essays in Cultural Criticism,* ed. Patricia Mellencamp, 222–239. Bloomington: Indiana University Press, 1990.

Douglas, Mary. *Purity and Danger: An Analysis of Concepts of Pollution and Taboo.* New York: Routledge, 1991.

Durham, Scott. "From Magritte to Klossowski: The Simulacrum, between Painting and Narrative." *October* 64 (Spring 1993): 17–33.

Durning, Simon, ed. *The Cultural Studies Reader.* New York: Routledge, 1993.

Dyer, Richard. *Heavenly Bodies: Film Stars and Society.* New York: St. Martin's Press, 1986.

———. "White." *Screen* 29, no. 4 (Autumn 1988): 44–64.

Edelman, Murray. *Constructing the Political Spectacle.* Chicago: University of Chicago Press, 1988.

Eisner, Joel, and David Krinsky. *Television Comedy Series: An Episode Guide to 153 TV Sitcoms in Syndication.* Jefferson, NC: McFarland & Company, 1984.

Ely, Melvin Patrick. *The Adventures of Amos 'n' Andy: A Social History of an American Phenomenon.* New York: Free Press, 1991.

Entman, Robert M. "Modern Racism and the Images of Blacks in Local Television News." *Critical Studies in Mass Communication* 7 (December 1990): 332–335.

Faludi, Susan. *Backlash: The Undeclared War against Women.* New York: Crown Publishers, 1989.

Ferguson, Russell, Martha Gever, Trinh T. Minh-ha, and Cornel West, eds. *Out There: Marginalization and Contemporary Culture.* New York and Cambridge, MA: New Museum of Contemporary Art/MIT Press, 1990.

Feuer, Jane. "The Concept of Live Television: Ontology as Ideology." In *Regarding Television: Critical Approaches—An Anthology,* ed. E. Ann Kaplan, 12–21. Frederick, MD: University Publications of America, 1983.

———. "MTM Enterprises: An Overview." In MTM: "*Quality Television,*" ed. Jane Feuer, Paul Kerr, and Tise Vahimagi, 1–31. London: British Film Institute, 1984.

Fiske, John. *Power Plays, Power Works.* London: Verso, 1993.

———. *Media Matters: Everyday Culture and Political Change.* Minneapolis: University of Minnesota Press, 1994.

Flitterman-Lewis, Sandy. "Psychoanalysis, Film, and Television." In *Channels of Discourse, Reassembled,* ed. Robert Allen, 203–246. Chapel Hill: University of North Carolina Press, 1992.

Foucault, Michel. *This Is Not a Pipe.* Trans. and ed. James Harkness. Berkeley: University of California Press, 1983.

———. "What Is an Author?" In *Foucault Reader,* ed. Paul Rabinow, 101–120. New York: Pantheon Books, 1984.

———. *The Care of the Self: Vol. 3 of The History of Sexuality.* Trans. Robert Hurley. New York: Vintage, 1986.

———. "The Ethic of the Care of the Self as a Practice of Freedom." In *The Final Foucault,* ed. James Bernauer and David Rasmussen. Cambridge, MA: MIT Press, 1987.

———. "On the Genealogy of Ethics: An Overview of Work in Progress." In *Ethics: Subjectivity and Truth,* ed. Paul Rabinow, trans. Robert Hurley and others. New York: The New Press, 1997.

Fraser, Nancy. "Sex, Lies, and the Public Sphere: Some Reflections on the Confirmation of Clarence Thomas." *Critical Inquiry* 18 (1992): 595–612.

Frazier, E. Franklin. *The Negro Family in the United States.* 1939. Reprint, New York: Dryden Press, 1948.

Freud, Sigmund. "Repression." In *General Psychological Theory,* ed. Philip Rieff, 104–115. New York: Collier/Macmillan, 1963.

Gianakos, Larry James. *Television Drama Series Programming: A Comprehensive Chronicle, 1959–1975.* Metuchen, NJ: Scarecrow Press, 1978.

Gitlin, Todd. *Inside Prime Time.* New York: Pantheon, 1985.

Glazer, Nathan. *Affirmative Discrimination: Ethnic Inequality and Public Power.* New York: Basic Books, 1975.

Gooding-Williams, Robert. *Reading Rodney King/Reading Urban Uprising.* New York: Routledge, 1993.

Gray, Herman. "Television, Black Americans, and the American Dream." *Critical Studies in Mass Communication* 6 (December 1989): 376–386.

———. "The Endless Slide of Difference: Critical Television Studies, Television and the Question of Race." *Critical Studies in Mass Communication* 10, no. 2 (1993): 190–197.

———. *Watching Race: Television and the Struggle for "Blackness."* Minneapolis: University of Minnesota Press, 1995.

Grossberg, Lawrence, Cary Nelson, and Paula Treichler, eds. *Cultural Studies.* New York: Routledge, 1992.

Hall, Stuart. *The Hard Road to Renewal: Thatcherism and the Crisis of the Left.* London: Verso, 1988.

———. "The Whites of Their Eyes." In *The Media Reader,* ed. Manuel Alvarado and John O. Thompson, 7–23. London: British Film Institute, 1990.

Hamamoto, Darrell Y. *Monitored Peril: Asian Americans and the Politics of tv Representation.* Minneapolis: University of Minnesota Press, 1994.

Harper, Phillip Brian. "Nationalism and Social Division in Black Arts Poetry of the 1960s." *Critical Inquiry* 19, no. 2 (1993): 234–255.

Heath, Stephen. "Representing Television." In *Logics of Television: Essays in Cultural Criticism,* ed. Patricia Mellencamp, 267–302. Bloomington: Indiana University Press, 1990.

Heath, Stephen, and Gillian Skirrow. "Television: A World in Action." *Screen* 18, no. 2 (Summer 1997): 7–59.

Hoffman, Frederick. *Race Traits and Tendencies.* 1896.

Houston, Beverle. "Viewing Television: The Metapsychology of Endless Consumption." *Quarterly Review of Film Studies* 9, no. 3 (Summer 1984): 183–195.

Huyssen, Andreas. "Mass Culture as Woman: Modernism's Other." In *Studies in Entertainment: Critical Approaches to Mass Culture,* ed. Tania Modleski, 188–208. Bloomington: University of Indiana Press, 1986.

Jhally, Sut, and Justin Lewis. *Enlightened Racism: The Cosby Show, Audiences, and the Myth of the American Dream.* Boulder, CO: Westview Press, 1992.

Johnson, Hillary, and Nancy Rommelmann. *The Real Real World.* New York: MTV Books/Pocket Books/Melcher Media, 1995.

Jones, LeRoi. *Blues People.* New York: William Morrow, 1963.

Joyrich, Lynne. "Critical and Textual Hypermasculinity." In *Logics of Television: Essays in Cultural Criticism,* ed. Patricia Mellencamp, 156–172. Bloomington: Indiana University Press, 1990.

Katz, P., and D. Taylor, eds. *Eliminating Racism: Profiles in Controversy.* New York: Plenum Press, 1988.

Killens, John Oliver. "Our Struggle Is Not to Be White Men in Black Skin." *TV Guide,* 25 July 1970, 6–9.

Kim, Elaine H. *Asian American Literature: An Introduction to the Writings and Their Social Context.* Philadelphia: Temple University Press, 1982.

Kim, Ha-il. "Minority Media Access: Examination of Policies, Technologies, and Multi-Ethnic Television and a Proposal for an Alternative Approach to Media Access." Ph.D. diss., University of California, Los Angeles, 1992.

Kovel, Joel. *White Racism: A Psychohistory.* New York: Columbia University Press, 1984.

Leab, Daniel. *From Sambo to Superspade: The Black Experience in Motion Pictures.* Boston: Houghton Mifflin, 1975.

Lipsitz, George. "From Chester Himes to Nursery Rhymes: Local Television and the Politics of Cultural Space in Postwar Los Angeles." Unpublished paper, n.d.

Lotringer, Sylvere, ed. *Foucault Live.* New York: Semiotext(e), 1989.

MacDonald, J. Fred. *Who Shot the Sheriff: The Rise and Fall of the Television Western.* New York: Praeger, 1987.

———. *Blacks in White TV: African Americans in Television Since 1948.* Chicago: Nelson-Hall, 1992.

Modleski, Tania. *Loving with a Vengeance: Mass-Produced Fantasies for Women.* New York: Methuen, 1982.

Morreale, Joanne. *A New Beginning: A Textual Frame Analysis of the Political Campaign Film.* Albany: State University of New York Press, 1991.

Morrison, Toni, ed. *Race-ing Justice, En-gendering Power: Essays on Anita Hill, Clarence Thomas, and the Construction of Social Reality.* New York: Pantheon, 1992.

Morrison, Toni. *Playing in the Dark.* New York: Vintage, 1993.

Morse, Margaret. "Talk, Talk, Talk: The Space of Discourse in Television News, Sportscasts, Talk Shows, and Advertising." *Screen* 26 (1985): 2–15.

Myrdal, Gunnar. *An American Dilemma: The Negro Problem and Modern Democracy.* Twentieth Anniversary ed. 1944. Reprint, New York: Harper & Row, 1962.

Naficy, Hamid. "Mediawork's Representation of the Other: The Case of Iran." In *Ques-*

tions of Third Cinema, ed. Paul Willeman and Jim Pines, 227–239. London: British Film Institute, 1990.

———. *The Making of Exile Cultures: Iranian Television in Los Angeles.* Minneapolis: University of Minnesota Press, 1993.

Negt, Oskar, and Alexander Kluge. *Public Sphere and Experience: Toward an Analysis of the Bourgeois and Proletarian Public Sphere.* Minneapolis: University of Minnesota Press, 1993.

Norback, Craig T., Peter G. Norback, and Editors of *TV Guide. TV Guide Almanac.* New York: Ballantine, 1980.

Omi, Michael, and Howard Winant. *Racial Formation in the United States: From the 1960s to the 1990s.* 2d ed. New York: Routledge, 1994.

Otis, Johnny. *Upside Your Head! Rhythm and Blues on Central Avenue.* Hanover: Wesleyan University Press, 1993.

Owens, Craig. "The Allegorical Impulse: Toward a Theory of Postmodernism." In *Beyond Recognition: Representation, Power, and Culture,* 52–87. Berkeley: University of California Press, 1992.

Pinkney, Alphonso. *The Myth of Black Progress.* Cambridge, UK: Cambridge University Press, 1984.

Postman, Neil. *Amusing Ourselves to Death.* New York: Penguin, 1985.

Rainwater, Lee, and William Yancey, eds. *The Moynihan Report and the Politics of Controversy.* Cambridge, MA: MIT Press, 1965.

Reeves, Jimmie L., and Richard Campbell. *Cracked Coverage: Television News, the Anti-Cocaine Crusade, and the Reagan Legacy.* Durham, NC: Duke University Press, 1994.

Robbins, Bruce, ed. *The Phantom Public Sphere.* Minneapolis: University of Minnesota Press, 1993.

Roth, B. M. "Social Psychology's Racism." *The Public Interest,* no. 96 (winter 1990): 26–36.

Said, Edward. *Orientalism.* New York: Vintage Books, 1978.

Scott, Joan Wallach. *Gender and the Politics of History.* New York: Columbia University Press, 1988.

Shannon, A. H. *The Negro in Washington: A Study of Race Amalgamation.* 1930.

Shohat, Ella. "Ethnicities-in-Relations: Toward a Multicultural Reading of American Cinema." In *Unspeakable Images: Ethnicity and the American Cinema,* ed. Lester D. Friedman. Urbana: University of Illinois Press, 1991.

Simmons, Jon. *Foucault and the Political.* New York: Routledge, 1995.

Sowell, Thomas. *Affirmative Action Reconsidered: Was It Necessary in Academica?* Washington, DC: American Enterprise Institute for Public Policy Research, 1975.

Spigel, Lynn, and Michael Curtin, eds. *The Revolution Wasn't Televised: Sixties Television and Social Conflict.* New York: Routledge, 1997.

Spillers, Hortense. "Mama's Baby, Papa's Maybe: An American Grammar Book." *Diacritics* 17, no. 2 (1987): 65–81.

Spurr, David. *The Rhetoric of Empire: Colonial Discourses in Journalism, Travel Writing, and Imperial Administration.* Durham, NC: Duke University Press, 1993.

Stam, Robert. "Television News and Its Spectator." In *Regarding Television: Critical Approaches. An Anthology,* ed. E. Ann Kaplan, 23–40. Frederick, MD: University Publications of America, 1983.

Takami, David. *Executive Order 9066: Fifty Years Before and Fifty Years After.* Seattle: Wing Luke Asian Museum, 1992.

Taylor, Ella. *Primetime Families.* Berkeley: University of California Press, 1991.

Terrace, Vincent. *The Complete Encyclopedia of Television Programs, 1947–1979.* 2d ed., rev. Vol. 2. South Brunswick: A. S. Barnes & Co., 1979.

Thomas, William Hannibal. *The American Negro: What He Was, What He Is, and What He May Become.* 1902.

Turner, Patricia A. *Ceramic Uncles and Celluloid Mammies: Black Images and Their Influences on Culture.* New York: Anchor Books, 1994.

U.S. Department of Labor. *The Negro Family: The Case for National Action.* Washington, DC: Government Printing Office, 1965.

Watson, Mary Ann. *The Expanding Vista: American Television in the Kennedy Years.* Durham, NC: Duke University Press, 1994.

West, Cornel. *Prophesy Deliverance! An Afro-American Revolutionary Christianity.* Philadelphia: Westminster Press, 1982.

White, Mimi. "Rehearsing Feminism: Women/History in *The Life and Times of Rosie the Riveter* and *Swing Shift.*" *Wide Angle* 7, no. 3 (1985): 34–43.

Williams, Raymond. *Television: Technology and Cultural Form.* New York: Schocken Books, 1974.

Young, Robert. *White Mythologies: Writing History and the West.* New York: Routledge, 1990.

Yúdice, George. "Marginality and the Ethics of Survival." In *Universal Abandon: The Politics of Postmodernism,* ed. Andrew Ross. Minneapolis: University of Minnesota Press, 1988.

CONTRIBUTORS

Stephen Michael Best teaches in the Department of English at the University of California, Berkeley. He is currently at work on a book called *The Subject of Property*, about property, race, and mechanical reproduction in American culture at the turn of the nineteenth century.

John Caldwell teaches digital video production and television studies in the Department of Communication at the University of California, San Diego. "Negotiating Race in the L.A. Rebellion" is an excerpt from his book, *Televisuality: Style, Crisis and Authority in American Television* (1995).

Phillip Brian Harper, Associate Professor of English at New York University, is the author of *Framing the Margins: The Social Logic of Postmodern Culture* (1994). "Extra-Special Effects" is excerpted from his latest book, *Are We Not Men? Masculine Anxiety and the Problem of African-American Identity* (1996).

Brian Locke is a graduate student in the Department of American Civilization at Brown University, where he works on racial representation and U.S. history.

José Esteban Muñoz teaches in the Department of Performance Studies at New York University. His latest book is *Disidentifications* (forthcoming).

Hamid Naficy is Associate Professor of Media Studies at Rice University. His publications include "Phobic Spaces and Liminal Panics: Independent Transnational Film Genre," in *Global/Local: Cultural Productions and the Transnational Imaginary,* edited by Rob Wilson and Wimal Dissanayke (1996), *The Making of Exile Cultures: Iranian Television in Los Angeles* (1993), and *Otherness and the Media: The Ethnography of the Imagined and the Imaged,* coedited with Teshome Gabriel (1993).

Jimmie L. Reeves teaches in the School of Mass Communications at Texas Tech University, and is the author, with Richard Campbell, of *Cracked Coverage: Television News, the Anti-Cocaine Crusade, and the Reagan Legacy* (1994).

Sasha Torres is the Richard and Edna Salomon Assistant Professor at Brown University, where she teaches television, film, and cultural theory in the Department of Modern Culture and Media. She is an editor of *Camera Obscura* and is currently working on a book called *Black, White, and In Color,* about U.S. television's production of race relations and national subjectivity since 1963.

Mimi White is Professor of Radio/TV/Film at Northwestern University. She is the author of *Tele-Advising: Therapeutic Discourse in American Television* (1992) and the co-author of *Media Knowledge: Popular Culture, Pedagogy, and Critical Citizenship* (1992).

Mark Williams teaches in the Department of Film Studies at Dartmouth College. His book on early Los Angeles television is forthcoming.

Pamela Wilson recently completed her dissertation, *Disputable Truths: The American Stranger, Television Documentary and Native American Cultural Politics of the 1950s,* at the University of Wisconsin, and is now teaching at Robert Morris College in Pittsburgh. She has published articles on cultural studies and media in *South Atlantic Quarterly,* the *Historical Journal of Film, Radio, and Television,* and *Quarterly Review of Film and Video.*

Library of Congress Cataloging-in-Publication Data

Living color : race and television in the United States / edited by
Sasha Torres.

p.   cm. — (Console-ing passions)

Includes bibliographical references and index.

ISBN 0-8223-2178-5 (cloth : alk. paper). — ISBN 0-8223-2195-5
(pbk. : alk. paper)

1. Minorities in television — United States.   2. Television
broadcasting — Social aspects — United States.   I. Torres, Sasha.
II. Series.

PN1992.8.M54L58   1998

302.23'45'08900973 — DC21   97-31459   CIP